TWENTIETH CENTURY VIEWS

The aim of this series is to present the best in contemporary critical opinion on major authors, providing a twentieth century perspective on their changing status in an era of profound revaluation.

Maynard Mack, *Series Editor*
Yale University

THE THEATER OF
BLACK AMERICANS

VOLUME I

THE THEATER OF
BLACK AMERICANS

VOLUME I

Roots and Rituals: The Search for Identity
The Image Makers: Plays and Playwrights

A COLLECTION OF CRITICAL ESSAYS

Edited by
Errol Hill

Prentice-Hall, Inc.   A SPECTRUM BOOK   *Englewood Cliffs, N.J.*

Library of Congress Cataloging in Publication Data

Main entry under title:

THE THEATER OF BLACK AMERICANS.

   (Twentieth century views) (A Spectrum Book)
   Bibliography: p.
   CONTENTS: v. 1. Roots and rituals. The image
makers. v. 2. The presenters. The participators.
   1. Afro-American theater — Addresses, essays,
lectures. I. Hill, Errol.
PN2270.A35T48   792'.0973   79-16658
ISBN 0-13-912717-8 (v. 1)
ISBN 0-13-912709-7 (v. 1) pbk.

Editorial/production supervision by Eric Newman
Cover illustration by Stanley Wyatt
Manufacturing buyers: Cathie Lenard and Barbara A. Frick

10 9 8 7 6 5 4 3 2 1

PRENTICE-HALL INTERNATIONAL, INC. *(London)*
PRENTICE-HALL OF AUSTRALIA PTY. LIMITED *(Sydney)*
PRENTICE-HALL OF CANADA, LTD. *(Toronto)*
PRENTICE-HALL OF INDIA PRIVATE LIMITED *(New Delhi)*
PRENTICE-HALL OF JAPAN, INC. *(Tokyo)*
PRENTICE-HALL OF SOUTHEAST ASIA PTE. LTD. *(Singapore)*
WHITEHALL BOOKS LIMITED *(Wellington, New Zealand)*

Contents

Acknowledgments

Excerpts from *Shuffle Along* are reprinted with permission. © 1921 Warner Bros. Inc. Copyright renewed. All rights reserved. Used with permission.

Excerpts from *A Land Beyond the River* are published through the courtesy of Pioneer Drama Service, Box 22555, Denver, Colorado 80222, holder of performance rights for this play.

Excerpts from *Purlie Victorious* are reprinted by permission of Samuel French, Inc. © 1961 by Ossie Davis.

Excerpts from *Happy Ending* and *Day of Absence* are reprinted with permission. © Copyright, 1966, by Douglas Turner Ward. Reprinted by permission of the author and of Dramatists Play Service, Inc. Caution: *Happy Ending* and *Day of Absence,* being duly copyrighted, are subject to a royalty. The amateur acting rights are controlled exclusively by the Dramatists Play Service, Inc., 440 Park Avenue South, New York, New York 10016. No amateur production of the plays may be given without obtaining in advance the written permission of the Dramatists Play Service, Inc., and paying the requisite fees.

Excerpts from *A Raisin in the Sun* are used with permission. *A Raisin in the Sun* by Lorraine Hansberry. Copyright © 1958, 1959, 1966 by Robert Nemiroff as Executor of the Estate of Lorraine Hansberry. Reprinted by permission of Random House, Inc.

Excerpts from *The Amen Corner* are used by permission of the author. Copyright © 1968 by James Baldwin.

Excerpts from *In the Wine Time* are reprinted with permission. *In the Wine Time* by Ed Bullins. From *Five Plays by Ed Bullins*, copyright © 1968 by Ed Bullins. Used by permission of the publishers, The Bobbs-Merrill Company, Inc.

A selection from *The River Niger* by Joseph A. Walker is used with permission. Copyright © 1973 by Joseph A. Walker. Reprinted with the permission of Hill and Wang (now a division of Farrar, Straus & Giroux, Inc.). Reprinted by permission of William Morris Agency, Inc., on behalf of the author. Copyright © 1973 by Joseph Walker.

Excerpts from *The Duplex* are reprinted with permission. Approximately 358 words from *The Duplex* by Ed Bullins (extracted from the essay "Structural Elements in Ed Bullins' Plays" by Samuel A. Hay). Copyright © 1971 by Ed Bullins. By permission of William Morrow & Company. William Morrow and Company, Inc., New York, 1971. *The Duplex: A Black Love Fable in Four Movements.*

Excerpts from *The Slave* are used by permission of The Sterling Lord Agency. Copyright © 1964 by LeRoi Jones.

Excerpts from *And We Own the Night* by James Garrett are reprinted by permission of the author and of Amiri Baraka (LeRoi Jones), editor of *Black Fire*, 1968.

THE THEATER OF
BLACK AMERICANS

VOLUME I

Introduction

by Errol Hill

Theatre is both an art and an industry; an expression of culture and a source of livelihood for artists and craftsmen; a medium of instruction and a purveyor of entertainment. The essays collected in this book attempt to view Black theatre in all these aspects, but the exercise goes beyond the purely academic. There is a sense of urgency that informs our inquiry. Black Americans today recognize, perhaps more clearly than at any other time in their history, that theatre as an institution can have a significant impact on the relentless struggle of a deprived racial minority for full equality and on the need for spiritual well-being of a people divorced from their ancestral heritage through centuries of degrading slavery. The trend is clearly marked in the spectacular growth of Black theatres across the country.

Widespread recognition of the theatre's potential for changing, healing, and restoring—a return, as it were, to the pristine function of the communal, ritual drama—has thrown the Afro-American theatre into a flurry of controversy. The positions taken by theorists and practitioners serve only to generate further questions that call forth still more manifestoes. What, for instance, should be the principal objective of Black theatre? Should its content be strictly defined by the overriding concern for Black liberation? To what audience should this theatre be addressed primarily? What form should it take? How may it express a Black identity, if such a characteristic does in fact exist? What price art in Black theatre when Black people are involved in a struggle for survival? What is the true role of the critic in this theatre? These and many similar crucial questions provide a salutary philosophical counterpoint to the proliferating and sometimes frenzied activities of Black theatre groups nationwide.

It is well to remind ourselves that these issues are not new to Black theatre, though they have never before had a national forum nor have they been voiced with such force and pressure, a force and pressure due in no small part to the Black revolutionary context in which they have lately been raised. Others in earlier decades—most notably during the period of the 1920s commonly referred to as the Harlem Renaissance—have wrestled with similar questions. But the rapid decline of European colonialism in Africa since the 1950s and the concomitant emergence of Black nation-states, the 1954 Supreme Court order requiring public school desegregation coupled with civil rights battles on the home front, and the rallying cry for immediate equality by outspoken leaders such as Martin Luther King and Malcolm X—all have contributed to the recent explosion of Black nationalist sentiment in the arts. Contributing too to a heightened concern with the nature and scope of Black theatre are the increased concentration of Black Americans in urban areas and the Black Arts movement with its emphasis on Black cultural centers in which revolutionary political action and community organization are paired with poetry, drama, and the arts. Culture in this context becomes central to the struggle rather than peripheral. The arts become the means for reaching the public, and as a result the theatre, being the most public of the arts, finds itself in the forefront of the nationalist movement.

Back in 1858 William Wells Brown chose the dramatic form for his public addresses against slavery. It was in 1915, however, that the programmatic use of Black drama as an instrument for social reform was begun by the National Association for the Advancement of Colored People. That year, the NAACP appointed a Drama Committee to study ways and means of utilizing the stage in the service of its cause. Chief among the members of this Committee was W. E. B. DuBois, who, in 1900, had predicted that the relationship between the darker and lighter races of man would be the chief problem of the twentieth century. A Harvard Ph.D. and Professor of Economics and History at Atlanta University, DuBois joined the NAACP in 1910 and founded its magazine, *The Crisis,* which he edited for twenty-four years. From this platform he led the militant wing of the Negro movement and spoke out fearlessly against racial discrimination of every kind. The intention of the Drama Committee was not simply to sponsor a rash of propaganda plays that spoke in one-sided accents of current social problems. DuBois was too much of an intellectual and statesman for such a simple-minded approach. He had earlier published *The Souls of Black Folk,* one of the first examinations of Black arts, and on the occasion of the 1913 Exposition to observe fifty years of emancipation from slavery, he had written and staged a pageant, *The Star of Ethiopia.* Two years later he reflected on that experience:

> In art and literature we should try to loose the tremendous emotional wealth of the Negro and the dramatic strength of his problems through writing, the stage, pageantry, and other forms of art. We should resurrect forgotten ancient Negro art and history and we should set the black man before the world as both a creative artist and a strong subject for artistic treatment.[1]

The urgent need, then, was to develop good Black dramatists writing about the Black experience and to assure them a hearing on the dramatic stage. In the first decades of this century, when Blacks were effectively shut out from the legitimate professional theatre, the Lafayette Players in 1915 courageously set up shop in Harlem to prove that Black actors were as competent at their craft as their White counterparts downtown. Hardly had the Players begun their long and noteworthy career of staging mostly Broadway revivals in condensed versions when protests began to flow from the pens of Black critics. The Broadway theatre might ignore honest portrayals of Black life and culture, but a Harlem-based theatre imitating alien Broadway fare was not to be silently tolerated.

Lovett Fort-Whiteman, drama editor of *The Messenger,* affirming that the stage for Negroes should be dominated by Negroes, demanded that "our society be reflected upon the American stage even if we have to call a mass meeting of Harlem's theatregoers and effect a boycott on the Lafayette Theatre."[2] The Players attempted to meet this harsh criticism by offering a prize for original Black plays, but there is no evidence that this action produced a radical change in their repertory. It was left to DuBois, as editor of the magazine *The Crisis,* to initiate the Krigwa Playwriting Contest in 1925, which resulted in the publication of several prizewinning short plays, the emergence of new Black playwrights, male and female, and the founding of the Krigwa Little Theatre intended as a nation-wide Black theatre movement.

This was in the midst of the Harlem Renaissance, when Black leaders spoke with a new assertiveness of their needs and aspirations.

---

[1] *The Crisis,* IX (April, 1915), p. 312.
[2] *The Messenger,* Vol. 1, No. 11 (November, 1917), p. 30.

In theatre, the sparkling Black musical comedy represented by *Shuffle Along* took Broadway by storm. Not all Blacks rejoiced at this conquest. Broadway, after all, was a White preserve patronized by White audiences, and the Black Broadway-type musical comedy for all its flair and vigor was still too reminiscent of the despised minstrel tradition for everyone's comfort. In 1926, having formed the Harlem group of Krigwa Players, DuBois enunciated his four fundamental principles for a Negro theatre. Such a theatre, he asserted, had to be *about us, by us, for us,* and *near us* (that is, located in the Black community).[3]

The Krigwa Players established themselves in the basement of the 135th Street Harlem Library, which they helped to convert into a pocket theatre for their productions and which was occupied by successive companies of Harlem theatres after the Krigwa group became inactive in 1930. Their first season opened with three one-act plays by prizewinning authors of *The Crisis* competition. They were careful to eschew the separatism and exclusivity that in the '60s hobbled the efforts of an important Harlem company and made it difficult for the group to command widespread support for its continuance when foundation funds were cut off. While addressing their plays to Black audiences, the Krigwa Players reserved a warm welcome "for all artists of all races and for all sympathetic comers and for all beautiful ideas."[4]

While DuBois was encouraging playwriting and sponsoring productions of Black plays for Black audiences, he and others were also concerned about both the content and the form of presentation of the nascent Afro-American theatre they were strenuously promoting. As early as 1916 DuBois had observed, in a statement prophetic of the current fascination with ritual as an appropriate model for Afro-American dramatic form, that throughout Africa "pageantry and dramatic recital are closely mingled with religious rites and in America the 'Shout' of the Church revival is in its essential pure drama."[5] Another perceptive theorist and spokesman for the Black theatre movement of the time was Alain Locke, then professor of philosophy at Howard University and renowned today for his intellectual leadership. Exemplary of the quality of that leadership

---

[3]"Krigwa Players' Little Negro Theatre." *The Crisis,* Vol. 32, No. 3 (July, 1926), pp. 134-36.

[4]Playbill for Krigwa Players' first season in Harlem, New York, May, 1926.

[5]"Drama Among Black Folk." *The Crisis,* XII (August, 1916), p. 169.

is his anthology. *The New Negro,* which not only includes much of the finest literary work of the Harlem Renaissance but which also attempts to analyze the aesthetic direction of the period.

Others had written disparagingly of the image of the Black performer as a song-and-dance comedian on the professional stage, but Locke saw hidden resources in the folk arts of Negro song, dance, and pantomime which could be exploited and transposed to the serious stage to provide what he called a "galvanizing stimulus." He called for Negro dramatic art to be liberated from the handicaps of both external disparagement and self-imposed limitations. He saw the need for experimentation in form and urged on Black theatre artists the courage to be original, to break with established dramatic convention of all sorts and develop their own idiom. Training and direction were indeed essential for Black artists, he maintained, but along the lines of their own instinctive patterns and idioms of expression, not superimposed from an alien source. Finally, Locke reaffirmed the importance of the African continuum in the arts of Afro-Americans. "One can scarcely think of a complete development of Negro dramatic art," he wrote, "without some significant artistic re-expression of African life and the traditions associated with it."[6] Continuing in this vein, he added these inspiring sentiments:

> If, as seems already apparent, the sophisticated race sense of the Negro should lead back over the trail of the group tradition to an interest in things African, the natural affinities of the material and the art will complete the circuit and they will most electrically combine. ... Here both the Negro actor and dramatist can move freely in a world of elemental beauty, with all the decorative elements that a poetical emotional temperament could wish.[7]

Central to the debate over the function and structure of Black theatre, then as now, is the prevailing view that the theatre of Black Americans should by definition be distinct from that of White America. The argument goes as follows. The two societies identified by the federal government's 1968 Kerner Report have, through their widely contrasting experiences, arrived at different conceptions of reality that seem to demand differing modes of creative expression. Black theatre that appears to be analogous in form to the established

---

[6]"The Negro and the American Stage." *Theatre Arts Monthly,* Vol. X (February, 1926), p. 119.

[7]*Ibid.*

Euro-American theatre is, therefore, deemed to be a thoughtless imitation of an alien culture and a betrayal of the true heritage of the race.

Addison Gayle, Jr., one of the more vocal proponents of the Black aesthetic, in the January/February 1977 issue of *First World* pinpoints the challenge confronting the Black artist who lives in a society where the very terms of existence are, in Mr. Gayle's words, "defined by persons and forces antithetical to his being." The Black artist must "hold on to his own sense of reality," affirms Gayle, "while vigorously denying that offered by the society." The argument is developed along these lines:

> For him, the overwhelming question is whether or not the reality of the oppressed and the oppressor are fundamentally the same; or whether the rigors of living in a tyrannical society do not force upon the oppressed experiences, perceptions, and ways of viewing man and the world that are contradictory to that of those who are not oppressed. ... The refusal to accept white American definitions of reality leads to a refusal to accept its definitions of such concepts as manhood, heroism, beauty, freedom, and humanism.[8]

If such concepts are in fact defined differently by Black people and White, it follows that theatre as an art form involved in expressing these concepts will likewise be different for the two societies.

It is here that theatre as an industry that must be financially viable if it is to function becomes a crucial issue. White American theatre represents the dominant culture. This cultural dominance is sustained not alone through numerical superiority or an unbroken Euro-American tradition, but in practical terms through economic control of the means of theatrical production. Professional theatre in America is and always has been in White hands. Even the so-called independent Black professional companies that exist today are dependent on regular handouts from White philanthropic foundations. Withdrawal of these grants is financially crippling and leads to almost certain demise.

In the past Blacks have sought to join the mainstream professional theatre to which they were first denied access, then grudgingly admitted, and finally allowed entrance on terms that perpetuated their image as song-and-dance clowns performing for the amuse-

---

[8] "Blueprint for Black Criticism." *First World,* Vol. 1, No. 1 (January/February, 1977), pp. 41-45.

ment of White audiences. Little wonder that the musical comedy theatre, generally conceded to be America's gift to the world stage, fell into disrepute among the very Blacks who had provided its genesis and contributed to some of its brightest days. Occasionally, nowadays, Black artists appear on Broadway in serious productions that offer some thoughtful insights into Black life and history; other actors go there to practice their craft on the rare occasions when they are tapped for a challenging role from the world theatre. In the main, however, those Black artists who remain on Broadway are in the business of entertainment, and while art and entertainment are not necessarily incompatible, the art of Black theatre on Broadway is unlikely to be fundamentally different from the established formulas and standards that apply to the Euro-American theatre and will continue to seem a weak echo of the dominant culture.

The fact is that Broadway is the wrong marketplace for the theatre experimentalist, Black or White. But whereas experiments in White theatre are departures from the norm and properly find a home on the fringes of Broadway or in community-supported regional theatres, Black experimental theatre is (or should be) the norm for Black artists, for all Black theatre that is not simply imitative is in the process of becoming and deserves an assured place in the cultural life of the nation. This is a condition that too few of the major drama critics are willing to concede, and, as a result, most critical response exhibits an intolerance of Black theatre productions that do not fall within readily categorized modes.

The task of forging a new Black theatre that would express in meaningful ways the true voice and vision of Afro-Americans cannot be carried out on Broadway. That is why practitioners of serious Black theatre have found it necessary, time and again, to turn to Black communities for sustenance and support. How have these communities responded to efforts to locate dramatic theatres in their midst? Recent years have witnessed a significant improvement in audience turnout to Black shows, but overall the record of support for community-based theatres remains discouraging. In Harlem alone, that metropolis of Black artistic talent, some eighteen or twenty attempts have been made in the last half-century to establish a strong resident theatre organization. All have failed. Few Harlem theatres exist today; none can claim to be flourishing.

The reasons for this continuing lack of support for the Black community theatre are easily adduced. Blame has been laid on the type of plays produced, which are too narrowly focused on polemical and political views not always shared by the community. Plays that uplift the mind and enrich the spirit are rarely seen. Paucity of entertainment, in the best sense of the word, has also been remarked. The Black urban community, plagued by high unemployment and economic depression, is not financially able to maintain a community theatre. The location and atmosphere of the theatre buildings have been criticized as uninviting if not downright forbidding. The lack of a theatregoing tradition among Blacks has also received its share of reproach. There is a modicum of truth in all these complaints, as well as in the fact that the Black press, despite an enviable record in defense of Black causes, has not always been as supportive of Black theatre as the need required.

In 1953 Miles Jefferson, theatre reviewer for the Atlantic University journal *Phylon,* complained that no Black newspaper or periodical in the Manhattan area carried a regular theatre column on Blacks in professional theatre written by a Black critic. His proferred services had been turned down on the excuse that readers of Manhattan's Black papers were not interested in the Broadway theatre. Commented Mr. Jefferson: "How may one appreciate and enjoy any art if he is not enlightened concerning it? And how may he be exposed to it better than through the Negro Press?"[9] Happily, the situation in recent times has changed for the better, but a tradition of theatregoing (or, preferably, theatre participation) is not instantly created; it is developed over years of exposure to the practice of theatre and to illuminating commentary on theatrical performance. It will take time before Black theatres reap the benefit of a more enlightened editorial policy by the press regarding theatre reviews.

The question of how to encourage and protect needed experimentation in the Afro-American theatre while retaining and expanding audiences who have been nurtured on standard theatre fare is the knottiest of all problems faced by responsible Black theatre practitioners. Most of them, concerned as much with survival as with aesthetic considerations, tend to adopt a pragmatic approach of using whatever form seems to work best for a particular production and are content to bequeath the search for a recognizable Afro-American theatre form to the pens of critics and theorists. Some others have turned away altogether from the staging of

[9]"The Negro on Broadway, 1952-53." *Phylon,* Vol. 14, No. 3 (1953), pp. 268-279.

static texts on a conventional stage in favor of a type of participatory theatre by players and audience in a shared space of interaction and celebration.

This kind of eclecticism is not necessarily wasteful or self-indul- gent. A variety of approaches is desirable in order that honest ex- perimentation may be carried out over a broad spectrum and pro- vided that such efforts are scrutinized in the searching light of informed criticism and public appraisal. It should be stated, how- ever, that serious experimental theatre cannot be successfully pur- sued on a part-time schedule, or by inadequately trained artists, or without appropriate and flexible plant and equipment. All of which brings us back to the question of money. The dilemma was evident to Theophilus Lewis, drama critic of *The Messenger* in the 1920s: "Without economic autonomy, the Negro stage can never become the flexible medium for the expression of the spirit of Negro people it ought to be."[10] Lewis was among the first of many writers to call for the founding of a permanent national Black theatre where the work of developing a theatrical identity for Afro-Americans could begin. He even went so far as to suggest that a monthly contribution from the five richest Black churches in New York city would enable a company to be formed that would be able to afford the services of the most talented artists.

Of all the expressions of Black theatre needs down through the years, the call for a national Black theatre has been the most per- sistent. Alain Locke emphasized the need early in the century when he asked that native talent be cultivated beyond the demands and standards of the marketplace, and in the protected housing of the art theatre where it could flower to the utmost perfection. Every decade since that time has heard the appeal repeated with growing insistence and has witnessed short-lived attempts to establish such an institution. That the absence of a national Black theatre is as keenly felt today as it was fifty and more years ago is manifest in the view of Ernie McClintock, respected leader of one of the more active and vigorous Harlem-based groups, the Afro-American Studio Theatre founded in 1966. Writing in the *Black Alliance Newsletter* of February 1978 on the problems confronting the Black theatre movement at the present time, McClintock cites first the lack of a

---

[10]Quoted in "Theophilus Lewis and the Theater of the Harlem Renaissance" by Theodore Kornweibel, Jr. *The Harlem Renaissance Remembered,* ed. Arna Bontemps (New York: Dodd, Mead & Co., 1972), pp. 171-89.

major theatre company that produces frequent quality productions and has captured the imagination and support of large numbers of Blacks, thereby setting a strong positive example for others. "Examples of artistic excellence in theatre are crucial," he says; "an involved and sincere effort to establish a true national Black theatre must be realized immediately."

This writer readily acknowledges that a single prestigious company of talented Black theatre artists working in a national house to explore, develop, and present the finest productions of Afro-American theatre is a desired goal. But a national Black theatre must be truly national. While training, research, experimentation, and skilled performance should proceed with a resident company, including actors, dancers, musicians, singers, and other types of entertainers, the national theatre should open its doors to productions from other Black theatres, which should be invited to present works there that are judged of value in helping to create and define standards of beauty and excellence pertinent to the Black experience. Conversely, productions of the national company would tour other theatres in order to share its discoveries and creations with the national Black community.

It cannot be a futile hope that America will one day build and support a House of Black Culture, including a National Black Theatre, situated in one of the major Black cities. Such an edifice should not be viewed as capitulation to a separatist ideology. On the contrary, it would help to unite the two societies by giving, for the first time, tangible recognition to the different cultural legacy of Afro-Americans, enabling them to approach the Euro-American culture as equals rather than as satellites. For in truth, Afro-Americans have contributed much from their culture to the greatness of America in the arts, as in other walks of life, and in return they have been left the poorer for their gifts. Elegant national and municipal cultural centers rise steadily around the country, all of them designed as symbols of the dominant White culture that, at best, is deemed tangential to the rich racial heritage of Black Americans. Amphitheatres are built for great symphonic summer festival productions that dramatize episodes from the saga of American history, but no open-air symphonic dramas of the Afro-American story are heard in the land. Instead, Black-controlled theatres, struggling ever for survival, occupy cramped basements and draughty lofts where gifted artists lurk around restively as if the shadows of slavery still hovered over their heads. In the revolutionary '60s the cry was: Black Theatre—Go Home! It is time now for Black theatre to come out of the shadows.

Throughout this book, the terms *Negro, Afro-American,* and *Black American* are used synonymously to refer to Americans of African descent. The word *Negro,* to which some opprobrium has lately been attached, is used only where historically appropriate.

I wish to acknowledge with gratitude the help of Mary Gould of the Drama Department at Dartmouth College in typing portions of the mansucript.

This book, Volume I of a two-part series on the Theater of Black Americans, covers "Roots and Rituals: The Search for Identity" and "The Image Makers: Plays and Playwrights." Volume II deals with "The Presenters: Companies of Players" and "The Participators: Audiences and Critics."

Some African Influences
on the Afro-American Theatre

by James Hatch

Blk Love Song #1 by Kalamu Ya Salaam begins with a Black woman intoning "Where is the seed of Africa? Where are the first men who walked the earth? Have they vanished?" The chorus answers, "They are gone to America. They are gone to the New World."

In the American theatre, the African seeds took root. Some produced great vibrant blossoms, visible, self-conscious imports known as *Neo-Africanisms;* these are the deliberate and conscious attempts by Black Americans to use African themes and materials. Other seeds transmitted *Africanisms,* fruit as familiar to Americans as yams in the grocery store, and because they are common as the earth, they are less visible and therefore unacknowledged.

The distinction between *Africanisms* and *Neo-Africanisms* is in part an artificial discrimination to speed the discussion, and no invidious value is attached to either term to imply that one is more genuinely "African" than the other.

Neo-Africanisms in Afro-American Theatre

Every tide of liberation for Black America has thrown up waves of renewed interest in folk customs of African origins. The respon-

"Some African Influences on the Afro-American Theatre" (originally "Speak to Me in Those Old Words, You know, Those La-La Words, Those Tung-Tung Sounds") by James Hatch. From *Yale/Theatre,* Vol. 8, No. 1 (Fall 1976), pp. 25-34. Reprinted by permission of *Theatre* (formerly *Yale/Theatre*) and the author with slight emendation by the author.

sibility for resurrecting and dramatizing these customs and beliefs of "our ancestors" has fallen to the intelligentsia, to the artists, and to the public platform of the theatre.

The 19th century saw several militant movements that advocated emigration back to Africa, especially to Liberia or to the island of Haiti, which was regarded as a free "African" state because its slaves had successfully rebelled against the French. William Easton, an Afro-American, used the Haitian revolution for the subject of his play *Dessalines* (1893), a rhetorical drama that may have been performed at the Haitian pavilion at the Chicago World's Fair (World Columbian Exposition, 1893). In the first scene of the play, Dessalines challenges a mulatto by throwing a dagger at his feet and saying in part, "Thou claimst race with those who rule, and I, a full blood African, dare thee to mortal combat." Dessalines then strangles the mulatto and tells the other slaves a tale of when he "was wont to hunt the great king of the jungles, whose roar is like the distant thunder and whose bite is death."

Although this may not be the first conscious alliance with the motherland published in an Afro-American drama, it is among the earliest extant. It's worth noting, however, that the first professional Black company acting in America, the African Company (1820-1827) worked in a Manhattan theatre, the African Grove; here they performed for the Black community exclusively until a partition was made "at the back of their house for the accommodation of the whites."

At the end of the century as the ragtime musical emerged, the minstrel show declined in popularity. A Neo-African emphasis appeared in a number of shows: *Senegamian Carnival* (1898), *The Sultan of Zulu* (1900), and of course, the famous shows starring Williams and Walker—*In Dahomey* (1902) and *Abyssinia* (1908). *In Dahomey,* billed as a Negro Musical Comedy by J. A. Shipp, Paul L. Dunbar, *et al.,* with music by Will Marion Cook, is the story of an old Southern Negro, Lightfoot, who is president of the Dahomey Colonization Society. He hires two detectives (Williams and Walker) to find a missing treasure, and they all end up traveling to Dahomey with the colonists. After comic mix-ups in which the colonists are nearly executed by the King of Dahomey, they decide there's no place like home.

In addition to its topical interest, the theme of colonization expresses a romantic longing for homeland, and the resolution in the play may have been the one chosen in life: one cannot go home again. The music is composed of marches, cakewalks, and songs, two of which concern the beauty of the African woman—"My Dahomian Queen" and "Brownskin Baby Mine."

Among the popular show writers of the era were Bob Cole and Rosamund Johnson whose "Under the Bamboo Tree" and "The Congo Love Song" were hits. A verse from another effort of theirs, "My Castle on the Nile," expresses the Afro-American's dilemma:

> Dere ain't no use in try'n to rise up in de social scale,
> less you kin trace yo' name back to de flood. You
> got to have ancestral halls an' den you mu'nt fail.
> To prove dere's indigo mixed in you blood, I done
> found out dat I come down from ole chief
> Bungaboo. My great gran'daddy was his great
> gran'chile an' so I'm gwinter sail away across de
> waters blue to occupy my castle on de Nile.

It might be inferred that the writers, who were both sophisticated gentlemen, are expressing more than comedy. The performance of Bert Williams, who excelled in the role of the sad clown, evoked laughter; it may have been a laughter too deep for tears.

In the decade that followed, the single greatest tribute to Africa was organized and written by Dr. W. E. B. DuBois. *The Star of Ethiopia* (1913), a pageant, was presented to audiences of 30,000 at the Armory in New York City. The Egyptian Art Temple was constructed in the center of the floor, and around it were shown the paintings, sculpture, and other works of art executed by "colored peoples." The pageant itself used 350 actors in six episodes. The spectacle was such a success that it was performed in other cities, and was revived in Los Angeles as late as 1925. Du Bois wrote that he chose a pageant because "All through Africa, pageantry and dramatic recital are closely mingled with religious rites."

When the First Great War to Save Civilization and its vast migration of Black folk to the industrial North ended, the disappointment of that "freedom journey" sparked the summer riots of 1919. With the return of the segregated Black troops, Black nationalism surged again. W. E. B. DuBois held four Pan-African Congresses between 1919 and 1927. Marcus Garvey organized the Universal Negro Improvement Association with its hope of owning a homeland in Black Africa; Afro-American writers like Countee Cullen asked "What is Africa to me?"

This was a serious question for the artists of the Negro Renaissance. The Cult of Primitivism presented the Negro as "An uncorrupted remnant of preindustrial man," which laid the double bind (damned if you do, damned if you don't) of American racism at the Black artist's door. As exploited by white writers like Eugene O'Neill, Carl Van Vechten, and Ronald Firbank, the idea smacked of Tarzanism with its images of savagery, superstition, and illiteracy; in the sometimes uncertain hands of Black playwrights, the image was meant to be one of nobility, innocence, and ancestral wisdom, a creature unspoiled by European decadence. If Whitey said the Negro had rhythm, the Black perceived a pejorative intent; when the Afro-American artist claimed a superior élan for rhythm in his people, he was asserting a positive political shibboleth of racial identity with Africa. Professor Alain Locke sometimes supported this latter view by asserting his people had something special, an "almost naive reflection of poetry and folk feeling of a people who have, after all, a different soul and temperament from that smug unimaginative industrialist and self-righteous and inhibited Puritan."

Professor Locke proposed using "ancestral sources of African life and tradition. No one," he maintained, "with a sense of dramatic values will underestimate the rich resources of African material in these respects. Not through a literal transposing but in some adaptation of its folklore, art-idioms and symbols, African material seems likely to influence the art of drama. ..." Professor Locke may have had in mind two one-act plays, both produced at Howard University in the twenties — *The Death Dance* (1923) by Thelma Duncan and *Sadhji* (1927) by Richard Bruce. Both are tales of love and death in an African village, both use African names for their characters, and both center about a "Medicine Man" and a beautiful female dancer. Both use dance and drums as theatrical and dramatic spectacle. *The Death Dance* is subtitled "An African Play," *Sadhji* is described as "An African Ballet." In addition, the latter boasts a ballet score by Grant Still and a chanter who recited "actual proverbs of the Azande of the South-Central Congo." Example: "Those who pick berries in the same wood do not love each other." These two plays, to use Locke's phrase, are "adaptations of art-idioms and symbols"; they express an Africa researched more in imagination than in the village. The plays are dramatic parallels to the lyrical African figures drawn by Aaron Douglas who illustrated the printed texts.[1] They deliberately employ ethnic material in a positive assertion of cultural value to reveal the "beauty which prejudice had buried."

The double bind of racism with its double vision of the African as a noble/savage is apparent in the commercial theatre of the time; a good example is the show number "Mozambique" from *Blackbirds of 1930* written by Flournoy Miller, Eubie Blake, and Andy Razaf. "Mozambique" featured the song "Jungle Moon" and was set in a Rousseau-style jungle painted with a touch of Disney. Seventeen women in belly dance costume and tail feathers à la the Folies-Bergère rolled their bellies, eyes, and palms as they shook their blond Afro-wigs. These "jungle bunnies" were pure Broadway.

The decade of the thirties saw a serious number of non-commercial efforts employing African themes. Just earlier, in 1920, John Matheus and composer Clarence Cameron White wrote an opera on Dessalines, *Ouanga*. The Cleveland Opera series of 1932 produced the three act opera, *Tom Tom,* with music and libretto by Shirley Graham (Du Bois). She stated that her brother had brought the African situations and rhythms from Liberia.[2]

In 1935 Black playwrights Willis Richardson and May Miller published the book *Negro History in Thirteen Plays,* which contained several dramatizations of African history, heavily romanticized. The Federal Theatre Project used its Negro units to stage Orson Welles' Haitian *Macbeth.* The Italian invasion of Ethiopia inspired Theodore Ward to write *Falcon Of Adowa;* however, like white playwright Arthur Arent's stage documentary *Ethiopia,* Ward's play was never staged.

Perhaps the strongest boost to Neo-African theatre came when Asadata Dafora, a native of Sierre Leone, created a dance opera, *Kykunkor: Or Witch Woman* (1934), which employed authentic drums and dances. This much acclaimed New York production stimulated a continuing interest in African dance and theatre. In 1935 Katherine Dunham traveled to the Caribbean, and in 1948 Pearl Primus sailed to Monrovia; both brought back ethnic dances that were to appear in concert halls and Broadway shows over the

[1]Alain Locke and Montgomery Gregory, *Plays of Negro Life* (N.Y.: Harper and Brothers, 1927).

[2]Interview with Shirley Graham (DuBois), May, 1975. Hatch-Billops Collection, New York City.

next thirty years. Nonetheless, for some the double vision of Africa remained. Loften Mitchell reports that a revival of *The Emperor Jones* in Harlem with Jules Bledsoe running through the stage bush was greeted by the audience with some derision, "Man, you come on outa that jungle. This is Harlem."[3]

With few exceptions the African heritage on the American stage in the thirties and forties was embodied in the musical, not only because music and dance were an intrinsic part of African culture, but because the musical, opera, and dance-drama were forms that lent themselves to romantic feelings about un-particularized African characters. In 1959 Lorraine Hansberry took a giant step toward creating a particularized African.

Joseph Asagai, from Nigeria, walked into the Younger family's flat in Chicago, bringing the African into serious drama. Somewhat self-consciously and with an acute historical perspective, he asked Beneatha Younger to go "home" with him.

> *Asagai.* Yes...three hundred years later the African Prince rose up out of the seas and swept the maiden back across the middle passage over which her ancestors had come.
> *Beneatha.* Nigeria?
> *Asagai.* Nigeria. Home. I will show you our mountains and our stars, and give you cool drinks from gourds, and teach you the old songs and ways of our people.

The forest prince, a Nigerian intellectual, had come to awaken the urban princess from a sleep of 300 years. Eleven years later, Ms. Hansberry's *Les Blancs* placed Tshembe Matoseh on stage. This African leader, a product of missionary humanism, must seize independence for his own nation by tossing Shakespeare into the River Niger and by killing Whitey. In his agony, he kills his own revolutionary brother, but for no purpose. History sweeps past him. The Afro-American stage has kept its double bind with a new double vision. The more Ms. Hansberry succeeded in particularizing the African, the more perfectly he spoke the King's English; the more she dispelled romanticism, the more the kinship of the American Express Card superseded ethnic ties.

As the African nations achieved independence and U.N. membership in the sixties, an ever-growing number of Afro-Americans made their "hajj" to the homeland, first to North Africa, to Egypt;

[3]Loften Mitchell, *Black Drama* (N.Y.: Hawthorn Books, 1967).

later to Nkrumah's Ghana, where the patriarch of Pan-Africa, W. E. B. DuBois, spent his last years assembling the *Encyclopedia Africana.* The result: By the end of the decade, more Afro-American artists had had firsthand experience with nationhood than ever before. Upon returning to the U.S. they found others hungry for knowledge of their roots. Many dropped their "slave" names, Imamu Amiri Baraka (LeRoi Jones) the most in evidence among them. His Black Arts Movement in Harlem (1965) set in motion a Black theatre revival that was to develop a strong mythic and ritual wing based in African religious and secular life. Contemporaneous with Imamu's chants, rituals, and neo-myths performed at Spirit House in New/Ark, New Jersey,[4] were the manifestoes and productions of rituals at the New Lafayette Theatre (NLT) in Harlem (1967-1972).

NLT's director, Robert Macbeth, announced in *Black Theatre Magazine #3* his intention to visit Africa for three months and "study with the Brothers. I think at that point we can really begin to learn some things about the ritual." Marvin X told Macbeth, "I'm just wondering if the new rituals aren't over here."

MACBETH: They are, they are. See, wherever the rituals come from, more of their vibrations still exist there. Now all I'm interested in is to become more in tune with the vibrations of the rituals. ... I'm afraid to do the rituals—it's a difficult environment to do the rituals in, so I need strength, I need some more support in doing the rituals. So, to be able to say, yes, I saw the Brothers doing them...it reassures me of the value of the rituals, and allows me to know that as we perform them they will be true, they will be real, as they should be. It's again a step away from any other kind of theatre that we would know about. You see the difficulty even now as we talk about them, is that I'm certain you understand what I'm saying, but I'm sure that nobody else would have the faintest notion of what we're talking about.

In its 1969-70 season the NLT created three major rituals, *Ritual To Bind Together and Strengthen Black People So That They Can Survive the Long Struggle That Is To Come* (August-Sept. 1969); *To Raise the Dead and Foretell the Future* (March-April 1970); *A Black Time for Black Folk; A Play Without Words* (August-Octo-

---

[4]Woodie King in 1972 produced a record with Motown entitled *It's Nation Time.* On this disc the Spirit House Movers and other groups can be heard in Baraka's ritual chants.

ber 1970). Richard Wesley, then an administrator of the theatre, issued a statement in 1971 that described them: "music, art, drama, and dance are all combined in a totality"; the distinction between audience and performer is destroyed; space and time are available for improvisation and personal exploration in the event; the theatre group, in and out of performance, lives a tribal collective life; the group is an "organic part of Harlem, the African Nation in the West!"[5]

Except for the last statement, one of non-European identity, the manifesto is similar to those conceived by Richard Schechner at that time. Whether the NLT rituals were truly African in form and/ or content need not be discussed here, but the conscious intent of the group to employ ancestral ceremony for *efficacious* purpose rather than for entertainment is relevant. Schechner's incisive distinction between ritual and theatre is pertinent.[6]

Although NLT blended some ritual qualities with theatre, the ritual raised the Black consciousness and created spiritual and psychic energy. A note in the fourteen page ritual *To Raise the Dead and Foretell the Future* warns the participant:

> Do not conjure this spirit unless you feel pure and righteous, for it is told that when this deity is summoned it never returns where it comes from without a soul, and if the caller is not righteous in the way of his people then his dearest loved one will be taken back to the land of the dead to return never again.

The participant-audience varied in reaction from "Y'all got to

[5]"The New Lafayette Theatre." Mimeograph paper.

[6]*Efficacy*	*Entertainment*
(Ritual)	(Theatre)
results	fun
link to an absent Other	only for those here
abolishes time, symbolic time	emphasizes now
brings Other here	audience is the Other
performer possessed	performer knows what he's doing
audience participates	audience watches
audience believes	audience appreciates
criticism is forbidden	criticism is encouraged
collective creativity	individual creativity

Richard Schechner, "From Ritual to Theatre and Back: The Structure/Process of the Efficacy-Entertainment Dyad," *Educational Theatre Journal* (December 1974).

be kiddin','" and "Hey man! What's this here? I came to see a play, Man!" to Larry Neal's comment that the spirits and ancestral ties of Blacks could be raised, but "not by using vague pseudo-African rituals rather than rituals created by their mothers and fathers."·

It was this last concept, that of using the Afro-American styles that had evolved from the African over the last three centuries, that Barbara Ann Teer has sought to develop in her National Black Theatre (NBT), founded in 1968. Any facile summary of her theories is unfair. However, one point can be made here. Ms. Teer has traveled to Nigeria and has worked with a number of Africans in her theatre on 125th Street, not to impose Yoruba rituals on Black Americans, but rather to develop eclectic forms based on close examination of Black life in America with its intuitive and acquired rhythms and rituals of the street, church, bar, school, and family. All offer form, content, and style that can be used to raise the consciousness of Afro-Americans as to who they are, and who they can be. "Our institution is not really a theatre; it's an institution of re-education, a temple of liberation; we're a family organization, and we happen to use theatre as a vehicle to perform, to teach, to educate."[7] The thrust, then, is not to superimpose Africanisms on Afro-Americans, but to discover these Africanisms in the group and in the self.

This concept is similar, as we shall see, to Paul Carter Harrison's "African Sensibilities in an African Continuum"; the major difference is that Mr. Harrison uses a prepared text, a play script much closer to "theatre" than does Ms. Teer. However, both agree that the Black American of the seventies has in him a spirit passed on not by his environment alone, but by blood and bone from his ancestors. This idea can be seen in Joseph Walker's *The River Niger* (1972). The poem the father writes in praise of the river Niger is a self-conscious Neo-Africanism; the rituals that he and his family live by contain African Sensibilities.

Africanisms in the Afro-American Theatre

Orlando Patterson has identified three main currents in the writing of Black history: catastrophism, contributionism, and

[7]Interview with Barbara Ann Teer, January 3, 1973. Hatch-Billops Collection, New York City.

survivalism. The first current is composed of historians who deny that any significant African culture survived the infamous Middle Passage of slavery. The second group of writers concentrate upon the contributions of. Black scientists, inventors, and artists to the American mainstream. The third, the survivalists, maintain that a considerable number of cultural, spiritual, and material artifacts did survive and that these have had extensive influence upon American life. Black historians like J. A. Rogers, John Hope Franklin, and John Henrik Clarke have had a continuing battle with uninformed and Anglocentric writers who stripped the Afro-American of his accomplishments. Typical of this racist denial of African contribution is George Pullen Jackson's elaborate study of white and Negro spirituals. He concludes,

> I do not deny the possibility that there are, in American negro religious folk songs, certain hangovers. I would merely state that I haven't found any yet, nor do I know of any other who has found any. I have found what seems to be an American negro racial emphasis, nothing more. Others may in the future be more successful because more intent on finding the Ethiopian in the song-fuel heap.[8]

One such man "more intent" was LeRoi Jones, whose book *Blues People* traces the African influence in American music. Although racists were able to deny Africa's influence in the arts in America, it was more difficult to deny it in South America and the Caribbean. (The Cuban ritual drama *Shango De Ima* contains the Yoruba pantheon with many Yoruba words and chants. This play has been in repertory at the Afro-American studio in Harlem.) Because of the work of cultural anthropologists like Herskovitz, Jahn, Thompson, Turner, and others, there is hard evidence in the arts that African culture, though greatly modified, has not only survived but flourished. How it has been transmitted and transmuted is still debated. Those who argue that it is learned have until recently held an edge over those who assert that cultural memory can be inherited.

An example of artifacts passed on can be found in a script by William Wells Brown, an escaped slave who wrote a play, *The Escape: Or, A Leap for Freedom* (1858), in which he presented some aspects of plantation life including a slave wedding in which the mistress of the house marries the slave couple by having them "jump the

---

[8]George Pullen Jackson, *White and Negro Spirituals* (Locust Valley, N.Y.: J. J. Augustin, Publisher, 1943).

broomstick," a custom common in slave days. Mrs. Gaines, the mistress, says:

> Now, Dolly, you and Susan get the broom, and get out in the middle of the room. There, hold it a little lower—a little higher; there, that'll do. Now, remember that this is a solemn occasion; you are going to jump into matrimony. Now, Cato, take hold of Hannah's hand. There now, why couldn't you let Cato take hold of your hand before? Now get ready, and when I count three, do you jump. Eyes on the *broomstick!* All ready. One, two, three, and over you go. There, now you're husband and wife, and if you don't live happy together, it's your own fault.

Dolly, the house servant who held the stick, then comments after her mistress has left the room, "When I get married, I is gwine to have a preacher to marry me. I ain't a-gwine to jump de broomstick. Dat will do for fiel' hands, but house servants ought to be 'bove that."

What once seemed to be a slave owner's depreciation of Black marriage may be the remnant of an African ceremony. A late 18th-century watercolor, "On the Plantation," pictures a slave entertainment that may be a wedding in which not only the broomstick appears but a stringed instrument identified as the *molo,* and a drum called *gudu gugu,* as well as the Yoruba head ties worn by the women.[9] An examination of the stick in the painting suggests that it is not a broomstick but a "conjur stick," a ceremonial cane whose power is symbolic and actual, a simple version of the juju cane that Paul Carter Harrison places in his play *The Great MacDaddy* (1974):

> a heavy wooden cane bedecked like a fetish and shaped like an elephant's head at the top. It has the appearance of a carved tree branch. The object is a cane inherited from his father; MacDaddy's juju stick. He moves down to hold up the juju cane for inspection of its power. Confident, his attitude locked into place, he now looks out into the audience as if confronting the dangers in the world lurking behind their eyes.

At the play's climax, the Great MacDaddy invokes the power that resides in the stick, the power of African sensibility, and exorcises Scag and bad times; he then invokes a communal celebration with

[9]Judith Wragg Chase, *Afro-American Art and Craft* (N.Y.: Van Nostrand Reinhold Company, 1971).

the audience that is a revitalization through music, song, drum, and dance. "We gonna rise up this mornin'/We gonna stay up all day," to reconstruct a harmonious balance for the American Black man with his universe. The playwright states, "The intention of the ritual, then, is to identify rather than simulate African sensibilities."[10]

Although this use of the juju stick is a conscious Neo-Africanism, the author suggests that there is a larger sensibility, an innate Black aesthetic. He has set forth these theories in two books, *Nommo* and *Kuntu Drama,* an anthology, in which he advocates the Continuum of African Sensibilities based in part on racial memory. His premises are taken from Jahn's *Muntu,* an anthropological study that posits that the world (cosmic) view of the Bantu peoples is one held generally by Africans south of the Sahara. This philosophy perceives that everything is everything; that is, the universe is not a series of dichotomies of good/bad or spirit/material but is a vast intricate harmony of man, nature, cosmos, God—each having some element of spiritual as well as material being; and man, because he has consciousness and the invocative power of the spoken word, is responsible for maintaining the balance between man and nature. If this balance be violated through stupidity, greed, or folly, man must expect to suffer. In the proverb of the Yoruba, "He who shits on the road will meet flies on his return." The song of the babalawos, fathers of the secrets, tells us,

> Enjoy the world gently
> if the world is spoilt
> No one can repair it
> Enjoy the world gently.[11]

If the Black world of America be spoilt, the theatre event of the African Continuum can at least engage "the body/spirit, thereby testifying to our continuation as an African people on this continent." Mr. Harrison asserts that his theatre will find a response in the racial memory of Afro-Americans, through the Neo-African structure they have constructed to preserve this life view: the Black

[10]For a discussion of the Nigerian diviner staff in the Western Hemisphere, see Robert Farris Thompson's essay "An Introduction to Transatlantic Black Art History: Remarks in Anticipation of a Coming Golden Age of Afro-Americana."

[11]Bakare Gbadamosi and Ulli Beier, *Not Even God Is Ripe Enough* (London: Heinemann Educational Books, Ltd., 1968).

church, the social rituals of story-telling in beauty parlors and bars, the language and gestures of Black people wherever they gather away from "profane eyes."

In a more specific case, Robert Farris Thompson has identified what he calls the "aesthetic of the cool" as a subsaharan characteristic that has not only survived in Afro-Americans but which in turn has helped them to survive.

> In a strict West African sense...mystic coolness is an ancient charter for entire black civilizations passing through fire and passing through heat (African wars, slavery, imperialism, colonialism, racism, hate) to affirmation and self-determination.

He insists that he is not speaking of the western *sang-froid* of Cool-Hand-Luke, the existential loner who challenges the mountain because "it is there." Rather the Black master of cool

> shares his heroism by leaving his performance where possible with humor and other invitations to audience participation, even in the process of being challenged. He more than keeps his head; he has the presence of mind to direct both audience and enemy in a crisis situation.[12]

(Consider the public performances of Muhammad Ali!)

If an aesthetic may be defined as a dialectic of production and appreciation,[13] there is a Black style, a Black sensibility, and it is one that has now been traced directly to African philosophy and social behavior.

How then is this aesthetic manifested in behavior? The cultural anthropologists give us clues. Examples: (1) Subsahara Africans impregnate the universe, animate and inanimate, with a life force that can metamorphose, under proper conditions, from form to form or from material to spiritual and back again. (2) Words and the art of using them are a special power that can summon and control spirit. (3) Africans often treat a part of the body or personality as if it had a separate existence of its own. (4) They are given to "projecting" human behavior onto animals and insects, etc., and then laughing at that behavior. (5) Afro-American behavior acknowledges a sense of community that manifests itself by assuming

---

[12]For a discussion of the concept of cool, see Robert Farris Thompson's "Aesthetic of the Cool," *African Arts* VII, 1 (Autumn).

[13]This definition is from Prof. Dan Rose of Temple University.

familiarity and complicity with anyone of their color. There are more. The question now is how these characteristics are distinct from, say, Irish-American or Chinese-American ones? The answer: the mode. For clearly there is an Afro-American life style (which is not to say all Africans or Afro-Americans behave in the same way!); however, parts of the African continuum can be identified in many Afro-American plays.

In addition to those compiled by Mr. Harrison in his anthology, others come to mind. In Jean Toomer's *Balo* (1924), a lyric one act, a sensitive young man finds the spirit amid the social quiet of his neighbors and family; in *Funnyhouse of a Negro* (1964), and nearly all of Adrienne Kennedy's plays, the characters metamorphose from identity to identity and even objects change form; in *Divine Comedy* (1938) by Owen Dodson, church, leader, chorus, and response; the rap (urban version of the southern sermon) is found in *No Place To Be Somebody* (1969) by Charles Gordone; in *Run Little Chillun* (1933) by Hall Johnson, the uses of music and church ritual; in *Natural Man* (1937) by Theodore Browne, its collective energy of song and spirit versus the steam machine; and finally, the plays of Langston Hughes, particularly *Mule Bone* (1930), which he wrote in collaboration with Zora Neale Hurston, contain African elements. This play, set in the street and on the porch of a general store in a tiny Black Southern town, is a treasury of folklore, filled with proverbs, riddles, dance, song, story-telling, call-response, children's games, and a language rich in imagery and polyrhythms. ("I wouldn't give a poor consumptive crippled crab a crutch to cross the River Jurdon [sic] ." Or, in response to a woman walking past, a man says, "Mama throw it in the river, papa come get it!"[14]) The "it" is more than the woman's undulating ass; "it" is the quintessence of femaleness that the man *detaches* from the person of the woman. The "it" has a life of its own in much the same way a Black person who commits a *faux pas* might say, "I'm goin' outside and have a talk with my mouth." This form of detachment is a quite different mode from the sophism that Euripides put into Hippolytus's mouth: "It was my tongue that swore the oath, not I."[15]

[14]Langston Hughes and Zora Neale Hurston, *Mule Bone* (Typescript: Hatch-Billops Collection).

[15]Dan Rose, "Detachment: Continuities of Sensibility Among Afro-American Populations of the Circum-Atlantic Fringe." In *Discovering Afro-America*, Roger D. Abrahams and John F. Szwed, eds., (Leiden, Holland: E. J. Brill, 1975).

All of the plays mentioned above share the African Continuum of Sensibilities not only in content, but in form and style. They are: (1) by nature anti-well-made plays, assuming the Scribe-Sardou-Ibsen formula to be a special European characteristic. The "plots" of the Afro-American plays "meander" in circuitous association, returning at key moments to the center (altar) of the action. The stories are much like the courtship of a male pigeon: he circles the female, doubles back, walks away, plumes himself, pecks at the earth, struts back, circles her again, all the while burbling, cooing, clucking various songs in a slowly developed dance, which for all its apparent diversion still has but one purpose to be fulfilled when the female is ready. (2) This style of writing is quite different from the straight line, build-to-a-crisis at the end of the scene, Western formula, which is complementary to the capitalist mode: Time is money; ergo, jump it, fuck it, and get back to the office! In fact, these two conflicting life styles and life views are presented by Alice Childress in her beautiful play *Wine in the Wilderness* (1969) in which a hustling Black artist has to relearn what the spirit of African Continuum is.

The concept of African sensibilities is a large and complex set of ideas, which, at its extreme edges, allows room for fuzziness of criticism and for political chauvinisms; however, its central thesis demands the re-evaluation of American and Afro-American theatre history. For example, minstrelsy, which important theatre historians like Richard Moody claim is America's first and most original contribution to world theatre, now reexamined by Amiri Baraka, Eileen Southern, and others, can be seen as an African creation that Daddy Rice, Dan Emmett, and thousands of other white men ripped off. The beautiful wrist-articulated hands of an African dancing the *Adowa,* a festive dance of Ghana, immediately suggest that if a pair of white gloves were placed on them, we would see the classic minstrel gesture. Or again, the shuffle, which has been so denigrated as a sign of subservience, is an African step commonly used in the New World when slave masters suppressed dancing, which they defined as one foot crossing in front of or behind the other. The "ring-shout," a common element of African dance, can be seen as the "walk around" of the minstrel show.

It is often said, and never really documented, that the best plays of Ed Bullins are structured like jazz, with theme line and space for improvisation; certainly their productions at the New Lafayette Theatre in Harlem emphasized this characteristic as each play was

allowed to take its own time and run for over three or more un-
interrupted hours. The claim that Afro-Americans have developed
their stories like their music (in an African manner), is a claim that
in the mouth of a Western-oriented critic is still a damning cliché.
That an Afro-American play is "loose" doesn't make it a genuine
African theatre piece, but it does suggest that it be judged by other
standards than those of European sensibility alone. The last decade
of theatre reviews from LeRoi Jones' *Toilet* to the Black production
of *The Wiz* is strewn with white misjudgments based on ignorance
of Black aesthetics. The pleas for Black reviewers has more merit
than providing work for a few intellectuals; nor is the cry one of
mere chauvinism: Black critics are often more severe on their
brothers and sisters than white critics. The need is for what lies
beneath the skin—an African sensibility.

The particular manifestation of these sensibilities in drama may
often appear to be identical or congruent with that of other cultures.
For example, other ethnic groups have proverbs or leader-chorus
responses, but the philosophical intent as well as the mode and feeling of performance may be quite distinct. Hence the need for Black
directors, actors, designers, and even theatre architects.

In this decade there are influences at work whose results we cannot yet know. Since 1972, at least three books on African theatre
have appeared in English. Anthony Graham-White reports that 148
African plays are available to English readers, not including works
of white Africans like Athol Fugard whose recent and successful
plays *Sizwe Banzi Is Dead* and *The Island* were developed with
two South African actors—John Kani and Winston Ntshona. Among
Black African playwrights Wole Soyinka's plays (*Kongi's Harvest,
A Dance of the Forests,* etc.) have been the most widely produced
in this country. A variety of authentic African musicians and dance
troupes have toured here. Finally, those Black African scholars who
a generation ago attended British and French universities are now
in residence here. What all this imports may be glimpsed in an
annotated bibliography of Afro-American plays listing nearly 100
of the more recent scripts with African titles, characters, or stories.[16]

For the last 150 years Afro-American theatre has been drawing its
energies from both sides of the hyphen, sometimes consciously,
sometimes intuitively. As acquaintance with things African grows,

[16]James V. Hatch and Omanii Abdullah, *Black Playwrights, 1823-1977: An
Annotated Bibliography of Plays* (N.Y.: R. R. Bowker, 1977).

as the essential and difficult work of tracing Africanisms in American culture continues, we will come to know how really vast and invisible the African influence on all American theatre has been. The ancient juices have mingled with the new. The next few years may be vintage ones for the Afro-American theatre. In the words from Camille Billops' picture poem, "Go well, world, you Mama and Papa La-la."[17]

---

[17]The [original] title of this article and the concluding words are taken from a picture-poem by Afro-American artist Camille Billops.

Notes on Ritual
in the New Black Theater

by Shelby Steele

The New Black Theater, which I will define as that theater initiated by Imamu Amiri Baraka and dedicated to a Black nationalistic perspective, represents a very severe break from contemporary American drama. Beyond the very obvious differences in material, perspective and emphasis, there are even more fundamental and far-reaching differences that reflect two conceptions of the nature of art which are as antithetical as the colors black and white. Moreover, these differences seem so culture-bound as to make an eventual coming together increasingly unlikely.

One of the most salient characteristics of the New Black Theater that maintains its separation from mainstream American drama is its ritualistic aspect. By ritualistic, I mean the strong presence of *symbols, characterizations, themes* and *language styles* which are frequently repeated from play to play and over a period of time, with the result that easily recognized patterns are established which have the function of reaffirming the values and particular commitment of the audience for whom the plays are written. The term *ritual* is used here in the modern sense, which is looser than the traditional religious view of ritual as a rigidly prescribed unvarying pattern of spiritual observance. As one writer says in reference to the Blues, "We are dealing here with substitute rituals."[1] From the breakdown in our society of the traditional religious rituals

"Notes on Ritual in the New Black Theater" by Shelby Steele. From *Black World,* Vol. XXII, No. 8 (June 1973), pp. 4-13, 78-84. Copyright © June 1973 by *Black World.* Reprinted by permission of Johnson Publishing Company and Dr. Shelby Steele.

[1]M. G. Cooke, *Modern Black Novelists* (Englewood Cliffs, N.J.: Prentice-Hall, 1971), p. 50.

(especially for younger Blacks), other more secular rituals have emerged.

Several contemporary Black dramatists have openly embraced the idea of ritual in modern Black drama, and many have advertised certain of their plays as ritualistic drama. Ed Bullins calls his play, *Bees Dat Way,* a "ritual," and Kalamu ya Salaam's play, *The Destruction of the American Stage,* was published under the label, "A Black Ritual."[2] Many of Imamu Baraka's plays, in both title and content, strongly suggest ritual as a controlling concept. His play, *Madhearts,* is subtitled "A Morality Play," while another is simply titled *Bloodrite.* Larry Neal, one of the first to discuss ritual in the New Black Theater, says in his well-known essay, "The Black Arts Movement," in reference to an important Baraka play, "*Slave Ship*'s energy is, at base, ritualistic."[3] Later, he refers to the same play as: "...ritualized history. That is, history that allows emotional and religious participation on the part of the audience. And, like all good ritual, its purpose is to make the audience stronger, more sensitive to the historical realities that have shaped our lives and the lives of our ancestors."[4] Ron Milner's essay "Black Theater—Go Home!" is probably the most explicit in this regard. He defines the New Black Theater itself as, "...the ritualized reflection and projection of a unique and particular way of being, born of the unique and particular conditioning of Black people. ..."[5] As a means of presenting the Black experience through a nationalistic perspective, ritual has emerged as a predominant force, both in the thinking of several Black playwrights and in the nationalistic theater they have created.

This ritualistic aspect points to a conception of art that is fundamentally opposed to the Western concept of "art for art's sake." In this view, art must be functional; it must serve an end beyond itself. Functional art becomes a means to an end rather than an end in itself. The artifact is inspired by and created for a particular purpose which exists outside the artifact. In many African societies, for example, where art was cultivated only in a functional sense, the mask or statue makers created works of art for use in religious

[2]*Black World* (April, 1972), p. 3.
[3]Addison Gayle, Jr., *The Black Aesthetic* (Garden City, New York: Doubleday & Company, Inc., 1971), p. 269.
[4]*Ibid.*
[5]Gayle, *The Black Aesthetic,* p. 288.

ceremonies or as objects through which one could communicate with the spiritual world. When these artifacts were not being used to fulfill the function for which they were created, they were thought of as little more than worthless pieces of wood.[6] There was no separation between the artifact and its function.

The conception of art which the playwrights of the New Black Theater have relied upon is not far removed from this view. "Art for art's sake: is incest!" says Ron Milner, "...Black people desperately need a healthy natural art form: art coming from an intercourse with life!"[7] As this statement suggests, the central problem faced by the Black dramatist was that he was dealing with an art form around which his own culture had developed very few traditions. Unlike Black-American music (Blues, spirituals and jazz), which is wholly a creation of Afro-American culture and an integral part of its most important traditions, Black drama has had to take the dramatic form and reshape it to meet the peculiar needs of the Black community. The position that drama should serve a specific function beyond itself represents a first step in this reshaping process.

With the matter of functionality resolved, the next question is simply what function Black drama should serve. By the Black nationalist playwrights, with whom this article deals exclusively, this question has been answered in the political and social terms of Black nationalism. "Black art is the aesthetic and spiritual sister of the Black power concept," according to Larry Neal. "Both concepts are nationalistic."[8] In this respect, the function of the New Black Theater is the development of a revolutionary and nationalistic consciousness, the creation of a Black frame of mind which ultimately redefines the world in the self-interest of Black people. Ron Karenga expresses this function with penultimate directness, "Black art must expose the enemy, praise the people, and support the revolution."[9]

With this wedding of Black art and Black power where, as Neal says, "...your ethics and your aesthetics are one," the function of the nationalist playwright himself also becomes quite clear.[10] Un-

[6]Janheinz Jahn, *Muntu* (New York: Grove Press, 1961), p. 157.

[7]Gayle, *The Black Aesthetic*, p. 293.

[8]Gayle, *The Black Aesthetic*, p. 257.

[9]Abraham Chapman, *New Black Voices* (New York: Mentor New American Library, 1972), p. 478.

[10]Gayle, *The Black Aesthetic*, p. 260.

like the traditional Western artist, many of the parameters of his literary involvement are already defined for him. His own vision must be exercised within those parameters.

With the function of the New Black Theater essentially determined, the matter of how that function is achieved becomes increasingly important. In religious ceremonies, where the imperative of reaffirming a particular system of values is roughly the same, the use of ritual has been traditional. However, in these ceremonies, there has been little or no concern for drama *per se,* so that religious rituals can remain the same each time they are performed. The ritual of communion in the Catholic church is an example. But, in drama, there must be some variance from performance to performance or else the element of suspense is lost and there is no drama. The New Black Theater has gotten around this dilemma by dramatizing the values it seeks to reaffirm from play to play rather that using a single play (ceremony) repeatedly. Suspense and drama are maintained through variations on themes, so that the message is the same but the form through which it is communicated varies from play to play. Although no single play may include a comprehensive statement of all the values, certain patterns emerge over time and from play to play which do accomplish such a statement. Ritual in the New Black Theater is achieved through the repetition of patterns, symbols and values from drama to drama rather than the traditional religious method of repeating a single ceremony until it becomes ritual.

Six important literary devices which have been used to achieve ritual in the New Black Theater are: *allegory, symbol, characterization, recurring themes, language styles,* and *repetition.* (In the case of allegory, symbol, and characterization, there is some natural overlapping so that the terms are often interchangeable in the context of a given play.) Again, it is important to emphasize that all these devices do not appear in every play from the New Black Theater, but rather from play to play.[11]

It is difficult to find in this theater a play which could be called

---

[11]The plays that will be discussed in this section are, in some cases, the lesser known plays of the authors mentioned. This is because many of their better known plays have been thoroughly discussed in several other places and because the lesser known works have often been avoided precisely because of their ritualistic structure. Also, I will try to refrain from long listings of relevant plays and would refer the reader instead to the *Black Drama Anthology,* edited by Woodie King and Ron Milner (New York: Signet New American Library, Inc., 1972).

an allegory in the strict sense; however, there are several that could be termed allegorical. Imamu Baraka's play, *Great Goodness of Life (A Coon Show)*, is an example. Reminiscent of Kafka's *The Trial*, a middle-aged postal employee (bureaucrat) named Court Royal is arrested and charged by an anonymous voice (omnipotent Whiteman) which never reveals itself. The characters, some visible and some not, all represent something beyond their surface roles. Court's lawyer, for example, appears on stage with wires attached to his back and a huge wind-up key stuck in the side of his head. He babbles, slobbers, and grins as he recommends in exaggerated sheepishness that Court simply plead guilty and accept his fate without resistance. He is the overdrawn mimicked symbol of the Uncle Tom who stands ready to sell Court down the river at the mere suggestion of the anonymous White Voice. On the surface, he is a lawyer, but there is a second and more important meaning to be read beneath and concurrent with the surface story. This second meaning is made obvious to the audience through the use of blatant symbols like the wind-up key in the side of the lawyer's head, which tells us immediately that he is really the Uncle Tom of the story.

As the lawyer exits, another character variously named Young Voice, Young Boy, and Young Man enters. He is strong, young, and Black, and speaks tough and cryptically. He wears only Black. He, like the lawyer, demands that Court plead guilty, but for entirely different reasons. To Young Voice, Court is a "guilty, stupid nigger" because he has worked hard all his life and caused no trouble. Young Voice, who is obviously the play's militant antagonist, is also a captive of the unseen White Voice. In the end, Court is asked by that voice to shoot Young Voice in a blood rite that will set him free and turn his soul "white as snow." After only a brief hesitation, he shoots Young Voice, who dies, but not before saying in his last breath that Court is his "Papa." Court is stunned for a second, but quickly recovers, singing that his soul is "white as snow."

On the surface, we have the story of a weak man who kills his own son rather than resist the pressures of an evil power. In the second and concurrent meaning, we have a middle-aged Black, a representative of an older generation, who is so intimidated and filled with fear of the white man that he is unable to stand up for the life of his own son. Filicide, an unthinkable sin, becomes preferable to resisting the omnipotent white man. Through allegory, the play achieves the suspense of drama as well as the implicit communication of a nationalistic value system.

Allegory lends itself to ritual by giving concrete form to such intangible things as political stances, ideas, degrees of militancy, races (*i.e.,* an intangible conception of a race), countries, *etc.* When these things are made concrete, they become convenient symbols that can be repeated again and again. The capacity of allegory to concretize and regularize the dramatic world of a play into commonly recognized symbols and patterns makes it the natural partner of ritual.

The symbols in the New Black Theater are usually presented in the form of characterizations. These characterizations are repeated from play to play so that they become almost immediately recognizable. An example is the frequently seen white woman, who is fundamentally evil, and who taunts the Black male with her perverse sexuality. She often symbolizes the relationship of America to the Black man. In Ed Bullins' play *The Gentleman Caller,* this figure is a central character. Her name is symbolically Mrs. Mann, and we first hear her offstage "warbling 'America.'" On stage, she is dressed typically in only a thin dressing gown, which she opens in the Black gentleman caller's face in an effort to reduce him to the sex object of race mythology. Always with sexual overtones, she manages to utter every racial slur and epithet imaginable. She is the temptress, but it is understood that if the Black male consummates the relationship she teases him with, he will be compromised, violated, and lost to his people forever. She is a figure that must be either spurned or raped by the militant Black male; no middle ground is possible.

In this symbolic characterization, the white woman is always seen as the "Ultrafeminines" of Eldridge Cleaver's *Soul on Ice.* Mrs. Mann is dressed in frills and draped in blond locks that mark her as frivolous and superficial, innocent, yet unknowingly capable of causing great destruction—the vain Southern belle who undresses in front of the stable boy and then tells her "Daddy" that he peeked. She is a woman-child, playing a game with the Black male in which her position affords her the privilege of never losing. Lula in Baraka's *Dutchman* is at first only a self-indulgent and pretentious "poetess," who toys with Clay for nothing more than sport. Guessing at his name, she says in the style of the New York dilettante, "Lloyd Norman? One of those hopeless colored names creeping out of New

Jersey." As the play moves to its climax, Clay, at Lula's hateful prodding ("...you're just a dirty White man."), loses his defensive innocence in a deadly rage, revealing a deep race consciousness and impassioned sense of self. But it is too late. She stabs him, as Clayton Riley says, "When her provocation has brought out of him that essential part of his being Lula (America) knows must be destroyed."[12]

There are a great number of other characterizations that serve as symbols in the New Black Theater. There is the white male, for example, who is often seen as homosexual or "faggish." In *The Gentleman Caller,* Mr. Mann is "made up much like Mrs. Mann, except that he has on shorts that are cut from the American flag." In *The Toilet,* by Baraka, the White boy, Karolis, writes a love note to Foots, a Black youth, that results in his being beaten in the high school toilet by Foot's cruel friends.

There is also the Black youth who is strong, noble, and relentless in his pursuit of revolutionary goals. The hero in Herbert Stokes' *The Man Who Trusted the Devil Twice* is a high school student who leads a revolt against the school's principal, who is also his father, and an irredeemable Uncle Tom, who trusted the devil (White man) twice. The play, *Growing into Blackness,* by the young woman playwright Salimu, offers the female version of this characterization. A young Black girl is asked by her mother to get rid of her Afro or leave the home. After considerable inner struggle, she leaves home to live with a group of revolutionaries in a gesture of revolutionary solidarity.

The symbolic characterizations themselves are often established by the use of other symbols. The Uncle Tom, as in *Great Goodness of Life (A Coon Show),* usually wears a suit and a tie to represent his identification with the White man's system, while the revolutionary youths wear dashikis, Afros, and black clothes. White characters, as in *The Gentleman Caller,* may be dressed in the American flag or played by Black actors in white-face. If music is involved in the production, often it is of the Archie Shepp type, which has come to represent a revolutionary trend in Black music. Finally, the names by which characters are called, as in mixed or explained allegory, are often open statements of what the character represents. A humorous example is seen in Ben Caldwell's play, *The Family Portrait,* which has three characters, named Farthest From the Truth

[12]Ben Caldwell, Ron Milner, Ed Bullins and LeRoi Jones, *A Black Quartet* (New York: Signet New American Library, 1970), p. xiii.

(father), Nowhere Near the Truth (mother), and Sunshine on the Truth (son). In Marvin X's play, *Take Care of Business,* only the heroes have proper names. The White character is called only "Devil." This is a common technique and has the effect of dehumanizing the "bad guys" so they become nothing more than what they symbolize.

Beyond allegory, symbol, and characterization, the writers of the New Black Theater use other techniques which have the effect of regularizing and ritualizing their drama. One very important one is the use of recurring themes. The conflict between generations, which sometimes goes to the point of patricide and matricide, as in Jimmy Garrett's play, *We Own the Night,* is one such theme. The conflict almost always arises from the parents' inability to understand the newfound militancy of the son or daughter. In this play, Johnny, the leader of a group of young men in the midst of an actual rebellion, shoots his mother dead when it becomes apparent that she is too ingrained in the white man's ways to adapt to the new order for which he is fighting. "We're...new men, Mama... Not niggers. Black men," he shouts at her, and then fires the gun.

The student leader in the Herbert Stokes play mentioned above kills his father for collaborating with the repressive white authorities. After being arrested for the killing, he is liberated from the white man's court as a hero. In other plays, like Ron Milner's *Who's Got His Own,* the generational conflict is the central theme, but is treated from a more sympathetic point of view. Still, the conflict is a predominant theme in the New Black Theater and represents a significant shift in the way in which the older generation is viewed in recent Black literature generally. As Larry Neal observes, "In Afro-American literature of previous decades, the strong Black mother was the object of awe and respect. But in the new literature, her status is ambivalent and laced with tension."[13]

Murder, itself, whether in or out of the family, is another recurring theme which appears in several of these plays. However, the use of murder is most often symbolic. There is rarely killing simply for the sake of killing. The murder is usually committed in the name of revolution, in which case the white person or Uncle Tom is killed because he has become an obstacle to the revolution. Other times, as in some of Baraka's earlier plays (like *Dutchman* and *The Slave*), the murder symbolizes the futility and brutality of America's inhuman

[13]Gayle, *The Black Aesthetic,* p. 271.

racial dilemma. Still, in most plays, the murder usually has an affirmative effect. The murder of Mrs. Mann by the Black maid in the Bullins play affirms the maid's Blackness and consummates her transition from a foot-shuffling house nigger to a proud Black woman. The use of murder in this way corresponds closely to Frantz Fanon's view, which sees the violence of the oppressed as redemptive and self-affirming. (Baraka has even titled one of his highly ritualistic plays *Bloodrite*.) The reaffirmation of self in terms of clearly delineated value sets is the central concern of all ritual, and so it is not surprising that murder and violence, as symbols of Black reaffirmation and reavowal, should predominate in the New Black Theater.

A recurring theme, which is often tied closely to the theme of murder, is that of personal transformation. Here the character begins the play identifying closely with the white man's world view and the values that view represents. However, in the course of the play, something happens which causes that view to crumble in the character's eyes. He, or she, is forced at some crucial moment to see things as they really are, to feel the depths of humiliation, and to finally rise with the recognition that revolution and resistance are the only way. The murder of a character previously identified with the white man's system often consummates this epiphany. Mrs. Mann is finally shot by the Black maid, whom we first see as a hideous symbol of Black humiliation. After she kills the white woman, she is cleansed and pure again, dressed in her own self-styled African garb. Her former self is unrecognizable.

In Ben Caldwell's *Prayer Meeting or, The First Militant Minister,* this theme receives a humorous treatment. A Black burglar, who happens to manifest a strong revolutionary point of view, breaks into the home of a Black minister who has preached restraint to his people after the murder of a Black man by a white policeman because the minister assumed that was what God wanted. When the preacher comes home before the burglar is finished, the burglar hides in the closet of the bedroom. The preacher comes in, not knowing the burglar is present, and drops to his knees entreating the Lord to stop his people from resorting to violent retribution for their brother's death. But, from the closet, the burglar poses as the Lord himself, and shouts at the minister in disgust, "...Get up off your knees! And stop tryin' to bullshit me!" By convincing the preacher that he is the Lord answering his prayer, he shames him into a conversion. Soon he is prepared to lead his people in a protest march against the murderers of the Black man. He removes a revolver from his drawer and places it on the bedstand beside his Bible. He then says, "Brothers and Sisters, I had a talk with the Lord last night. He told me to tell you that the time has come to put an end to this murder, suffering, oppression, exploitation. ..."

Another less imposing, but still everpresent, theme in the New Black Theater is anti-Semitism. This is especially so in the works of Baraka and Bullins. The white female bitch figures in the plays of both men are often Jewish. Lula in *Dutchman,* a classic bitch goddess figure, thinks of plantations as being surrounded by wire. This projection, reminiscent of German concentration camps, labels her Jewish in Clay's eyes. Sharon Stover in Bullins' *The Pig Pen* is also both a bitch figure and Jewish. The use of anti-Semitism is usually very subtle and restrained. (I can think of no play in which it serves as the predominant theme.) Like most racial or ethnic aspersions, there is rarely an accompanying explanation. It is simply assumed that the meaning of a line like this one from Baraka's play *Police,* "Blonde Jewish freaky softee," will be understood by the audience.

This may have to do with the traditional illusions encouraged among the Jewish people as brothers in suffering to the Black man. Both groups have suffered, yet their responses to that suffering have been quite different, leading to the development of cultures that are almost antithetical. Leslie Fiedler, in his essay, "Negro and Jew: Encounter in America," suggests that the Jew is actually the founder of Western culture and the most European ethnic group in contemporary American society. ("The Jew is the father of Europe; the Negro, only the adopted child.")[14] The roots of Black culture, of course, go in the opposite direction, deep into African culture; yet, because of their common suffering, the dominant Anglo-Saxon culture, typically superficial regarding ethnic and racial groups, has tended to disregard culture and view both in the same light on the basis of their common heritage as outcasts. The expectation of commonality was aroused even when there were few cultural grounds for it ever being realized. This fundamental problem, coupled with the strong economic (but not otherwise) presence of the Jew in the

[14]Leslie A. Fiedler, *No! In Thunder* (New York: Stein and Day, 1972), p. 237.

Black community, has been the source of great tension between the two groups, especially in the New York area where there is the country's largest concentration of Jews.

Whatever the source of tension, the anti-Semitic theme has often appeared in the drama of the New Black Theater. The Jew has emerged, somewhat like the police or "pigs," as a symbolic antagonist closer to the Black hero than most whites (in some cases, his women), because the society has thrown them together, but always in opposition, always the irritant that triggers the hero's rage.

The use of language is yet another device tending to ritualize the plays of the New Black Theater. A particular style of language has emerged that is used almost universally in this theater, except with white characters and squares, who are often baffled and confused by it. Its most obvious and important characteristic is its reliance on the Black-American (Northern and urban) street argot. The hero is always someone who talks "real." He is "hip," but not "jive." His aim is to tell it precisely as it is, but with a style and emphasis that insinuates on his part a broad and fundamental awareness or hipness. This style is essentially functional and emanates from the urban street world of pimps, prostitutes, poolroom sharks, confidence men, pushers, and hustlers of all types. In this world, survival is dependent on a clear understanding of what is going on around oneself. Slip-ups in this regard can be, and often are fatal. Because the stakes are often nothing less than life and death, there is no room in this world for squares or people who are not fully aware of what is happening around them. The square is a traditionally despised character in the Black community for the very simple reason that he is dangerous. If, for example, he gets high and blurts it out to a stranger in some bar that he got his nickel bag from Joe, the pusher, then Joe's livelihood is endangered. The square simply threatens the very delicate balance this world depends upon.

As most linguists suggest, one of the important functions of language has always been to differentiate between classes of people. By the manner of speech alone, one can often determine the class background of an individual. This differentiation process also functions in the urban street world of the Black community. Because the square is dangerous, there must be a way to spot him. Certainly one such way is by his language, although there are several others. The street world develops its own parlance, and those who are not familiar with it are squares and outsiders; people to be carefully watched.

The New Black Theater, with an ideology that impels it to identify with the masses of Black people, has come to adopt the street world parlance as its predominant mode of expression. However, added to it is the rhetoric of Black nationalism. This hybrid language, like the street language it comes from, also has the function of differentiating, but in the New Black Theater, the square is the person who is unaware of the revolutionary ideology and the language which expresses it. He is dangerous in this context because his ignorance is an obstacle to revolution. The character of Len Stover in Bullins' *The Pig Pen* is such a square. Statements like the following, made to the play's revolutionary hero, quickly reveal Len as a square: "Now, it may seem a bit irregular under these circumstances, but we must keep in mind the individual life styles that are being expressed here." On the other hand, the ability of the hero in the same play to say in one breath, "The fact remains that the White man still oppresses us," and in another, "White port and lemon juice...comin' up," reveals him to the audience right away as the character who represents the ideal hybrid of street wisdom and elevated revolutionary consciousness. Other symbols must be present, also, before this identification can be complete, but the hybrid language style is essential.

The use of this language in the New Black Theater from play to play has regularized it into a symbol for a certain frame of mind (revolutionary consciousness born of the harsh circumstances of raw street life) that is a central goal of this theater and the nationalist movement generally. The language becomes a part of the overall ritual by differentiating the characters and by pointing, through its own hybrid structure, to the desired revolutionary frame of mind.

The final and most obvious device used in the New Black Theater that contributes to its ritualization is simply repetition. The symbols, characterizations, themes, and styles of language must be repeated from play to play with enough frequency for them to develop into patterns which can be quickly recognized by the Black audience. It is precisely because these things have been repeated with great frequency that one can speak of this theater as ritualistic.

The criticisms of the New Black Theater have been repeated to the point of becoming almost ritualized themselves. That the characters are only one-dimensional representatives of an ideological point of view, that the plays themselves evoke only a self-gratifying hatred, that the symbolism and language are often unnecessarily vulgar, and that the violence is only vengeful and without redeeming social or aesthetic value are only a few of these criticisms. Much of this criticism has been unfair and motivated more by an aversion to the values the New Black Theater has sought to project than by the drama itself. Some of it has also been fair. In any case, the nature of the criticism necessarily depends on the particular aesthetic values of the critic. If he requires that art be functional, as the playwrights themselves do, then certainly his comments will be friendlier, and *vice versa*. However, giving the New Black Theater its assumptions regarding the functionality of art, there still seem to be certain natural limitations to the ritualistic-dramatic form which should be discussed.

One such limitation emanates from the very heavy reliance on symbols, particularly symbolic characterizations that are peculiar to ritualistic drama. The symbolic characters, such as the young revolutionary and the Uncle Tom, are so immediately recognizable in many cases that they are deprived of any sense of personal mystery. When the personality of the characters in a drama is predictable, then at least one important source for creating drama is made unavailable to the author. He is limited because his characters are limited. He must rely on the suspenseful juxtaposition of character types, dramatic action, and other devices to achieve the dramatic suspense that his characters lack.

This reliance on symbol also tends to obscure or override the actual drama of a play. Because the symbolic characters are defined for us by things outside the play, they are not dependent on the play itself to establish their character. It has already been established in other plays and in the mythology of the nationalist movement. In this sense, the symbolic character types, like the white female temptress, exist independent of the particular play they may be in. Because we already know them and all the things they represent, the power of their dramatic action is often diminished.

Another limitation has to do with the codification of experience that is necessary for the kind of ritualized drama in which the New Black Theater is involved. Again, from play to play, certain patterns are established which evolve into a kind of code that is both inclusive and exclusive, depending upon one's knowledge of the symbols of the code. If one is aware that "White port and lemon juice" attributes knowledge of street life to the character who says it and that the same character's ability to speak fluently about the

oppression of his people means that he exemplifies the right combination of street experience and political sophistication that is
the goal of the nationalist movement, then one is sufficiently aware
of the symbols of the code to be included. If, on the other hand, one
has no feel at all for the implications of such a combination, then
the code becomes exclusive. Likewise, if one cannot recognize the
symbolic characterizations, then a full involvement in the dramatic
experience becomes difficult.

However, the drawback of such codification is not so much that
it excludes some from a full involvement in the drama of the New
Black Theater, but that it may encourage a certain shallowness in
approaching the drama as well as the values the drama projects.
Because the code is exclusive, there is the implied suggestion that
a mere familiarity with its symbols is sufficient for participation in
the drama and the nationalist movement from which it comes. This
is an unavoidable limitation of the ritualistic dramatic form which
makes room for the well-known "right-on" man who masters completely the language and symbols of the code but has no understanding of their real meaning. Such a person wishes to be "in," but
without responsibility; he plays the theater and the movement
cheap by reducing their deepest values to a hollow code that can
be acted out at will. The "right-on" man might well appear at the
theater with a flask of white port and lemon juice in one hand and
a copy or "The Quotable Karenga" in the other, but, if asked to
interpret the play he was watching, would either spew forth rhetoric
or turn suddenly mute.

A final limitation of the ritualistic form has to do with what might
be called the life expectancy of the overall ritual itself. An essential
characteristic of ritual is simply repetition. Ritual is achieved only
through the repetition of patterns, symbols, *etc.* However, it is
only natural to ask the question of how long any ritual may be repeated and still have meaning for those who participate in it. At
a certain point, there will have been enough repetition of patterns
and symbols for them to be established as ritual. Certainly the New
Black Theater has reached this point. From here on, it becomes a
question of how long the ritual can continue being repeated without becoming trite.

The real problem with ritual in this regard is that it involves a
certain absolutism which seems almost impossible to maintain in a
world that changes as fast as our own. The values which the New

Black Theater ritualizes in its drama are repeated from play to play as though they are absolute and will always have relevancy. But, we know that times change and that what is good today may not be tomorrow. Political values seem particularly tenuous in this period of our history. If, for example, the goals of the nationalist movement began to be achieved, the need for certain values would be eliminated and the need for others created. Because ritual projects values as absolute, it would be difficult for the ritualistic dramatic form to accommodate the necessary alterations. In this respect, the life expectancy of ritual is further limited by the life expectancy of the values it ritualizes. ·

However, the absolutism of ritual may pose another problem. By maintaining through ritual that its values are absolute, the New Black Theater may be forecasting for itself a very hard and painful death. When values and styles are projected in ritual as absolute, they arouse in their adherents an emotional commitment that cannot be changed without substantial inner turmoil. This makes it extremely difficult for a ritual to simply merge with or transform into something else when it has run its natural course. A casting out or purging process is usually necessary. The process is similar to that experienced by an individual who ceases to participate in the rituals of his religious faith because they have lost their meaning for him. His separation is inevitably painful and often involves a wholesale rejection of the former faith. The ritualization of the New Black Theater, with its underlying absolutism, may suggest that its inevitable passing may be somewhat turbulent, at least for those who have been most involved. This, of course, is primarily speculation and is not meant as a prophecy. Still, the emotional involvement in concepts which are projected as truth is usually quite intense and often makes separation from them very difficult.

However, the limitations of the ritualistic dramatic form do not preclude the possibility of good drama, as many suggest. The medieval morality plays, which are certainly as ritualistic as the drama of the New Black Theater, are still read and appreciated, and the values they projected are still thought to be an essential aspect of Western culture. If the situation for Black people in America remains as it is today, the drama of the New Black Theater, along with its nationalistic value system, may have substantially more staying power than many critics suspect.

Two Afro-American Contributions
to Dramatic Form

by Eleanor W. Traylor

I, who am borne away to become an orphan, carry my
parents with me. For Rhythm is she not my Mother and
Drama is her man? So he groaned aloud in the ship and
hid his drum and laughed.

ZORA NEALE HURSTON,
Jonah's Gourd Vine.

I

The oral traditions of Black slaves in America provided the
motif and substance of the only distinctively indigenous American
dramatic form. When, in the first two decades of the twentieth century, those traditions, embellished by the genius of Negro composers, librettists, dancers, actors, musicians, and arrangers,
appeared on the professional stage, an authentic Afro-American
theatre was born. Thus, when Harold Cruse, writing in 1968, complains that since 1921 "there has not been a worthwhile Negro production in the musical genre"[1] he certainly does not mean that
excellent plays by Black writers featuring excellent performers in
all dramatic genres since that time are lacking. They are not. He
means, simply, that the period, described by James Weldon Johnson
in *Black Manhattan,* which engendered the ragtime musical, the

"Two Afro-American Contributions to Dramatic Form" by Eleanor W. Traylor.
First published in *Indigene,* ed. James Spady (Philadelphia: Black History
Museum, 1978). Reprinted by permission of the author and with slight alterations
by the author.

[1]*Crisis of the Negro Intellectual* (New York: William Morrow and Company,
1967), p. 69.

cake-walk, hoe-down, tap-dance motifs, the "signifyin'" language, the "highlifin'" movement, the splendid array of color-drenched costume, and the peacock style of production has not since been equalled. That period brought to the stage much that formed…"a demonstrably interior cohesion…a complete neutrality to exterior mores and norms,…a…mediation of opposing motion."[2] But by no means did the Harlem Renaissance, even nearly, exhaust the materials or the shaping devices which constitute the masking-miming traditions of the original progenitors or their heirs.

Afro-American critics, writing for *The Messenger* (1917-1928), *Opportunity* (1923-1949), and *The Crisis* (1910-), begin as early as 1917 critical discussion regarding the question of the basis of a Negro theatre. Definitive issues of that discussion continue to the present day. As one playwright, in many ways representative of artistic effort by Black playwrights in the decade of the sixties, has phrased it:

> We don't want a higher form of White art in Black face. We are working toward something entirely different and new that encompasses the souls and spirit of Black people.[3]

Another facet within the continuum of critical discussion is expressed by a critic as late as 1977:

> If we rely on our creativity—on trial and error rather than on the attitude that we will impress whites and "teach" blacks via our admirable exercise in European forms—then we can arrive at "a Black" theatre which has far more meaning and impact than the mere fact that the performers are Black. That is, if we really want to deal with the substance of lives of Black people in America.[4]

Critical voices, early and late, have described the state of the Black stage at various times during its development, have indicated its ostensible failure, have praised its success, have prescribed for its behavior, and have even prophesied its future directions. Moreover, some have recognized Black theatre as having little to do at all with stage plays:

[2]Henry Louis Gates, "Dis and Dat: Dialect and the Descent," an unpublished paper read at the MLA Summer Seminar on Afro-American Literature: "From Critical Approach to Course Design," Yale University, June 8, 1977. He paraphrases Wole Soyinka.

[3]Marvin X, "Interview with Ed Bullins," Ed Bullins, ed., *New Plays from the Black Theatre* (New York: Bantam, 1969), p. xxi.

[4]Tom Dent, "Southern Black Cultural Alliance Festival: Theatre," *First World*, 2 (March-April, 1977), pp. 42-43.

> To those who want to institute the Negro theatre, let me say it is already established. It is lacking in wealth, so it is not seen in the high places. ... The real Negro theatre is in the jooks and the cabarets. Self-conscious individuals may turn away the eye and say, let us search elsewhere for our dramatic art. Let 'em search, they certainly won't find it. Butter Beans and Susie, Bo-Jangles and Snake Hips are the only performers of the real Negro school it has ever been my pleasure to behold in New York.[5]

Despite the valuable insights which form the continuity of critical discussion on Afro-American drama, there remains a consideration not often illumined. First, the *source* of all that can be called representative American theatre is Aframerican.[6] Second, long before 1917, two Afro-American stylistic forms had developed; certain aspects of an artistic process found in these are pervasive in artistic expression by Afro-American artists to the present day. It is upon these two forms, the minstrel show and the slave narrative, that this discussion shall focus. Theatrical productions mounted by Black artists on stage, despite their orientation, have historically contained certain aspects of an artistic process begun in America by African peoples. Whether one may speak of consistent consummate stage productions containing all aspects of that artistic process is a question which this survey may raise but which ultimately extends beyond its scope.

In 1845, Frederick Douglass in his *Narrative,* explains, "I was myself within the *circle;* so that I neither saw nor heard as those without might see or hear."[7] The power of that annunciation echoes through a more recent critical observation: "Once a mythology is formed, a *temenos* or magic circle is drawn around a culture, and literature develops historically within a limited orbit of language, reference, allusion, beliefs, transmitted and shared tradition."[8] When one probes the Afro-American "*temenos* or magic circle" of

---

[5] Zora Neale Hurston, "Characteristics of Negro Expression," Nancy Cunard, ed., *The Negro: An Anthology* (London: Frederick Ungar, 1934), pp. 24-31.

[6] James Weldon Johnson's term.

[7] *Narrative of the Life of Frederick Douglass* (1845; rpt. New York: New American Library, 1978), p. 31. Italics added.

[8] Northrop Frye, "The Critical Path: An Essay on the Social Context of Literary Criticism," *Daedalus* (Spring, 1970), pp. 268-342. My attention was first called to this essay and its implications by Robert Stepto in his paper "The Reconstruction of Instruction," at the MLA Summer Seminar on Afro-American Literature: "From Critical Approach to Course Design," read at Yale University, June 6, 1977.

creation, one discovers certain essential ingredients of a distinct shaping-process. That process does not seem to yield the same structures of tragedy, comedy, realism, expressionism, surrealism, or absurdity as those modes are understood within the European context. The process which nourished the first American dramatic form (the minstrel show) created the Blues and offers the continuing vocabulary of new world dance. It arises from "a tradition of confrontation and improvisation,"[9] of "grace under pressure."[10] That process, which was forged in America by African peoples, offers modes or forms transcendent of those which it adapts and improvises.

The spiritual does not follow the same melodic line as the Anglican hymn. A rag is not a minuet, or a reel; jazz dance requires different movement than that of the ballet, and the mask of the blues hero signifies differently from that of the tragic protagonist. The angle of vision from which life is seen, the rhythm of movement by which life is expressed, and the beat of the sound by which life is heard are the shaping devices which determine the hermeneutic of any cultural artifact. The hermeneutic of an Afro-American theatre is to be illumined not so much in "the substance of the lives of Black people" as in the design and shape and sound and movement of *forms* that those lives have created. For those shapes and rhythms and sounds have ordered the screams of anguish and the shouts of triumph of a people. They have also, as great art does, revealed dimensions of humanity otherwise inaccessible. But a great theatre not only requires majestic form but also majestic subject. The minstrel show, in itself, is a majestic form; it also embodies other majestic forms. Great subjects and forms are also the particular gifts of the folk tales and narratives which emerge out of the Afro-American cultural calabash.

II

> Of all the artifacts out of Africa, it is the mask which most compels. ... Obatala, the Yoruba sculptural God, is not the artist of Apollonian illusion; he is the artist of inner essence. The Yoruban mask remains only a piece of carved

[9]Albert Murray, *The Omni-Americans* (New York: Outerbridge and Dienstfrey, 1970), p. 18.

[10]Albert Murray, *Stomping the Blues* (New York: McGraw-Hill, 1976), p. 63.

wood without iwa, or character...without the
artist who bears it before his choral audience. In
all African art, the audience is chorus, and the
mask is wood until it becomes mask-in-motion.
The Western concept of "mask" is meaningless...
to the Yoruba. Precisely because "the doll in wood"
cannot itself signify. Once [in motion], the mask is
vehicle for the primary evocation of a complete
hermetic universe...a world autonomous, one
marked both by a demonstrably interior cohesion,
as well as by a complete neutrality to exterior
mores and norms. The mask with its immobilized
features all the while mobile, itself is a metaphor
for dialectic—say rather, itself contains the media-
tion of opposing motion.[11]

HENRY LOUIS GATES, "Dis and Dat:
Dialect and the Descent."

When the lore, songs, dance, and masking rituals of African slaves
made their entrance on the stage, a native American dramatic form
was born. "Something new and entirely different" entered dramatic
history in the nineteenth century: the minstrel show. Its history and
form are revealing. The visible history of minstrelsy, available to
any student of the theatre, is a history of performance by white
actors in corked-black-face, burlesquing what they perceived as the
speech, behavior, artifacts, and masking rituals of Afro-American
slaves from whom they burgled all aspects of the form they enacted.
An icon called *Negro,* assigned to the realm of the ridiculous,
emerged in the minstrel performance. This icon regaled American
theatre audiences (whose taste was apparently appeased by aspects
of the bizarre rather than by those of the authentic—at least so far
as that audience's appreciation of Black culture was concerned) for
well over fifty years. The character types, inaugurated by the minstrel show were, of course, caricatures. Caricatures are appropriate
to farce and the minstrel show employs farce. Unfortunately, the
minstrel caricatures survived beyond the context of theatrical performance; they became, in the racial fabric of American life, indices

---

[11]James Weldon Johnson in his "Preface" to *The Book of American Negro* Poetry,
1969, expresses a similar idea. More recently, Wole Soyinka in *Myth, Literature,
and the African World,* 1976, anatomizes and strenuously clarifies this idea.

by which to beguile and bemuse some and to humiliate and distract others.

The minstrel caricature, the icon called *Negro,* was created by white comedians shuffling, grinning, slurring, and rolling their eyes while singing, tale-telling, or pantomiming their versions of Negro idiom. Regrettably, it is this image, rather than the brilliance of an Afro-American-inspired artistic form, or the long line of brilliant performance by Black minstrels preceding Bert Williams and George Walker and certainly continuing after them, which has enjoyed popularity. The minstrel caricature has, undoubtedly, obscured the value of the minstrel stage. Thus even the success and fun of the latter-day Silas Green show became the gall and dross of Black America whose daily drama, though brilliantly enacted, bore no resemblance to the minstrel caricature in whose image it felt itself regarded. Moreover, the minstrel caricature has enjoyed longevity and even dominance over artistic forms created or inspired by Black Americans in the United States. Richard Long's observation is undeniable: "Black folk entered the larger American consciousness in artistic form, dubiously, only at the end of the twenties in the nightly series *Amos and Andy,* performed by two white vaudevillians who prospered so mightily that in the twilight of their years, they were golf companions of General Eisenhower, then President."[12]

Reaction against the minstrel caricature by Black Americans needs no justification. Social, political, and economic racism in the United States has made the reaction not only understandable but necessary. Artistically, however, defensive preoccupation with the minstrel caricature, rather than serious study of the shaping elements of the minstrel show obscures the importance of an Afro-American dramatic form, the potential of which has not yet been fully explored by Afro-American artists working in the theatre. Examination of those shaping elements could yield that precious "something" which "encompasses the soul and spirit of Black people." For "the drum hidden away on the ship" was (if we permit the wonderful metaphor) to intone the only cultural forms, beginning in an oral folk tradition and continuing to emerge in artistic refinement, native to the American place. In order to construct the precise features of the original slave form which came to be called

[12]"The Outer Reaches: The White Writer and Blacks in the Twenties," *Studies in the Literary Imagination* (Fall, 1974), pp. 65-71.

the minstrel show, a far more extensive probe and elaboration than this initial foray is able to offer is, of course, required. Yet a few suggestions seem appropriate.

The minstrel show, "born out of plantation playtimes around the Negro cabins,"[13] was a masking ritual. Its *invisible* history, like a ruin, must be re-visualized. For that history will inform the conception and practice of masking and miming, deriving from a specific "orbit of language, reference, allusion, beliefs, transmitted and shared tradition,"[14] which define Afro-American cultural forms. What white performers spied down-field, up-field, or around the slave cabins was a masking performance. They "borrowed" the masking feature but not the signification of the mask. Moreover, they observed a performance not dependent upon a *static* text. What they saw was an *ecstatic* performance guided by a fluid text. They "borrowed" the illusion, severing that from the reality which shaped it. In addition, they observed that to be "well-made," a "play" need not necessarily develop character, plot, or theme in "logical" dialogue. The voyeurs observed an elastic form: free enough to admit the unexpected, yet tight enough to require and achieve total coherence. They observed a theatrical form which, in essence, was choral and improvisational. Many sacred and secular Afro-American forms contained the choric improvisational call-and-response motifs. A single voice might utter a resonant call, thereby establishing a contextual theme:

> Steal away!

to be answered by a quartet of voices, harmonizing the thematic line:

> Steal away home!

followed then by a full chorus expressing the desire of the many as one, and adding another dimension:

> I ain't got long to stay here!

Finally, they observed song and dance; they heard language as lore. Recent scholarship has clarified the extent to which the *voyeurs* borrowed:

[13]Edith J. R. Isaacs, *The Negro in the Theatre* (New York: Theatre Arts Incorporated, 1947), p. 19.
[14]Frye, pp. 268-342.

...the first blackface act to win widespread fame, was also the first clear instance of a minstrel using an Afro-American dance.... Minstrels made extensive use of humor, fantasy, and animal fables that they almost certainly derived from Afro-American folk song and narrative, which relied heavily on animal symbolism, used indirection and guile to voice protests or attack adversaries, and featured victories of the weak over the strong.[15]

The masking-miming rituals created by enslaved Africans on American soil was "something entirely different and new" to the American ethos. Edith J. R. Isaacs' reflection speaks directly to that point:

To perceive the significance of the Negro in American theatre, it is well to remember that a native art grows only on native roots. The Anglo-Saxon founders of American life were a stern-minded folk to whom the theatre was nothing less than "the ante-chamber of the devil" and actors were "caterpillers of the commonwealth." They commanded that all signs of theatre in the new world should be uprooted ruthlessly.... When later, English theatre did come freely into the country, it came by the back door.... Yet, gradually, plays came and found an audience and new men came from other European lands who brought their theatre with them...and this *borrowed* theatre—English, French, German, Spanish—is the base of our [American] commercial theatre.[16]

Moreover, maintains Miss Isaacs, "every art must go back to the soil for refreshment from time to time."[17] Thus, she concludes, "we [Americans] continue to build on a base with little folk foundation, and almost no peasant drama of the kind from which a 'cultural' theatre would normally grow. And that is the main reason why, in music and dance, in rhythm and comedy and pantomime, we [Americans] borrow so freely from the Negro theatre which has developed from the earth up."[18]

[15]Robert C. Toll, *Blacking Up* (New York: Oxford University Press, 1974), pp. 43, 48.

[16]*The Negro in the Theatre*, pp. 14-15. Italics added.

[17]*The Negro in the Theatre*, pp. 14-15.

[18]*Ibid.*

III

> The fact is, nothing great or enduring…has ever
> sprung full-fledged and unprecedented from the
> brain of any master; the best that he gives to the
> world he gathers from the hearts of the people,
> and runs it through the alembic of his genius.
>
> James Weldon Johnson,
> *Autobiography of an Ex-Colored Man*

When the oral accounts of run-away slaves entered literary history, a native American narrative mode developed. "Something new and entirely different" happened to the art of story telling: several genres enmeshed and a new way of relating experience manifested itself in the slave narrative. Not merely an autobiography, eschewing the precise chronology of a history, substantively not a novel; not conventionally an epic; structurally not a romance; neither epistolary nor picaresque nor homiletic; if gothic, not as an imaginative device, the slave narrative may encompass the ingredients of all these but is still something else. The slave narrative disturbed existing generic distinctions. It extended the act of language; it inceased the nature of written expression in English. It entered into the history of experience the panoramic struggle of a particular people at a particular time in their historical development.

By 1845, the slave narrative had become a powerful literary mode no better practiced than by Frederick Douglass; and, by 1858, had become a distinctive and highly refined literary device, first employed by William Wells Brown whose dramatic narrative, *Escape: or A Leap for Freedom,* became the first extant Afro-American dramatic text (script).

The 1845 *Narrative* of Frederick Douglass serves as an outstanding revelation of the great form and the great subject inherent in the slave narrative as an Afro-American modal genre. In it, a new literary voice (Aframerican) announces itself; a distinct sensibility is illumined. A particular myth asserts itself, and a hero experiencing a unique initiation, undertaking a specific quest, and dramatizing a certain view of existence emerges.

Aesthetically, Douglass' *Narrative* is a lyric evocation—a poem. The first person voice, speaking in reflection, orders the chaos of experience. The voice speaks calmly, almost casually, as it begins to relate the strange circumstances of its birth:

> ...I know nothing; the means of knowing was withheld from me.
> (*Narrative*, p. 22)

Continuing reflectively, the speaker not only describes experience but provides a consistent metaphor by which to characterize that which defies ordinary expression:

> It was the blood-stained gate, the entrance to the hell of slavery, through which I was about to pass.   (*Narrative*, p. 25)

Inchoate anguish is ineffable; the speaker finds in his environment an objective correlative by which to make the ineffable palpable:

> ...the dense old woods, for miles around, reverberate with their [slaves'] wild songs revealing at once the highest joy and the deepest sadness. They would compose and sing as they went along, consulting neither time nor tune. ... The thought that came up, came out—if not in the word, in the sound;—and as frequently in one as in the other. They would sometimes sing the most pathetic sentiment in the most rapturous tone, and the most rapturous sentiment in the most pathetic tone.   (*Narrative*, p. 31)

Indebted to the lesson of the songs, the speaker pays tribute:

> to those songs I trace my first glimmering conception....
> (*Narrative*, p. 32)

The imagery which the speaker employs in the service of clarity, for example, is markedly not employed in the service of the thrill:

> My feet have been so cracked with the frost that the pen with which I am writing might be laid in the gashes.   (*Narrative*, p. 43)

Thus, the *Narrative* intones a different sensibility from that which Mario Praz describes as "the state of sensibility [in Europe and America] which came to flower toward the end of the eighteenth century":[19]

> For the romantics, beauty was enhanced by exactly those qualities which seem to deny it, by those objects which produce horror; the sadder, the more painful it was, the more intensely they relished it. ... The discovery of horror as a source of delight and beauty ended by reacting on men's natural conception of beauty itself: the horrid, from

[19]*The Romantic Agony* (New York: Oxford University Press, 1970), p. 27.

being a category of the beautiful, ended by becoming one of its essential elements and the "beautifully horrid" passed by insensible degrees to the "horribly beautiful."[20]

The *Narrative* of Douglass employs imagery in the service of an altogether different aesthetic sensibility from the one described by Praz. The imagery of the *Narrative*, poetic in its intensity, dislodges the horrible from the category of the beautiful and places it into the category of the evil, the disgusting, the contemptible, and the decadent:

> The louder she screamed, the harder he whipped; and where the blood ran fastest, there he whipped longest. He would whip her to make her scream, and whip her to make her hush; and not until overcome by fatigue, would he cease to swing the blood-clotted cowskin. ... I shall never forget it whilst I remember anything. ... It was the blood-stained gate, the entrance to the hell of slavery, through which I was about to pass. (*Narrative*, p. 25)

On the other hand, by employing the imagery of synthesis and of association, the speaker in the Narrative exhalts the heroic and renders the "thrilling" petty by comparison:

> I was myself within the circle; so that I neither saw nor heard as those without might see and hear. ... The songs of the slave represent the sorrows of his heart; and he is relieved by them, only as an aching heart is relieved by its tears. ... Those songs still follow me, to deepen my hatred of slavery, and quicken my sympathies for my brethren in bonds. (*Narrative, p. 32)*

But the lyric quality of the *Narrative* is not its only strength. Rhetorically, the *Narrative* is a sermon for its intent is to exorcise evil and bludgeon it as unerringly and as fatally as the word can bludgeon. Its purpose is persuasion, not mere contemplation. It is a call to action for which a response is required that is different from the repose of reading and listening. The particular response for which the speaker calls is not left for inference. He specifically exults that his efforts are designed toward

> hastening the glad day of deliverence to the millions of my brethren in bonds—faithfully relying upon the power of truth, love, and justice, for success in my humble efforts—and solemnly pledging myself anew to the sacred cause,—I subscribe myself, Frederick Douglass, Lynn, Mass. April 28, 1845. (*Narrative*, p. 126)

[20]*The Romantic Agony,...* p. 27.

In addition, the *Narrative* is a paradigm of language and its uses; it is a comment on language itself. In this century, Ernest Hemingway was to snarl his "embarrassment" at the dissociation of sensibility revealed by the contrast between ameliorative language and barbarous reality. In the nineteenth century, Douglass defines the dissociation. In the *Narrative,* words like "just," "free," "liberty," "pursuit of happiness" enter the category of the hideously ironic, of the grotesquely absurd, not by reason of authorial lambast, but simply by reason of contextual juxtaposition.

Finally the *Narrative,* though a record of the actual, achieves the realm of myth. We know the first person narrator to be Frederick Douglass, an historical personage; yet, we feel the distance that the presence of the great and mighty commands. A man of sorrow, acquainted with grief, vulnerable in the extreme, dreadful in his suffering, awesome in his mightiness of heart, glorious in his triumph, his purpose obdurate, his passion awful, his perception emancipating, he is the hero. In this heroic dimension, the personal voice of Douglass assumes the mighty resonance of the multitude. This hero, the personal/collective voice of a great people in a moment of magnitude definitive of their history, undertakes the journey perilous. From "the blood-stained gate" through "the dense old woods," across the rivers of fire toward "deliverance" is the rite of passage dramatized in the *Narrative.* The rhythm of the rite and its essential substance, translated in the century since, forms the *mythos* of the main tradition of Afro-American literature.

The *Narrative* of Douglass was available to William Wells Brown when he created *Escape: or A Leap for Freedom.* Both texts stand at the fore of Afro-American fiction and Afro-American drama. Brown performed *Escape* from a pulpit podium; thus, the pulpit became the first stage setting on which the first extant Afro-American "play," a slave narrative, was presented. The "production" premiered as a one-man show in which Brown "signified," "surrendipidized," and "read" his audience as he juxtaposed "the most pathetic sentiment in the most rapturous tone." Despite the author's protestations that "the play, no doubt abounds in defects, but as I was born in slavery, and never had a day's schooling in my life, I owe the public no apology for errors,"[21] the performance apparently suffered no lack of dramatic power. In fact, "The Opinions of the Press," appended

---

[21]"Preface," *Escape: or A Leap for Freedom* (Boston: R. F. Walcutt, 1858).

to the 1858 first edition printing of the play, reveal something of its critical reception. The reviews report that the play was "informative upon the most interesting questions of the day" *(Seneca Falls Courier)*, was "in itself a masterly refutation of all apologies for slavery... abounding in wit, satire, philosophy, argument and facts, all ingeniously interwoven into one of the most interesting dramatic compositions of modern times" *(Auburn New York Daily Advertiser)*, "gave the greatest satisfaction to an intelligent and appreciative audience," and as "well executed and delivered" *(Philadelphia Morning Times)*. Of the dramatist himself, the reviewer from the *Seneca Falls Courier* adds that "Mr. Brown exhibits a dramatic talent possessed by few who have, under the best instructors, made themselves famous on the stage. He evinces a talent for tragic and comic representation rarely combined."

Brown's play had been inspired by the actual escape of a man and his wife, but Brown saw in the oral account all the dramatic intensity of the ages-old rite of passage tale; he also saw in the material a mode of powerful persuasion, which the dramatic art could serve. While Brown may not have known that his play was the first manifestation of an explicit American subject in an explicit American form drawn from an explicit American folk traditional nexus, he did know that on his landscape there was no greater suffering, no greater overcoming, no greater manifestation of complex humanity, no greater endurance, or courage, or will, or resources, or magnitude, or high seriousness than was the struggle of his people bound to be free.

But the actual material of his inspiration was not enough. Brown knew his duty to be an act of imagination which would deliver the actual not only as glorious as in itself it is, for that is not the work of art; that is the work of life which the people have already accomplished. His job was to render the actual in extraordinary terms, and thereby to make splendid in language, and therefore to record, that which may have passed unnoticed and uncelebrated. If that is the duty of artistic rendering, Brown took it up. For that work, he needed process. He found it in the oral traditional material available to him in Afro-American creative forms. His narrative works in the tradition of the tall tale; it employs the double blade of humor which in Afro-American tradition carves the smile as it spears the tear, suggests one focus as it comments upon another. Though his language is often imitative of the florid style of eighteenth-century diction, yet, of all the shaping materials within the black continuum, Brown shaped the delivery of his text upon the example of performed language at his behest: the oratorical tradition of the Black preacher—a cultural form beginning, according to Carter G. Woodson, as early as 1773 and continuing to the present day.

IV

Brothers and sisters, this morning...I intend to explain the unexplainable...find out the undefinable...ponder over the imponderable and unscrew the inscrutable.

(Folk traditional recorded by James Weldon Johnson)

"The old-time negro preacher," says James Weldon Johnson, "was a master of all the modes of eloquence...."

He knew the secret of oratory, that at bottom it is a progression of rhythmic words more than anything else.... He often possessed a voice that was a marvelous instrument, a voice he could modulate from a sepulchral whisper to a crashing thunder clap.... His imagination was bold and unfettered.... He had the power to sweep his hearers before him; and so himself was often swept away. At such times his language was not prose but poetry.... Above all [he was] an orator, and in good measure an actor.... It was through him that the people of diverse languages and customs who were brought here from diverse parts of Africa and thrown into slavery were given their first sense of unity and solidarity."[22]

Brown's debt to the function of or to the oratorical tradition of the preacher, and the debt of Black dramatists after him to this day, need no belaboring. Neither does his debt, nor that of those succeeding, to the ceremonial ritual that distinguishes Black American religious expression from Anglican or Roman or White American need belaboring. Yet, a point of emphasis regarding both may be useful. One of the continuities defining the tradition and marking out the history of Afro-American literature is the portrait of the preacher. The folklore, early and late, figures him; the most distinguished fiction of the literate tradition—dramatic and nondramatic—employs the portrait. The roles of the preacher-figure vary: he is sometimes serious protagonist or comic antagonist. Yet, whether fool, trickster-jester, pious or impious scapegoat, griot-

[22]"Preface," *God's Trombones* (New York: Viking Press, 1927), p. 3.

poet, communal voice, or warrior, his force — his power (in literature and in life) — is his mastery of "the modes of eloquence."

On the other hand, "the modes of eloquence," by which religious ceremonial expression has nourished Afro-American cultural forms, are not limited to language or its presentment. Religious expression has nourished every other element of dramatic presentation: music, dance, and spectacle. In Afro-American religious expression, setting, language, music, and movement cohere in a committed choric performance guided but unrestricted by a static text. The preacher carefully establishes his text, but "the unscrewing of the inscrutable" is the grand improvisational act which admits the spirit and calls the worshipers to the mighty choric response which is the heart of the ceremony. Likewise, the *mambo* and *houngan* of Voodoo ceremony meticulously draw the *vévé*, but the *rite de possession* signalling the entrance of the spirit is the grand extra-textual improvisational act responsive to the call of the spirit.

V

> Slip the yoke
> and
> Change the joke.
>
> Ralph Ellison, *Shadow and Act*

We do not know the exact signification of the masking-miming ritual which obtained in the slave quarters, but we know something of the form which it inspired. That form is unfettered by elements of stage setting which restrict life to parlors, kitchens, or bedrooms. It is an elaborate form allowing for the coherence of all the modes of eloquence arising and outpouring from within the Afro-American magic cultural circle. We do not know what exact ingredients the *voyeurs* of that early masking ritual left out, but we do know the nature of cultural forms which have developed historically within the "limited orbit of language, reference, allusion, beliefs, transmitted and shared tradition" which define the Afro-American *"temenos."* We know the stuff and form of narratives told by slaves; we know the powerful imagery of the dramatic monologues which are the sorrow songs:

> Just when I thought
> I was lost

> My dungeon shook
>   And my chains fell off.

We know the blues and, thus, we know the grand double vision that can admit the hard facts of existence and at the same time greet the spirit which exorcises them:

> Good mornin' Blues
> Blues how do you do
> I'm feelin' fine, Blues
> How do you do.

We know that the blues hero puts on a particular vestment. While the tragic hero dresses in the blood-stained cloak of nobility, destined for certain defeat, and while the comic hero wears the mantle of ordinary humanity, muddling in pedestrian concerns, the blues hero puts on the cloak of irony which shields him not from the wound of nobility nor from the foibles of the ordinary, but prepares him for the task of endurance which is his ordeal.

The consummate cultural forms of the Afro-American *temenos* have offered the dramatic modes for which those who eschew "a higher form of white art in black-face" strive. The minstrel show, not the caricature, and the slave narrative shot through with the modes of eloquence developed within the Afro-American cultural continuum are two major dramatic forms which African Americans have given the world.

The Aesthetic of Modern Black Drama:
From *Mimesis* to *Methexis*

by Kimberly W. Benston

> The Revolutionary Theatre must take dreams and give
> them a reality.
>
> AMIRI BARAKA,
"The Revolutionary Theatre."

I

The emergence of a dynamic and articulate Afro-American
theatre movement in the past decade and a half has been noted by
many commentators. Apart from sharply-focused comments on individual playwrights, scholarly criticism has tended to be concerned with the drama's nationalist values[1] or with the evolution of
its moral and narrative topoi.[2] However, little regard has been paid
to the structural dimension of the playwrights' work.

"The Aesthetic of Modern Black Drama: From *Mimesis* to *Methexis*" by Kimberly W. Benston. Reprinted by permission of the author.

[1] See, for example, "Bullins, Baraka, and Elder: The Dawn of Grandeur in Black
Drama," by Lance Jeffers, *CLA Journal* 16, no. 1 (September, 1972), 32-48; "The
Cultural Revolution in Black Theatre," by Lloyd W. Brown, *Negro American
Literature Forum* 8, no. 1 (Spring, 1974), 159-64; and "Anger and Contemporary
Black Theatre," by Robert J. Willis, *Negro American Literature Forum* 8, no. 2
(Summer, 1974), 213-15.

[2] See, for example, "LeRoi Jones and Contemporary Black Drama," by Louis
Phillips, in *The Black American Writer, Vol. II*, edited by C. W. E. Bigsby (Baltimore, 1969), pp. 203-17; "Black Theater," by Toni Cade, in *Black Expression,*
edited by Addison Gayle, Jr. (New York, 1969), pp. 134-43; "Notes on Ritual in the
New Black Theater," by Shelby Steele, *Black World* 22, no. 8 (June, 1973), 78-84;
and "Visions of Love and Manliness in a Blackening World: Dramas of Black Life
from 1953-1970," by Darwin T. Turner, *The Iowa Review* 6, no. 2 (Spring, 1975),
82-99.

This neglect is indeed ironic for, as is the case with Afro-American music—the primal ground of all modern Black art—the self-conscious development of organizing principles in Black drama is the very essence of its visionary quest. The inattention to structural factors may be understandable when one considers that exegesis of Black drama, even more than that of Black poetry and fiction, has been forged in a climate of politicized rhetoric and hence has too frequently limited itself to ideological issues. Scrutiny of the playwrights' own statements on the new drama, however, reveals a continuous struggle to imagine theatrical forms capable of containing revolutionary content.

Abiodun Jeyifous, in a recent historical critique of Black writings on Black drama, acutely defined the change in the modern (post-1963) era as a shift from the canon of "Negro Sensibility," which he describes as a blend of "Western bourgeois esthetic criteria and a sentimental racial awareness," to the advocation of Black "consciousness" evident in an avowed synthesis of dramaturgical and ideological presuppositions.[3] As Jeyifous suggests, this desire to unite a radical theatrical idiom with a new political vision caused modern Black playwrights to direct their theoretical as well as their practical efforts toward developing what Amiri Baraka first termed a "post-American *form.*" It is this little explored area of theoretical form— what might be accurately termed the *aesthetic* of Black drama—that I should like to examine for I believe that an analysis of the Black theatre movement's major speculative documents will reveal just how ideological and formal innovations have been necessarily intertwined.

My specific thesis is that the path of modern Black drama's aesthetic describes a curve which moves dialectically from quasi-naturalism and overt rage against Euro-American institutions toward the shaping of uniquely Afro-American mythologies and symbolisms, flexibility of dramatic form, and participatory theatre within the Black community. Spiritually and technically, this movement is one from *mimesis,* or representation of an action, to *methexis,* or communal "helping-out" of the action by all assembled. It is a process that could be described alternatively as a shift from *drama*—

---

[3]"Black Critics on Black Theatre in America," *TDR* 18, no. 3 (September, 1974), 34-45. While Jeyifous surveys the writings of black critics from the Harlem Renaissance to the present, he is centrally concerned with the earlier criticism, particularly that of Alain Locke.

the spectacle observed—to *ritual*—the event which dissolves traditional divisions between actor and spectator, between self and other. Through this process, the Black beholder is theoretically transformed from a detached individual whose private consciousness the playwright sought to reform, to a participatory member of tribal or, in this case, national ceremony which affirms a shared vision.

II

The increasing visibility and influence of drama among Afro-American arts in recent years has, I think, a clearer etiology than is usual in aesthetic evolution. During a period of expanding Black consciousness when the rhetoric of identity was quickly translated into stunning, often violent action, the Afro-American artist naturally sought a mode imbued with the structure of cummunal, if not directly political, activity. In such an atmosphere, the rapid development of theatre, an extremely political because pre-eminently social medium, was inevitable. As Black artists soon recognized, the very essence of theatre is its manifestly collective experience and, in very practical terms, its affirmation or challenge of the audience's codes of conduct, of their mechanisms of survival, their shared necessity, outrage, and vision.

Theatre can tap and redistribute custom and ceremony; it can generate violent energy (the French Revolution is sometimes said to have really begun when the opening-night audience of Beaumarchais' *Marriage of Figaro* reacted angrily to the depiction of aristocratic life) or neutralize the impulse toward action. In political terms then, when skillfully employed theatre can become a powerful weapon for regulation of communal values or, conversely, for radical change. Unlike literature, it makes no demands on its audience of literacy or privacy; as the proliferation of community-center/theatres attests (National Black Theatre of New York; Concept East of Detroit; East Cleveland Community Theatre; La Mont Zeno Community Theatre of Chicago; Free Southern Theatre of New Orleans; Mafundi Institute of Los Angeles, to name but a fraction), it may become an enlivened synecdoche of a unified national culture envisioned by its practitioners.

Considering the long-observed *will to drama* embedded in Afro-

American life and traditional art—the "poise for drama" (Zora Neale Hurston) displayed in minstrelsy, the Dozens, toasts, the call-and-response pattern of musical and religious performance, and the signifying improvisations of the street—we might have expected an untroubled flowering of dramatic innovation set in motion by contemporary political exigencies. However, especially in light of their need to articulate a specific, often didactic message, Black dramatists could not avoid the complexities of revolt against conventions governing the artistic medium they sought to exploit.

The modern Afro-American drama movement emerges, in fact, from the struggle with an inherited ·theatrical tradition, one in which audience and performer are rigidly separated, in which character is explored as either exemplification or mockery of an historic faith in individual destiny. This tradition's affirmation (as in the tragic continuum from O'Neill to Miller) is of a painfully earned autonomy; its revolt (as in Expressionist or Absurdist drama) is a self-deprecating gesture of alienation, at base another form of willed isolation. Long fueled by the energy of revolt,[4] modern Western drama has yet to proceed from dislocation, from exploration of incoherence within traditional paradigms of dramatic experience, to restoration of what Yeats called "the ritual of a lost faith." We might say that modern Black playwrights seek an idiom of the communal self that is prior to individual expression, a ritual of faith not lost but suppressed, burdened, and variously displaced.

Inevitably, then, contemporary Afro-American theatre's iconographic, thematic, and narrative concerns have led to inquiries into the nature of the dramatic experience itself. It is the continuity of dramatic *theory,* in fact, which allows us to see the apparently contrasting genres of the movement, such as didacticism, naturalism, various kinds of allegory, serious and comical rites, and, especially, numerous syntheses of these, as necessary and interdependent elements in a general reform. It is perhaps fitting, in light of the growing scepticism toward received modes, that the first significant manifesto was written by a figure with an already established reputation as poet, novelist, and essayist. Amiri Baraka's "The Revolutionary Theatre"[5] self-consciously enunciated the guiding principles for a radically new drama. Its tone, in typically Barakan fashion, is at

[4]See Robert Brustein's study, *The Theatre of Revolt* (Boston, 1962).

[5]*Home: Social Essays* (New York, 1966), pp. 210-15. "The Revolutionary Theatre" was written in 1964.

once prophetic, apocalyptic, and hortatory. While foreseeing a theatre "peopled with new kinds of heroes," the essay principally advertises the revolutionary theatre as a "theatre of Victims" which will force upon the Black onlooker images that kindle anger and liberating violence:

> The Revolutionary Theatre must EXPOSE! ... It should stagger through our universe correcting, insulting, preaching. ... [*It*] must Accuse and Attack anything that can be accused and attacked.

Baraka's call is for a theatre of uncompromising "assault" upon all that appears inimical to realization of Black power. Above all else, such a theatre requires narrative clarity and precision as it seeks to identify the exact institutional causes and effects of present conditions. The violence it espouses and would depict is a product of its uncompromising Manichean distinctions between victimized good and oppressive evil and of its apocalyptic program for liberation. The drama Baraka here envisions is therefore a drama of the unambiguous and pedagogical *word*.

At the heart of the revolutionary theatre is the pragmatic thrust of the then uncanonized "Black aesthetic":

> ...what we show must cause the blood to rush, so that pre-revolutionary temperaments will be bathed in this blood, and it will cause their deepest souls to move, and they will find themselves tensed and clenched, even ready to die, at what the soul has been taught. We will scream and cry, murder, run through the streets in agony, if it means some soul will be moved.

Baraka's essay is implicitly aimed toward creation of a unified Black audience from the disparate fragments of "pre-revolutionary temperaments." The heroes of his theatre, like the Afro-Americans who are to observe them, are seen as "victims" whose redemption lies in shocked recognition of their own privation. Yet Baraka simultaneously abjures the tragic possibilities inherent in the notion of an aggrieved heroism, the amoral pathos of inescapable and intolerable personal catastrophe. His "new kind of heroes" are not to be "the weak Hamlets." Having set in motion the bloody spectacle of victimization, Baraka recoils from the possibility of emotional commitment to the character who dies which would deflect attention from the action in which he dies.

Baraka fears the establishment of a rhythm of tragedy in which the ceremony of sacrifice is drowned more in pity than in blood. He

fears, that is, the dissolution of revolutionary theatre into the melodrama of liberal metaphysics. The hero (and the protagonists of
Baraka's own early plays, *Dutchman* and *The Slave,* are striking instances) therefore appears under a precariously double aspect. The
sense of wasted individuality is dispelled by a joyful, if ruthless
celebration of freshly conceived values. Self and group do not cohere; the latter's ethos survives as tacit compensation for destruction of the former. Thus while the essay is by implication a summons
to unification, its overt "preaching" to the Black victim finally produces an emotional distance between the theatre of assault and its
supposed beneficiaries.

This problematic view of the hero and his audience is accompanied by an apparent dualism with regard to form. Baraka clearly
desires a didactic and visionary theatre, yet he is also committed to a
kind of social realism, to a "preciseness [*of*] method" and "a social
theatre...where *real things* can be said about *a real world*" (my
emphasis). A rebel dramatist, he dreams of "World Spirit," and pro-
poses for his dream a violent test: Subjective passion and concrete
realism are the twin poles of his imagination. Baraka seems to sense
here that the more intense the desire for heightened vision, the
more one might be pulled back to confrontation with the tangible,
material world one scorns as "illusion." The key to this ambiguous
realism is Baraka's recognition that what one seeks is "a real world,"
a refuge from the stifling "appearances" (codes) of *the* real world.
"The revolutionary theatre" envisions landscapes of the "consciousness epic" which are yet contiguous with the agony- and blood-
drenched streets of its heroes: "it looks at the sky," Baraka tells us,
"with the victim's eyes."

Baraka's treatise (and the drama he wrote contemporaneously,
especially *Dutchman, The Slave,* and *The Toilet*) has had profound
effects upon subsequent theories. Of these, Ed Bullins' "The So-
called Western Avant-garde Drama"[6] and K. William Kgositsile's
"Towards Our Theatre: A Definitive Act"[7] are closest both chron-
ologically and ideologically to Baraka's piece. Bullins' essay shares
with "The Revolutionary Theatre" a near-obsessive preoccupation
with the dominant culture's reaction to the new Black drama (the
new theatre's enemies, Baraka concludes, are "most of you who are

[6]Printed in *Black Expression,* ed. Gayle, pp. 143-46 (written in 1967).
[7]Printed in *Black Expression,* ed. Gayle, pp. 146-48 (written in 1967).

reading this") and draws concrete comparisons between Euro-American and Afro-American "worldviews."

Bullins castigates modern Euro-American theatre for its concentration on Freudian and existential dilemmas which, in his view, hold a mirror up to its own tortured psyche but not to the world of significant actions. Their "reality" is, as Baraka had implied, no reality at all; it is a frightening projection of "disbelief" and, ultimately, of despair. This squandering of meaningful experience, Bullins asserts, has resulted in the drama's loss of "plot and story and character," by which he means a naturalism that supersedes the anxieties of self-alienation. Euro-American art is, above all, belated, an art in which a strange, dissipated action has supplanted the vital, if sometimes disturbing investigation of shared values. Bullins is thus essentially determined to assert the primacy of Afro-American theatrical experimentation; the tactile ferocity with which he concludes his essay conveys his desire for a new Black theatre that rejects the pervasive cultural decay and promotes a Black-oriented realism:

> To paraphrase Brother LeRoi Jones [Baraka]: It is a post-American form of Black theater we Black Artists should be seeking. It is Black Art that is like a dagger pointed at the vitals of America, and through the rips "we" (US) can enter the New Epoch.

Kgositsile's "Towards Our Theater" represents a significant departure from the concern with "mainstream" Euro-American values; its sentiments concern Black people only. Yet, like Baraka's, Kgositsile's program for Black theatre is based on a stringent critique of Black culture as presently constituted:

> The desired and desirable will be seen through elegant image and symbol abstracted from life. The undesirable, the corrupting, the destructive, will be portrayed in a grotesque manner, its sinister qualities driving us to the mercy killing of the villain.

This discourse, as announced by the essay's first word—*TESTIFYING*—is the homiletic exercise of a preacher whose text is dictated by narrowly defined nationalist principles. Though Kgositsile speaks briefly of a "theater of poetry" that combines "image, rhythm, and symbol," he clearly desires a wholly didactic, propagandistic drama that confronts the audience with appropriately idealized or demonized figures instead of soothing it with theatrical illusion or complex ("poetic") representation. In truth, Kgositsile desires a morality-play drama devoid of ("decadent") lyricism that castigates, worships, alienates, or affirms in unequivocal fashion. And a good deal of Black drama contemporary with "Towards Our Theater" illustrates the essence of the manifesto by being straightforwardly narrative, abstract, and emblematic.[8]

In these tracts, then, we perceive a clearly felt fear of dependence on the materialism inherent in pure realism. For in realism the hero's milieu takes a preponderant part in shaping his destiny; all actions, decisions, and feelings are enveloped by an awareness of extraneous determination, all sense of freedom is undermined and insulted. The hero, like Baraka's Clay in *Dutchman,* might declare the madness of reality, but reality must finally stand, little affected, above his "plight." The paradoxically didactic "realism" of Bullins and Kgositsile, like that of Baraka's more complex inspiration, is clearly not a concatenation of events so much as a movement of the psyche. Moreover, it does not affirm the activity of an individual but presents a more general action which all share by analogy. It is a realism that accepts the literal only to transcend it.

This theatre, which dominates its audience with programmatic images of "a real world," is truly the dramatist's objective correlative to a deeply subjective vision in which the call to liberation through violence threatens any concrete idea of "form." Indeed, as their apparently uncritical invocation of disparate techniques (naturalism, allegory, symbolism) suggests, these early manifestos cohere precisely in their passionate proclamation of the *primacy of content over form.* Their purchase on reality, the means by which they sought to depict a subject matter more "truthful" than that of either the conventional or avant-garde mainstream, was that of moral concern. That was both their strength and limitation. For such "realism," quite apart from any restriction of heroic action, could not advance its claims very far as long as it simply replaced superficial topicalities by a didactic seriousness. What was needed beyond thematic clarification and a rejection of available notions of form was a more complex realization of the structural implications of the new revolt. Hence, the didactic element had to be dampened, which meant not that it had to be eliminated but that it had to be grounded in something less nebulous than moral fervor. Never-

---

[8]See, for example, the plays collected in the anthology *New Plays from the Black Theatre,* ed. Ed Bullins (New York, 1969).

theless, the effect of the early, predominantly denunciatory theory was overwhelming: by opening up a vast new field of subject matter, by destroying dependence on current ideas of dramatic structure, those advocates of what we might call "moral mimesis" opened the floodgates for a spate of new *formal,* as well as thematic possibilities.

Not long after Kgositsile's and Bullins' declarations were published, several essays appeared which began a shift toward this more complex concept of Black theatre. In one sense, this sophistication was achieved by severe delimitation of purpose: following Kgositsile's lead, theorists of the Black theatre began to address themselves exclusively to the need for a drama of, about, and within the Black nation. Ron Milner, a leading playwright in the movement, struck a major chord with his plea for Black theatre to "go home" to the Black community both psychically and physically:

> This new theatre must be housed in, sustained and judged by, and be a useable projection of, and to, a black community! The community itself will be the theatre, and the black artist's house of drama like a weirdly fixed and pointed looking-glass, a light-prism casting warnings, directions, fruitful memories and marvelous imaginings on the walls of the doomed, or soon to be recreated buildings.[9]

In language no less urgent and vivid than Baraka's, Milner here challenges the Black playwright to draw his material from the people to whom he, in turn, communicates intensified and organized perceptions. Milner's Black theatre assumes a unified Black consciousness as audience; a theatre for the oppressed, it is yet not a "theatre of victims" but an expressive instrument of a struggling, cohesive nation. Though still announcing a drama of "warnings" and "directions," Milner now speaks of "marvelous imaginings," those "projections" of communal liberation that would free Black theatre from the bonds of realism, "assault," and preachment. Theatre is now no longer seen as a discrete institution addressing itself to a fragmented audience; nor is it simply within its chosen community: it and the community are enwapped synergically in mutually defining union. Here we verge on the transformation of drama into ritual; for Milner's theatre could not, like the theatre of assault, be the formalization of ideology into narrative or emblem. Rather, it would have to do with essences, fatalities and com-

[9]"Black Theater—Go Home!" in *The Black Aesthetic,* edited by Addison Gayle, Jr. (New York, 1972), pp. 288-94 (written in 1968).

pleted acts in which the destinies of self and group are indissoluble. It would, above all, move toward the simultaneous creation and expression of collectivity.

Larry Neal's "The Black Arts Movement"[10] which, along with Baraka's "The Revolutionary Theatre," is the most influential commentary on modern Black drama, joins Milner's manifesto in affirming "the integral relationship between Black Art and Black People." Indeed, Neal's article, which combines theory with an acute critical summary of the pre-1968 revolutionary drama, opens with the declaration that "the Black Arts Movement is radically opposed to any concept of the artist that alienates him from his community." Echoing Baraka's ongoing critique of Black literature as a whole, Neal emphasizes throughout his essay the need for an autonomous "symbolism, mythology, critique, and iconology" to facilitate the construction of a Black drama wedded to the history and desires of Afro-America. Neal was among the first writers to perceive the need for the Black theatre to develop new techniques and idioms to convey a new system of beliefs.

Milner, too, had perceived the formal requirements of a Black-oriented theatre, but in decidedly vague terms:

> I won't go into the demand for new dynamics, for a new intensity of language and form, that the material and the desired atmosphere will make on you; except to say that the further you go home, the more startlingly new and black the techniques become.[11]

To Milner's nascent awareness of structural demands, Neal added concrete suggestions for a formally viable Black aesthetic. He directed the playwright's attention to the cultural traditions of Afro-American and African societies.[12] Spirit worship, whether embodied in African orishas, Voodoo, or Afro-Christianity, could provide a source of emotive energy; jubilees, blues, spirituals, and dance would allow for rhythmic and lyric expressiveness; shamans, preachers, musicians, hustlers, conjurers, poets, and various other "survivors" would stock a theatre with a complex amalgam of heroes

[10]*TDR* 12, no. 4 (Summer, 1968), 29-39. The entire Summer, 1968 issue of *TDR* was devoted to plays, essays, and documents related to Black theatre and became, as Jeyifous points out, a kind of "collective manifesto" of the movement.

[11]"Black Theater—Go Home!," p. 291.

[12]In addition to "The Black Arts Movement," see Neal's "Some Reflections on the Black Aesthetic," in *The Black Aesthetic*, ed. Gayle, pp. 12-15.

and moral forces; and the collective folk consciousness in general would offer a plethora of responses to and transcendences of diasporic Black life. Neal and Milner together discerned that if Black drama is to be a vehicle of Black values, truly separate from the Euro-American mainstream, it must be shaped into new forms which are yet rooted in historically valid expressions of the Black people it serves. Thus what began with Baraka as a revolt against established conventions has become a revolutionary discovery of the need for convention on a deeper level; the early antipathy to form itself has metamorphosed into a discussion of the possibility of form. The focus of theoretical exploration has shifted from persistently ideological inquiry (which, after all, gave the initial impetus to Afro-American theatrical experimentation) to concern with the nucleus of the artistic transaction where ideology (content) and its theatrical embodiment (process) find their nexus.

The 1960s, then, saw a development in treatises on Black theatre from abstract, didactic discussion of existing institutions to an affirmation of unified Black strength and a fresh, more particularized dedication to constructing new traditions and new forms by reworking the best of the old. Since the early seventies, several theorists have offered blueprints for a distinctively Black theatrical event. Whatever their specific proposals, these writers share the belief that, as Clayton Riley expressed it, Black theatre should be "structured to take people away from basics, from fundamentals, into a special kind of chapel atmosphere for rituals."[13] As "ritual" has supplanted "message" as the key word in the theorists' rhetoric, religiosity, emotiveness, and style have overtaken didacticism as defining elements of Black theatre. And, quite naturally, the processes of performance, or ceremony, have replaced the particularities of text as the theatre's focal points.

Once again, Amiri Baraka initiated this change in tenor from anger to celebration with a call for plays which would show "how we triumphed."[14] Milner, however, was one of the first writers to outline the specific features and methods which might characterize such a theatre. He had already hinted at these in "Black Theater — Go Home!" when he asserted that "musicians are pointing out to

[13]"On Black Theater," in *The Black Aesthetic*, ed. Gayle, p. 309.
[14]"What the Arts Need Now," in *Raise Race Rays Raze: Essays Since 1965* (New York, 1971), p. 33.

us" the inevitability of innovative techniques in a distinctively Black art. Eight years later he declared:

> Everything is music. My whole basis for art—the only criteria or model I have. ... If you listen to the good lines in a show, and the show is moving right, it's moving like a piece of music, and it has to hit like a piece of music. ... If it doesn't do that, it just sits there and it's just a play.[15]

Most Black writers have claimed Black music as an inspiration to their efforts. Yet Milner presses this relation nearly to the point of identity. The essence of music, for Milner, is its affective quality, its ability to initiate the listener into its special cosmos. The call-and-response pattern characteristic of Afro-American music is a legacy of African ritual, that functional locus of communal wisdom which Milner identifies as the ur-theatre of Black culture. Thus Milner's Afro-American theatre will be a synthesis of African-rooted spirituality and Afro-American musical form, a secularized structuring of tribal ceremony:

> Black theatre is moving to the point where we've taken the ritual, passion, drama, and intensity of the church and put it into secular music so it can be a functional kind of thing; so you can use your catharsis, your collective energy and collective prayer in your every-day life. When Black theatre has incorporated those three ingredients —the church, the rock n' roll music dynamic and the drama—then it will be total and full.[16]

Milner's musical-ritual vision of Black theatre has found its practical realization in several impressive plays, particularly Milner's own *Season's Reasons* and Baraka's *Slave Ship*. Like African ceremony, this Afro-American theatre of music and dance has both purpose and meaning. At once visionary and functional—functional, in fact, *because* visionary—it elides passion and creation and equates creativity with significance. Milner's thesis exploits the pre-established symbiosis between Black audience and Black musician. He seeks thereby to free the Afro-American theatre from the shackles of the written narrative, to replace communication with manifestation. Re-presenting encoded modes of thinking as inscribed into a written script gives way here to improvisational action and

---

[15]Quoted in "We Are the Music: Ron Milner, People's Playwright," by Geneva Smitherman, *Black World* 25, no. 6 (April, 1976), p. 4.

[16]*Ibid.*, p. 6.

vocality. The perspectival relationship (and barrier) between seer and seen that is essential to traditional drama is dissolved into the im-mediacy of ritual flux. The dramatic event thus posited is one in which Black people can experience communal identity and solidarity during the theatrical happening itself.

This is the point from which succeeding Afro-American dramatic theorists have begun: How can the audience be even *more* actively involved? How can its experience become even more direct, even more *real?* For "realism," as a kind of metaphor of concrete aspiration, maintains its force even as the formal dialectic swings away from the pole of narrative coherence and mimesis. Free from narrow aesthetic prescriptions by virtue of a more rigorous commitment to the generative ideal of communal liberation, the playwrights have logically seized upon the form in which Afro-American conservatism and rebellion alike are rooted: religious ceremony.

Though religious in its implication of ritual celebration, Milner's theatre stresses its secular form as shaped by the rhythmic interactions of music, dance, tale, and poetry. Black ritual theatre as espoused by such artists as Barbara Ann Teer, Carlton Molette II, and Paul Carter Harrison utilizes these archetypal expressions in a more overtly religious framework. Molette, in stark contrast to the sixties' playwright's assault against the "Old Spirituality,"[17] has heralded the dynamic ceremonies of the Afro-Christian church as the basis for a spiritually invigorated communal drama.[18] As in the earliest manifestoes of the movement, Molette's model performer is the preacher. Yet, for Molette, the essence of the preacher's sermon "is not what he says...it is the way he says it." Molette is not eschewing verbal communication; rather, he is asserting the formative role of process in determining meaning, while recognizing the traditional Afro-American fusion of oratory and active response. In this "house of drama" (to appropriate Milner's phrase), the Apollonian compression of character is loosened by a Dionysian effusion of shared passions, motives, and moments. Molette's model is the Afro-Christian chanted sermon in which the biblical text is gradually subsumed into a communal ecstasy centered in spon-

[17]This is Neal's term for the Black Christian philosophy that stresses assimilation. Three plays which Neal singles out as particularly critical of the "Old Spirituality" are Milner's *Who's Got His Own*, Jimmy Garret's *We Own the Night*, and Ben Caldwell's *The Militant Preacher*.

[18]See "Afro-American Ritual Drama," *Black World* 22, no. 6 (April, 1973), 4-12.

taneous song, shout, and dance. In this "order of service," the preacher's use of oral techniques—repetition, rhythmic emphasis, variety of pitch—bends the relatively arbitrary textual content to the primary intention of "heightening emotional intensity." Church ceremony thereby creates, as Molette says, "a total spiritual involvement,...an affirmation of a sense of community." For the ritual-minded playwright, no longer embroiled in a confrontation with mainstream drama as were Baraka and Kgositsile, the chanting preacher is a more viable exemplar than the typical dramatist: through his agency (call), the audience/congregation encounters (responds to and realizes) the Other but is not other; it believes rather than appreciates; it creates through time yet abolishes time (the condition of true freedom); it is efficacious, not entertained.

The religious basis of Paul Carter Harrison's ritual theatre, while incorporating elements of Afro-Christian rites, is primarily African in influence and hence archeological and philosophical in character. Harrison's writings, the last to be considered in this exposition of Black theatre theories, constitute the most articulate dissertation on Black drama yet recorded. His theory begins in a critique of the agit-prop/sermonizing drama of the sixites. Though ostensibly designed to communicate with the Black masses, Black theatre which places dogmatic conceptions above the imaginative flexibility of the audience is, in Harrison's view, condescending and doomed to failure:

> The embattled brutha on the block finds it burdensome to wade through the heavy polemical prolixity...which tends to inhibit the necessary catharsis while whetting the radical palates of the white bourgeois intelligentsia. ... Street plays...tend to have an ephemeral effect on the brutha who eschews the realistic detailing of his immediate surroundings and which urge him to action that has consequences he is only too familiar with and which he is unwilling to be glib about.[19]

Harrison, quite unlike the Baraka of "The Revolutionary Theatre," assumes that the Black spectator is well aware of the injury to which he is daily subjected. What he seeks, therefore, is not a theatre of violent indoctrination but a mode of "spiritual release." He urges the Black dramatist to "move beyond material objectivity to form a

---

[19]Quotations of Harrison are from *The Drama of Nommo* (New York, 1972), unless otherwise noted.

nexus with our spiritual experiences." Toward this end he shares with Milner an advocation of "cultural continuity" or, more specifically, a veneration of Afro-American musical and religious conventions as appropriate vehicles of Black theatre ritual. At the same time, he shares with Molette a persistent emphasis upon the spiritual as opposed to the secular power of such models. But he departs from both Milner and Molette in finding within all potential elements of the Afro-American theatre dynamic an essential manifestation or memory of an ancestral African ethos.

Following Janheinz Jahn's analysis of traditional African and neo-African cultures,[20] Harrison outlines a theatre based on the specific terminology of Bantu cosmology. According to Bantu logic, *Muntu,* or all intelligible life including man, *Kintu,* or all objective phenomena, and *Hantu,* or the intersecting dimensions of time and space, all cohere as a single reality under the aegis of *NTU,* or Pure Being. *Kuntu,* or the modality and contextual origin of an image, and *Nommo,* or the image (Word) itself, are the forces by which man as *Muntu* brings himself into harmony with other enveloping forces. The precise emanations of these forces and their mutually sustaining relationships are very complex, and even Harrison has little use for the more esoteric aspects of the Bantu system. His citation of Bantu cosmology is, in fact, a clever rhetorical device by which he undermines the more "practical" and prosaic systems of nationalist ideologues, replacing them with a flexible lexicon of psychical and metaphysical dicta.

All Black theatre, according to Harrison, should be measured, not by a standard of realism or anger, but by its ability to "invoke the force of our ancestral spirits." Thus, the Baptist preacher, the bluesman, the modern jazz artist, the poet, and "even the Pimp peacocking in his colorful threads" are not simply historically interesting heroes but common purveyors of the Bantu traditions. And just as the various elements of the Bantu force-field form a synthetic whole, so the ultimate task of Black theatre ritual—the "Kuntu drama"[21] —is affirmation of a collective consciousness, a shared and traditional sensibility nurtured by spiritual vitality.

[20]See *Muntu* (New York, 1961).
[21]Harrison has collected a number of plays under this title (*Kuntu Drama:* New York, 1974) which he feels are representative of the new aesthetic of ritual. His own play, *The Great MacDaddy,* is probably the best exemplar of this aesthetic included in the anthology.

The Kuntu drama espoused by Harrison cultivates an audience whose members, "owing to African continuity, are not spectators by nature."[22] The distinctive aspect of this drama is theatrical energy, in regard to both performance technique and to the depth of lyrical-metaphysical content with which it deals. As in Barbara Ann Teer's Harlem-based National Black Theatre Company, which serves as an important model for Harrison's concepts, there are no *actors* or *spectators* in Harrison's drama, but instead *activators* (Teer employs the more adulatory term *"liberators"*) and *participators*. The improvisations of the theatrical event—activated by the leaders' invocation of traditional motifs, sounds, or words (Nommo)—becomes idealized content in the Kuntu drama. The end toward which each such occasion should move is destruction of any sense of theatre as spectacle and inclusion of the whole "congregation" in ritual activity. What the spectator at first watches he must ultimately become. Yet inclusion and participation are not mere metaphors; they are concrete physical acts. The audience must be permitted to control the space, to actually feel that it is their space just as the activators' images are, by ancestral right, the community's.

This is no small part of the reaction against the conventional Euro-American theatre, whose physical space, like the events within it, is compartmentalized and strictly contained—an accurate metaphor of the conceptual demarcations which give the Euro-American theatre its "meaning." By contrast, many Afro-American community theatres (Detroit's Concept East being a lively example) exemplify a resistance to the predeterminations of the proscenium and "round" architecture: they often allow the particular rite and its participants to define the playing space. Thus, as Harrison says, "the *event* becomes the context of reality, a force-field of phenomena which is ritualized."[23] The performance thereby rises out of the audience, develops through both open and closed audience permission, and finally flows into the communal will. It is this rhythm of dialectical stimulation and response that Harrison feels can fulfill the original and still essential aim of modern Black theatre:

> A vehicle should be sought that allows the experience to be confirmed by the intuition of the *participators,* be it uh-huh, a finger-pop, or

[22]"Who Knows What Beauty Rests in the Souls of Men? The *Shadow* Do!," in *Black Review No. 2,* edited by Mel Watkins (New York, 1972), p. 147.

[23]"Introduction," *Kuntu Drama,* p. 8.

a muted howl, so as to achieve totality. Perhaps then, theatre, as a secondary experience, will influence our primary experience: LIFE.

III

Theoretical concepts within the contemporary Black drama movement have been varied yet oriented toward unification of ideological, emotional, and aesthetic impulses. Contrary to general supposition, descriptions of Black theatre's character among its leading practitioners have been diverse and, taken together, intellectually progressive. Baraka was perhaps the most prophetic and cogent critic of the new movement when he wrote in the first sentence of his pioneering manifesto, "The revolutionary theatre should force change; it should be change."

The evolutionary path dictated by Black playwrights' ever-changing perspectives has led from an emphasis on naturalism and pedagogy to an equally passionate desire for ritual celebration of a common ethos. The primary aim of the Black theatre event has thus altered radically in the past fifteen years from "educating the people" to embracing the audience in collective affirmation of certain values, styles, and goals. If strictly ideological gestures have been curtailed, the theatre has become no less political, for the new forms cannot function without direct reference to the society in which they are embedded. Whether recalling the past or restructuring the present, Harrison's ritual performance, like Baraka's "revolutionary" realism, is essentially a prediction for a reordered future. Modern Black drama, at every point, pits an awareness of contingency against an assertion of control. The result has been not dramatic irony but the invigorating innovations of what Bullins has recently termed *Black dialectics:* "the dialectic of change and the dialectic of experience."[24] It is a dialectic pressing the dual claims of completion and renewal, seeking the image of Afro-America, as Sonia Sanchez has declared, "surviving yet not surviving but being."[25]

Black theatre itself has faithfully emulated its philosophical guides. Indeed, theory and practice have rarely been as sensitive

[24]"Introduction," *The New Lafayette Theatre Presents,* ed. Ed Bullins (New York, 1974), p. 4.
[25]"A Conversation with Sonia Sanchez," in *The New Lafayette Theatre Presents,* p. 163.

to each other as in the Black Arts Movement. The large body of theoretical criticism generated by the movement has been fundamentally necessary to its practical evolution. The energy of the theory's initial revolt from inherited idioms was the moving power; and the theory's intelligence ensured that it would pass, almost immediately, into construction and into creative development. Playwrights in the movement have instinctively recognized that the problem of collectivity—the keynote of all the manifestoes—is, in artistic terms, the problem of convention, and the revolt of their art against established social orders has become a revolution of form. The history of their theatre—a chronicle as yet unwritten—would thus be a tale of radical experiment and innovation. Whatever shape such a chronicle may take, it must be sure to locate the formal junctures of ideological prescription and poetic energy, and to discern their dialectical relation in the Black dramatists' search for a theatre of communality. The dramatists' own explorations demand nothing less.

America's Debt to the Language
of Black Americans

by Jim Haskins and Hugh F. Butts, M.D.

It would be ideal if, simultaneously with the recognition by white standard-English speakers of the legitimacy of black English and the learning of standard English by disadvantaged black children, there were to be a recognition by white America of its debt to the language of black Americans. Particularly in the area of informal language, this debt is great; but it is also considerable in literature and music and, to a certain extent, perhaps, also in the actual thought processes of white America. Such a recognition should not be difficult; one need only listen to American slang, for example, to know that it is largely black slang. One need only realize that in a situation where two different groups experience prolonged close sociocultural contact there is bound to be not only conflict but also cultural exchange. Arguments stressing the dominant position of whites and the subcultural and thus non-influential (upon whites) existence of blacks have no factual basis. Even a casual investigation into any analogous historical situation should reveal, as Wilhelm Reich has pointed out, that a subculture always has a proportionately larger impact upon a dominant culture than vice versa.

Many of the black language influences upon the American language have gone unrecognized because they have been slow and subtle. Many also have gone unrecognized because they were originally introduced by whites as conscious imitations of blacks to achieve humor or local color. The fact that in many cases these influences remained on their own terms is not acknowledged. This [essay] will treat a few examples in the areas of literature, music, and informal language.

Drama

Black dialects early found their way into American literature, much earlier than the nineteenth-century local-color movement, erroneously considered by many to have produced the first extensive use in writing of American black language. As early as 1721, Cotton Mather had recorded three words of the black dialect: *grondy* (many); *cutty* (skin); and *sicky* (sick). And about 1782 Benjamin Franklin inserted four or five lines of black dialect into his tract "Information to Those Who Would Remove to America."[1]

But it is in American drama that the black dialect first comes to the fore with any regularity or relevance. At least ten plays written before 1800 show this influence. The dialect in these plays was not written according to any literary tradition or formula. There can be little doubt that most of the black characters were drawn from life and that their speech is a crude, occasionally distorted, duplication of the sounds which the playwrights thought they had heard. There is very little consistency of spelling or syntax, even within the same play, but such variations are understandable. Not until much later did written black dialect assume literary conventionality. And uniformity was genuinely impossible in the eighteenth century; many slaves had only recently been brought from Africa and were struggling to learn English despite the interferences that their various languages produced.

According to Arthur Hobson Quinn, the first black character in American drama is the servant Ralpho in Robert Munford's comedy of elections in Virginia, *The Candidates* (written 1770, published 1798).[2] Ralpho does not speak in dialect (evidently), but his music of multisyllabic words would become typical of the comic black of later drama. "Gadso!" he says, "This figure of mine is not reconsiderable in its delurements, and when I'm dressed out like a gentleman, the girls, I'm thinking, will find me desistible."

[1]Cited in Allen Walker Reed, "The Speech of Negroes in Colonial America," *Journal of Negro History* 34 (1939), p. 248.

[2]Quoted in Jay B. Hubbell and Douglas Adair, "Robert Munford's 'The Candidates,'" *William and Mary Quarterly* 5 (1948), pp. 217-20.

The first positive use of black dialect in American drama was probably an anonymous play entitled *The Trial of Atticus, before Justice Beau, for a Rape* (1771). Caesar, a black comic, makes a brief appearance at the trial:

> *Justice.* Well, *Caesar,* did Mrs. Chuckle ever tell you anything about *Atticus'* abusing of her?
> *Caesar.* Yesa, Maser, *he* tell me that *Atticus* he went to bus 'em one day, and shilde [child] cry, and so he let 'em alone.
> *Justice.* How came she tell you of this?
> *Caesar.* Cause, Maser, I bus *him* myself.[3]

The author of the play considered Caesar's substituting the masculine for the feminine pronoun when referring to Mrs. Chuckle odd enough to be italicized, a fact that is helpful in tracing various features of black English in history.

Extensive use of black dialect is evident in the play *Occurrences of the Times,* written in 1789. Following is a typical speech by the black Debauchee, about a duel that did not take place:

> Ah! dat is—we didn't fite—twixt you and I, massa he no courage. Misser *Harcourt* he say—shentlemen preas to measus; and my massa say—shentlemen you no de law.[4]

Although the playwright took little care to render the dialect consistently (*assassinate* is written as *cisnate* in one passage and as *fascinate* in another), Debauchee's speech is quite convincing, and indeed, the playwright was quite faithful to a number of dialectical rules.

Some playwrights and other writers eventually brought black dialect to the point of near-unintelligibility. Samuel Low's *The Politician Out-witted* (written in 1788) is an example. When Humphrey offers to help his servant carry a trunk, Cuffy replies:

> Tankee, massa buckaraw; you gi me lilly lif, me bery glad;—disa ting damma heby. (Puts down the trunk.)—An de debelis crooka tone ina treet more worsa naw pricka pear for poor son a bitch foot; and de cole pinch um so too![5]

---

[3] Quoted in Richard Walser, "Negro Dialect in Eighteenth-Century American Drama," *American Speech* 30 (1955), p. 271.

[4] *Ibid.,* p. 272.

[5] *Ibid.*

As this is the only speech Cuffy makes, it is clear that Low employed the use of dialect purely for color—a very self-conscious device.

Despite the exaggerations, the oddities of spelling not warranted by the spoken language (e.g., *fite* for *fight*), and the comic intentions which caused the playwrights to overcolor the language in order to provide humor, these early dramatic efforts represent the first consistent attempts to translate the spoken sounds and sentences into written words. They mark the beginning of a literature of black dialect which eventually was to become characteristic of much of the best native American writing. When the local-color movement—the first truly American literary trend—arose in the nineteenth century, black life, black folklore, and most of all black dialect were major and determining aspects.

Folktales

White writers have borrowed heavily from black folklore. Gombo stories like the following are the source of Joel Chandler Harris's "Brer Rabbit" stories.

Before every Gombo story there was a ritual. The black narrator would call out "Bonne foi! Bonne foi!" in order to attract attention and give some validity to his story. The listeners would then answer in unison, "Lapin! Lapin!" to show they were just as smart as the storyteller and indeed would take the story with a grain of salt. Then the storyteller would launch into some tale like that of Compair Bouki (Friend Goat), who fired up his kettle and began to sing to attract the macaques (monkeys). After the simian tribe had gathered, Compair Bouki said, "I'm goint to jump in the kettle, and when I say 'I'm cooked,' take me out." They did as he ordered, but when the monkeys' turn came and they jumped into the pot and then asked to be taken out, Compair Bouki replied ironically, "If you were cooked, you wouldn't be able to say so." Only one little monkey escaped. Then Bouki tried the same trick with another group of monkeys. But the first little monkey had warned his kind, so when the goat, expecting to be taken out, said "I'm cooked," the macaques left him in the pot and chanted gleefully, "If you were cooked, you wouldn't be able to say so."[6]

[6]Tinker, *Gombo: The Creole Dialect of Louisiana*, pp. 12-13.

The relation of this tale to the "Brer Rabbit" stories is obvious, as is its relation to African stories like that of Minaba, a young girl who lived with her mother and two sisters in a poor village where there was little meat to be had. One day, after struggling to place a full bucket of water upon her head, she accepted the assistance of a kuku, a monkey-like animal, who had come to the water pipe to drink. Thinking how sweet and tender the kuku would be to eat but not wanting to share the food with her sisters, Minaba later sneaked back to the spot where she had met the kuku and killed it with her bow and arrow. Her sisters were angry with her when she returned with her prize. When the kuku was ready to be cooked, Minaba asked her sisters to help her prepare the pot and cook him, but the dead kuku sang, "Let Minaba cook the food alone because when Minaba came to the pipe I was the one who helped her," and the sisters refused. When the kuku was cooked, the sisters declined to join Minaba in eating the meat, saying, "Eat it yourself," and so Minaba ate the whole thing by herself. In a little while, Minaba began to feel sick and she asked her sisters to take her to a cool, shady place in the forest where she could lie down. But before the sisters could respond, the kuku inside Minaba's stomach began to sing, "Let Minaba go alone because when Minaba went to the pipe I was the one who helped her." Minaba had to go to the forest alone. She rolled on the ground in pain, and then suddenly the kuku ran out of Minaba's mouth and Minaba lay still, dead.[7]

The preceding stories show a worldly-wise understanding of character. At the same time they manage to relate to class consciousness and to make shrewd and exact observations of situations. Their appeal is great and they have exercised considerable influence upon American writers. The greatest tribute, perhaps, has been paid by Ambrose Gonzales, who not only wrote folktales after the manner of Gullah folktales but also wrote them in perfect Gullah dialect.

White Southern Speech

In order to acquire the intimate knowledge of the black idioms and dialects which they so skillfully use, both Gonzales and Harris

[8]Ann Sullivan Haskett, "The Representation of Gullah-Influenced Dialect in Twentieth Century South Carolina Prose: 1922-1930." (University of Pennsylvania Ph.D. Dissertation, 1964), pp. 238-41.

must have experienced them at firsthand for some time, probably since childhood.[8] Such experience was not at all uncommon in the South and indeed seems to have been sufficiently widespread to constitute another example of the influence of the black dialect upon standard English, at least southern standard English.

In 1746, G. L. Campbell, a British traveler to the American colonies, wrote of the southern white planters: "One thing they are very faulty in, with regard to their Children, which is, that when young, they suffer them too much to prowl amongst the young Negroes, which insensibly causes them to imbibe their manner and broken speech."[9]

In 1908, describing the Charlestonian aristocracy of his day, John Bennett wrote: "It is true that, up to the age of four, approximately, the children of the best families, even in town, are apt to speak an almost unmodified Gullah, caught from brown playmates and country bred nurses; but at that age the refinement of cultivation begins, and "the flowers o' the forest are a' weed awa!"[10]

A fairly common opinion is that Gullah is a dying dialect, now limited to the Carolina Sea Islands. There is abundant evidence, however, that it or a transitional dialect based on it, is still widely spoken, even in metropolitan Charleston, and even by some whites. It is useless to argue that it is natural for children to pick up the language but that once they reach adolescence they are immune to further influence.

Today, social conditions are such that communication between black and white children is not so intimate as it was in the days of plantation and plantation-like life. Nevertheless, those black dialect words and forms that the white children did imbibe in those days, though weakened through time, must still be assumed to exert an influence in the speech of whites in the onetime plantation areas.

Slang

The vital and increasing influence of black words and forms upon American slang need not be assumed. It obviously exists in the

[9]Quoted in William A. Stewart, "Continuity and Change in American Negro Dialects," *The Florida FL Reporter* (Spring 1968), p. 21, note 12.

[10] John Bennett, "Gullah: A Negro Patois," *The South Atlantic Quarterly* 7 (1908), p. 339.

speech of those whites who "dig" jazz, in that of whites who are associated with those who "dig" jazz, and in that of those young whites disillusioned with the dominant American culture who have absorbed the language of the black subculture. This language has been used by the young both as a defense mechanism and as an articulation of the revolutionary spirit, reasons that stand in sharp contrast to the original, slanderous imitation of the slaves' speech by white slaveholders or the "black-face" "black-talk" of white minstrels. Of course, vestiges of the original smirking use remain, but in most instances the usage is open, respectful, and conscious of the alternatives to the dominant culture intrinsic in black life and black language. But more important than this influence are the unconscious uses of black slang throughout the country and the open, conscious imitation of blacks. ...

Perhaps the most widely used slang form traceable to black origins is the term *O.K.* Attempts to trace the term to English, German, French, Finnish, Greek, and Choctaw sources have met with little success. *O.K.* can be shown to derive from similar expressions in a number of African languages and to have been used in black Jamaican English more than twenty years before its use by whites in New England.[11]

Some of the other "Americanisms" that appear to have an African or probably African origin are *jazz, jitter* and *jitter-bug, hep* (or *hip*), *banjo, boogie-woogie, jam* (as in *jam session*), *jive, to goose, to bug someone, to lam* (go), *to dig* (to understand or appreciate), *uh-huh* and *uh-uh* (for yes and no), *ofay* and *honkie* (names for the white man), *cocktail, guy,* and *bogus.* Many such words are direct-loan words from Africa; others are metamorphosed African words; and still others are direct translations.

Among the most interesting forms are those that express concepts oppositioned to the standard English usage: such as *bad* meaning good; *hard* having a positive connotation; *kill* to mean affect strongly, to fascinate; *love letter* to mean a bullet; and *murder* to express approval of something excellent. The source of these forms is not African; it is distinctly Afro-American, born of the need of blacks to change or "negate" the negative concept of blackness.[12]

---

[11]*New York Times,* August 25, 1971, p. 35.

[12]Clarence Major, *Dictionary of Afro-American Slang* (New York: International Publishers, 1970), pp. 13-14.

Music

Black jazz musicians were chiefly responsible for many black language influences upon American slang. They originated the vernacular of what is perhaps the most original and revolutionary art form in North America.

Black music per se may be said to occupy that unique position. The United States consumes a great deal of music, but as yet has not produced nearly so much as it consumes. Unlike most other nations, it does not have a wealth of native music. The only native music it can boast is black music, but American has not yet accepted that simple truth. Black music is the closest America has to folk music and as such black music is—or should be—as important to American musical culture as it is to the spiritual existence of blacks.

Folk Music. Folk music is produced without formal musical training; it is an emotional creation born out of deep suffering and its spiritual compensation in intense religious feeling. Black folk music comprises the spirituals. It evolved on the plantation, and because the plantation was far from theaters, music halls, and other sources of entertainment, it was encouraged by the whites. Through their blacks, the whites had entertainment, and black folk music thereby seeped into the skins of the southern aristocrats.

Popular Music. Popular black music is the black man's own natural return to gaiety and humor informed by sorrow and seriousness. For a long time this music was confined chiefly to the black community. However, in the years since World War II, with the recording business boom, popular black music has become popular American music. Black performers or white performers whose style is imitative of black styles head record-rating charts, and it is clear that if it were not for black popular music there would have been no such phenomenon in American musical culture.

Jazz. The third, or classical, type of black music is contemporary classical jazz, a derivation of the spiritual and folklore form, as is, for that matter, popular black music. Jazz is the child of an urban experience, while blues is that of a rural experience. As George Cain puts it in his novel *Blueschild Baby,* "Jazz is the city, only city niggers can feel this thing. I never liked it much, never listened really, hadn't been here long enough. To my country ear it was mad noise. But I'm a part of the tremendous pressure that generates that sound and I feel it so good now. Jazz is the black man's history."[13]

Or as Cecil Taylor says about his music in the liner notes of his *Looking Ahead,* "Everything I've lived, I am."[14] Music, like religion, is very much a part of the psychology of blacks in America. Like religion, it is black people's own special brand of worship and style, contributing much to the black man's perception and self-esteem.

But although it is a product of the unique black experience, jazz is also universal. Langston Hughes found this in his travels: "Everywhere, around the world," he noted in *I Wonder As I Wander,* "folks are attracted by American jazz. A good old Dixieland stomp can break down almost any language barriers, and there is something about Louis Armstrong's horn that creates spontaneous friendships."[15] This universality is intensified when jazz is analyzed in terms of its impact upon America. Increasingly urbanized, pervaded by the tension of a fast, ever-changing society, subject to "future shock," America in its entirety reverberates to the sound of jazz. Jazz—black jazz—is the expression of America.

The popularity of black music does not of course extend equally to all segments of American society. It applies chiefly to urbanized Americans, to rebellious Americans, and to young Americans in whom can be found at its greatest heights, the tension of America. It is for these people that the black musician and black music speak the truth. The musician and his music represent a breaking away from tradition and a turning to a new vision. They symbolize rebellion, and, at the same time change, at their heights. For urbanized Americans they are musical translations of life as well as means of escape from life. For rebellious Americans and for American youth, they are "underground" forms of communicating, and means by which to gain access to the black (real feeling and living) experience.

"Communication" is the important word here. Before man "advanced" to the literal stage, he lived in cultures where feelings were purely feelings and labels for them were not necessary. And it seems that today we may be finding our literal culture evolving back to

[13]George Cain, *Blueschild Baby* (New York: McGraw-Hill, 1970), p. 133.

[14]Cecil Taylor, *Looking Ahead* (Contemporary Records), liner notes.

[15]Langston Hughes, *I Wonder As I Wander* (New York: Hill and Wang, 1956), p. 114.

an essentially nonliteral one; witness the rock culture, in which noise and sounds seem to be enough to transmit the message of the "youth culture" to youth, and the thousands of sensitivity groups springing up around the country that emphasize touching as a chief means of communication. Perhaps because blacks in America have historically been thwarted in communicating verbally or literally, jazz is essentially nonverbal communication, on an emotional level. This is a kind of communication increasingly sought by alienated Americans. It has wedged itself deeply into the sensibility of black Americans, but also it has become more than ever before an extension of young or rebellious white persons' *conscious* communication apparatus.

Conclusion

Black language has exerted a strong influence upon the literature, informal language, and music of white America, not to mention the actual psyche of white America. It would behoove white America to realize this influence if it is ever in mature awareness to know itself.

An Origin For The Negro Spiritual

by Eileen Southern

The origin of the so-called Negro spiritual is lost in the past and shrouded with obscurity. It was not until 1867 that the first collection of slave songs was formally presented to the world in the book entitled *Slave Songs of the United States,* edited by William Allen, Charles Ware, and Lucy McKim Garrison.[1] By that date, however, spirituals had been sung by blacks for so many years that none could remember a time when spirituals were unknown. The student singers from the newly-established Fisk Institute, who set out on their first concert tour on October 6, 1871, included the singing of spirituals on their programs. These young people, called the Fisk Jubilee Singers, had had no contact with Allen's collection of 1867, but they sang some of the same songs that were in the collection. They had learned these songs from their parents, who had obtained the songs from *their* parents, who had learned the songs from yet earlier generations.

The Jubilee Singers carried the spirituals all over the nation, singing in churches and in concert halls, and then traveled abroad where they sang for the crowned heads of Europe. In the winter of 1872-73 a second group of student singers, from Hampton Institute, embarked upon a concert tour to raise money for the school by singing slave songs for the public. Everywhere people were enthralled by the beauty and "quaint charm" of these songs which, although new to the white public, were ancient among black folk.

In probing into the origin of a cultural phenomenon such as the Negro spiritual, several approaches are possible: the time of origin,

"An Origin for the Negro Spiritual" by Eileen Southern. From *The Black Scholar,* Vol. 3 No. 10 (Summer 1972), pp. 8-13. Reprinted by permission of *The Black Scholar* and the author.

[1]New York: A. Simpson & Co., 1867.

the place of origin, or the manner of origin. I will discuss all three approaches. Because of the paucity of historical evidence, theories with regard to any one of these three aspects will of necessity be speculative. Nevertheless, my research has uncovered a considerable amount of data, and it is possible to interpret this extant data, in such a manner as to throw new light upon what has been a controversial subject for many decades. Frequently statements have been made, orally and in print, that the slaves were taught spirituals by their slaveowners or that the spirituals were merely imitations of European folksongs.[2] Such statements represent utter nonsense, of course, but it will be of value to investigate the subject with the purpose of finding out what might have been the true state of affairs.

First, we should define the spiritual, for the term has been applied incorrectly to more than one song type during the course of music history. With regard to genre, the spiritual falls into the category of folk music; that is, it existed for a long period of time in oral tradition before being written down in musical notation. Generally, the name of the original author of a folksong has been forgotten. In any event, the people have taken over the song and reshaped it to such an extent over the years, that the song bears little resemblance to its pristine form, apart from the basic melodic structure and the essential message of the text. During the process of oral transmission, the song is adapted to the music taste of both performers and listeners. With regard to class, the spiritual represents religious or sacred folk music, often referred to as folk hymnody. In essence, the so-called Negro spiritual is the religious musical expression of black folk in the United States. It must be observed that the spiritual is to be distinguished from the "gospel song" which, although religious, is the invention of a *single* personality who provides a definitive version of his song by writing it in musical notation or by making a recording of it.

Our search for the origin of the spiritual necessarily begins with the year 1619 when black men first arrived on the shores of the mainland of the New World. Although Africans were brought here naked and in chains, they carried with them, nevertheless, an invisible kind of baggage—the rich cultural heritage of their homeland, especially with regard to music and dance. Olaudah Equiano, the first

[2]See, for example, the writings of George Pullen Jackson, particularly *White and Negro Spirituals*, New York: J. J. Augustin Publishers, 1943.

African to publish his autobiography in the English language, tells us in 1789:

> We are almost a nation of dancers, musicians, and poets. Every great event, such as a triumphant return from battle or other cause of public rejoicing, is celebrated in public dances, which are accompanied with songs and Musicke suited to the occasion. ...[3]

Numerous sources of the eighteenth century report upon the musical activities of the enslaved Africans in the colonies, singling out for special mention that the black folk sang songs in their native African languages and danced to the accompaniment of home-made instruments that resembled the traditional African instruments. In the northern colonies, the celebration of Pinkster holidays (the week following Pentecost Sunday) was turned over almost entirely to the blacks, slave and free, who revived African festivals as they had performed them in the countries of West Africa, the ancestral lands of most black Americans.[4] In New England, blacks sang and danced in the African manner during their so-called 'Lection Day festivities. In some places—for example, at Philadelphia—blacks found opportunities to relive the African experience during annual fairs. A local historian of Philadelphia reports:

> The slaves were allowed the last days of the fairs for their jubilees, which they employed in dancing the whole afternoon in the present Washington Square, then a general burying ground—the blacks joyful above, while the sleeping dead reposed below. In that field could be seen at once more than one thousand of both sexes, divided into numerous little squads, dancing and singing, "each in their own tongue," after the customs of their several nations in Africa.[5]

In the South, the African-style dances that took place in New Orleans became legendary. Hundreds of slaves assembled on Sunday afternoons in the public square called Place Congo, forming themselves into circular groups to dance the traditional African ring

[3]*The Interesting Narrative of the Life of Olaudah Equiano, or Gustavus Vassa, the African,* London, 1789, p. 3.

[4]See the articles by James Eights, Issac Stuart, and Benjamin Henry B. Latrobe in Eileen Southern, *Readings in Black American Music,* New York: W. W. Norton, 1971. Also Alice Morse Earle, *Colonial Days in Old New York,* New York: Empire State Historical Publications XVI, 1896, p. 195; James Fenimore Cooper, *Satanstoe,* New York, 1845, pp. 59-60.

[5]John Fanning Watson, *Annals of Philadelphia,* Philadelphia, 1830, p. 265.

dances to the accompaniment of drums and stringed instruments.[6] In the rest of the South the playing of drums was forbidden and, as well, the gathering of large groups of slaves for recreational diversion. Southern slaveholders lived in constant fear of slave uprisings, and with good cause, for there were several large scale revolts during the eighteenth and nineteenth centuries. Southern slaves did sing, however, at their work; and even the most brutal masters allowed time off for slave jubilees at least twice a year, for Christmas and Easter.

It was inevitable that over the years blacks would forget the African texts of their songs and begin to use the languages of the slaveholders. Just as inevitable was that the original melodies would be altered in the process of oral transmission. Basically, however, it was this repertory of music that evolved into the Afro-American folk music of the nineteenth century, producing a large variety of song types, such as the spirituals, worksongs, dance songs, field hollers and street cries, ballads, and blues. The spiritual differed from the other types in following a special line of development, for it was closely associated with the music of the Protestant Church.

As early as the seventeenth century some white Protestant clergymen took positive measures to Christianize a small minority of the transplanted Africans, teaching them to read the Bible and to sing psalms and hymns. Congregational minister Cotton Mather, for example, organized the Society of Negroes in 1693 and listed as one of its rules that "between the two prayers, a Psalm shall be sung." Missionaries of the Society for the Propagation of the Gospel in Foreign Parts (sent out by the Church of England) reported upon the slaves' fondness for singing psalms and hymns, particularly the hymns of Isaac Watts. Up until the last decades of the eighteenth century, blacks worshipped in churches alongside their white masters (although in segregated pews) and, consequently, sang the same psalms and hymns as the white members. Even outside the church, the slaves were encouraged to sing hymns while at work instead of their own folksongs. The Reverend Charles Colcock Jones wrote in 1842:

> ... it is proper to teach the scholars (i.e., the slaves) hymns and psalms, and how to sing them. They are extravagantly fond of music; and this taste may be turned to good account in their instruction. ... The tunes should not be intricate but plain and awakening. One great advantage

[6]See the article by Latrobe in Southern, *Readings*.

> in teaching them good psalms and hymns, is that they are thereby induced to lay aside the extravagant and nonsensical chants, and catches and hallelujah songs of their own composing. ...[7]

Jones was not the first white minister to observe that blacks were developing a distinctive repertory of religious folk music, not as a replacement for the official psalms and hymns of the church but as an additional source of sacred music. This practice was severely criticized by the white establishment, as Jones' words cited above indicate. Of all the critics, Methodist John F. Watson of Philadelphia was the most critical. In 1819 he wrote:

> We have too, a growing evil, in the practice of singing in our places of public and society worship, *merry* airs, adapted from old songs, to hymns of our composing...and most frequently composed and first sung by the illiterate *blacks* of the society. ...[8]

Here is a clue to the time and place of the origin of the spiritual! At the present stage of research, it appears that the earliest references to Negro spirituals are to be found in sources written during the early nineteenth century by persons active in the Philadelphia area. But why this particular period of time and why in Philadelphia, a northern city where few slaves were to be found because of Pennsylvania's abolition laws? Indeed, there were few slaves to be found anywhere above the Mason-Dixon line after 1830. One of the established myths about spirituals is that the songs were born on plantations of the South, invented by the slaves as they labored in the cottonfields under the blazing sun. To be sure, southern slaves *did* sing spirituals. But all evidence suggests that the song type originated in the independent black churches of the North where black congregations, freed from the supervision of white clergymen, could conduct their religious services as they wished.

It was during the 1770s and 1780s that black Christians first began to withdraw from white churches in protest against the discrimination they encountered there to form their own congregations. Most of these groups, which included Congregationalists, Episcopalians, Presbyterians, Baptists, and Methodists, maintained ties with the white mother churches and adhered to the official liturgies. But in Philadelphia, the fledgling African Methodist Episcopal Church

[7]Charles Colcock Jones, *Religious Instruction of the Negroes,* Savannah, 1842, p. 266.

[8]John Watson, *Methodist Error*...in Southern, *op. cit.,* pp. 62-63.

under the leadership of Richard Allen severed its ties with the
white parent church and thus prepared itself to become the first
independent black denomination in America.[9] The church ex-
panded rapidly, setting up congregations in other major cities, as
far south as Charleston, South Carolina. In 1816 its first General
Conference was held and Richard Allen was elected its first bishop.

But let us go back to the first group of protesting black Methodists.
Allen's church, called Mother Bethel, was dedicated on July 29,
1794. One of Allen's first tasks was to begin the compiling of a
hymnal for the exclusive use of his congregation, for he knew how
much his people loved music. In his hymnal he included the most
beloved hymns of his people, whether of Baptist, Methodist, Congregational, or even camp-meeting origin. The first edition was
published in 1801 with the long title customary during that period,
*A Collection of Spiritual Songs and Hymns Selected from Various
Authors by Richard Allen, African Minister.* Containing fifty-four
hymn texts, this hymnal is a landmark in the history of American
music. Within the same year a second, enlarged edition appeared,
*A Collection of Hymns and Spiritual Songs from Various Authors,
by Richard Allen, Minister of the African Methodist Episcopal
Church.* Ten hymns were added to the original corpus, making a
total of sixty-four songs. Typically for this period, Allen did not
indicate the authors of the songs in his hymnal, nor did he suggest
the tunes to which the texts should be sung. I have tracked down the
authors for some hymns by finding concordances in other eighteenth-century collections, but obviously some of the hymns were
written by Allen, himself, and by religious leaders in his church.
As for the tunes, we know from the evidence that congregations drew
upon various sources: hymn tunes in common circulation, folksongs and popular tunes, and original tunes that often were composed on the spot.

Bethel Church won wide recognition for its music; few visitors to
the city failed to visit the church, primarily to listen to the singing.
If some found the singing too exuberant for their taste—such as, the
Russian Orthodox Paul Svinin, who visited Bethel in 1811[10]—all
acknowledged that it was exotic. In the first place, according to con-

---

[9]See further in Charles H. Wesley, *Richard Allen, Apostle of Freedom,* Washington, D.C.: The Associated Publishers, Inc., 1935.

[10]Aburaham Yarmolinsky, *A Memoir on Paul Petrovich Svinin,* New York, 1930,
pp. 28-31.

temporary descriptions, the singing was in the African tradition with emphasis upon antiphonal performance, a loud strident vocal quality, and bodily movement during the singing. Second, and perhaps more important historically, unorthodox songs were used — songs that could not be found in Methodist hymnals. William Colbert, a white Methodist elder who visited Bethel in 1804, complained that he did not object so much to the sound of the singing as to the kinds of songs that were being sung. From the vantage point of the present, we are not surprised that Bethel should have used such songs; the title of Allen's hymnal indicated that it contained "spiritual songs" as well as hymns. To be sure, Allen was not the first person to use the term. As early as 1651, the title of a psalter published in the colonies included the words "spiritual songs," obviously in reference to the scriptural passage:

> Let the word of Christ dwell in you richly in all wisdom teaching and admonishing one another in Psalms and Hymns and Spiritual Songs, singing with grace in your hearts unto the Lord:
>
> [Colossians 3:16]

But Allen's hymnal seems to have been the earliest collection, to my knowledge, in which a distinction was made between hymns and spiritual songs. In some instances, hymns were turned into spiritual songs by the addition of refrains or choruses. Other songs apparently were originally composed as spirituals.

Undoubtedly, many of the songs sung in independent black churches, such as Bethel, and during camp-meetings were never printed in hymnals. These were the genuine spirituals! It is in order to discuss at this point our third approach to the origin of the spiritual — the manner of its origin. An analysis of a representative number of spirituals clearly reveals the compositional procedures employed. The anonymous folk composers selected verses from the Bible or verses from favorite Protestant hymns and added to these poetic materials verses of their own invention and refrains or choruses. Our critical Methodist churchman John Watson testifies to such procedures in his book:

> In the *blacks'* quarter [at camp meetings], the coloured people get together, and sing for hours together, short scraps of disjointed affirmations, pledges, or prayers, lengthened out with long repetition *choruses.* ... Some of these [tunes] from their nature (having very

long repetition choruses and short scraps of matter), are actually composed as sung, and are indeed almost endless.[11]

It is a simple matter to reconstruct the process. Here, for example, is the text of a favorite hymn of black folk at the beginning of the nineteenth century, No. 27 in Allen's collection:

1. *There is a land of pure delight*
   Where saints immortal reign
   Infinite day excludes the night
   And pleasures banish pain
2. *Sweet fields beyond the swelling flood*
   Stand dress'd in living green
   So, to the Jews, old Canaan stood
   While Jordan rolled between

This is one of Isaac Watts' most majestic hymns. One can readily understand why it became a favorite with the black Christians. But its ideas are couched in rather sophisticated terms, especially for a people newly freed from slavery who were, for the most part, illiterate. The folk composers caught the spirit of the wonderful old hymn, but fashioned a new song expressing the same ideas in their own language. The new version was more personal, more direct, more emotional, and easier to understand. Moreover, because it included refrains, all members of the congregation could join in the singing, even the illiterates. This is how they interpreted the hymn and thereby invented a spiritual:

Oh, brothers, you ought to been there
Yes, my Lord,
A sittin' in the kingdom
To hear Jordan roll.
Roll, Jordan, roll; roll, Jordan, roll
I want to go to heaven when I die
To hear Jordan roll.

According to all evidence, *Roll, Jordan, Roll* is one of the oldest spirituals extant. Its melody is characteristically West African with the use of the flatted seventh tone in a major scale (i.e., a "blue note") and syncopated rhythms. In the same way as this spiritual relates to the hymn *There is a Land of Pure Delight*, so do many other spirituals relate to Protestant hymns or Bible verses. In no way can the

[11]John Watson, *Annals*, p. 64.

spiritual be regarded as merely imitative of the hymn or Bible verses. Although the latter may have served as the inspiration for the spiritual and a source of isolated refrain lines or verses, the spiritual—once composed—becomes an independent creative work with its own characteristic language, mood, melody and rhythm. Allen's hymnal contains a large number of hymns that apparently inspired the invention of well-known spirituals. Some hymns generated large numbers of spirituals; for example, No. 10, in which the first stanza is:

> *Behold the awful trumpet sounds,*
> *The sleeping dead to raise,*
> *And calls the nations underground:*
> *O how the saints will praise!*

Space does not permit the citing of all the spirituals that relate to this hymn; one example is:

> *My Lord, what a morning,*
> *My Lord, what a morning.*
> *My Lord, what a morning,*
> *When the stars begin to fall*
> *You'll hear the trumpet sound*
> *To wake the nations underground*
> *Looking to my God's right hand,*
> *When the stars begin to fall.*

Here, the folk poet begins with his personal reaction to the importance of Judgement Day, then continues to build up his song using lines from the hymn at random (stanzas 4, 1, and 5). Among other spirituals related to this hymn are the well-known *In That Great Getting-Up Morning* and *Rocks and Mountains Don't Fall on Me.*

Not all spirituals, of course, would have been composed in this manner. Some obviously were created from new materials, and many came into existence as homiletic songs—the preacher or deacon inventing the verses and the congregation providing the refrains. As happens in the folk music tradition, the spirituals that appealed to the members of a congregation or a community were preserved, becoming a part of the musical repertory of the group, while those spirituals that lacked significance (poetic or musical) were discarded. Also, as is characteristic in the folk music tradition, the best spirituals would have traveled from one congregation to another, from one community to another, and from one region of the country to another, carried by the ministers as they were transferred from one congregation to another, by itinerant preachers, by the black "watermen" who worked on the boats that plied the Mississippi, the Ohio, and Missouri Rivers, and finally by the slaves when they were sold from one state to another. The phenomenon of "traveling folk music" would account for the fact that spirituals such as *I'm So Glad Trouble Don't Last Always* or *Swing Low, Sweet Chariot* were so widely dispersed all over the nation, although local versions often differed in minor details.

It is unlikely that the full story of the origin of the Negro spiritual will ever be explained to everyone's satisfaction. It is the way of folk music to resist clear logical explanations. My research has led me to the independent black congregations of Philadelphia at the beginning of the nineteenth century. But it well may be that future research will bring to light evidence from an earlier period of history about the origin of the spiritual.

An Aesthetic of the Cool:
West African Dance

by Robert Farris Thompson

Four shared traits of West African music and dance are suggested here, together with a fifth, which, although nonmusical, seems very relevant. These shared characteristics appear to be the following: the dominance of a percussive concept of performance; multiple meter; apart playing and dancing; call-and-response; and, finally, the songs and dances of derision.

The first phase, which is Alan Merriam's—the dominance of a percussive concept of performance—describes a core element. In the Western classic symphony, two tympani are outnumbered by some forty-three melodic instruments, which is symptomatic of an ascendancy of harmonic and melodic concepts and the relative unimportance of percussive traditions. But in tropical Africa even instruments outside the membranophone and idiophone classes will be played with percussive bias instead of in ways soft and legato. Africans do not traditionally bow fiddles legato, but pluck them energetically, with vigorous attack.[1] So striking is this emphasis upon percussive musical diction (which has to do with aesthetic choices and not the inevitable use of a drum or even hardwood sticks) that I am tempted to designate West Africa as a percussive culture. In fact, heaven itself has been portrayed by a West African poet in terms of percussive display and onomatopoeia:

> Let the calabash
> Entwined with beads

Extracted from "An Aesthetic of the Cool: West African Dance" by Robert Farris Thompson. First published in *African Forum*, Vol. 2, No. 2 (Fall 1966), pp. 85-102. Reprinted by permission of the author.

[1]Alan P. Merriam, "The African Idiom in Music," *Journal of American Folklore*, April-June, 1962, p. 127.

With blue Aggrey beads
Resound
Let the calabash resound
In tune with the drums
Mingle with these sounds
The clang of wood on tin:
Kentensekenken
Ken—tse ken ken ken[2]

In the West African world, it is one of the dancer's aims to make every rhythmic subtlety of the music visible.[3] When the master drummer of the Ijebu Yoruba rises in level of pitch, during a ceremony for the waterspirit named Igodo, the master dancer is said to rise, correspondingly, upon his toes. When a Thundergod drum choir of the Egbado Yoruba plays music expressive of the hot-tempered God of Iron, the master dancer immediately becomes explosive in her gestures to maintain an appropriate balance with the emotional coloring of the percussive patterns being rendered.

Surface appreciation of such procedures may mask the fact that it is West African *dancing* that is percussive, regardless of whether or not it is expressed with a striking of one part of the body against another (the chest whacking with the hands of Dahomean *Kpe*) or with stamping patterns and rattles. Percussive flavoring governs the motion of those parts of the body that carry no weight—the gestures—as well as the steps that do. Unsurprisingly, a good drummer in West Africa is a good dancer, and vice versa, although the degree of specialty and professionalism varies with each individual.

The mnemonic retention of dance steps shares the same verbal basis of drummers who are attempting to impart the memory of a given drum pattern to an apprentice drummer. This verbal basis often consists of drum syllables:[4] They are used when a dancer wishes to speak out the drum or bodily rhythms of a particular dance

[2]Francis Ernest Kobina Parkes, "African Heaven," in *New World Writing No. 15* (New York: Mentor, 1959), pp. 230-232.

[3]Marshall Stearns, "Is Modern Jazz Dance Hopelessly Square?" *Dance,* June, 1965, p. 33.

[4]An excellent discussion of the verbal basis of Akan drumming may be found in Nketia's *Drumming in Akan Communities of Ghana* (London: Thomas Nelson and Sons, 1963), pp. 32-50. In addition, an interesting colloquium, "Drumming Syllables in Five Traditions: South India Colonial North America, Arabic Countries, Japan, and West Africa," held at the New England Chapter Meeting of the American Musicological Society at Boston University on March 5, 1966, furnished fresh

in order to make clear the duration of the gestures and steps and the contrasts with which a particular movement is built. To return to the master dancer of Ajilete, Nigeria, we note that she pays close attention to the syllables enunciated by the drums, and when she hears the pattern *gere gere gere gekan,* she swings her hands across her body during the first six syllables. Each time the last two syllables sound, she draws her hands up to her breasts with a simultaneous inhalation of breath.[5]

Thus, West African dances are *talking dances,* and the point of the conversation is the expression of percussive concepts. This gift reappears in the Negro New World: Marshall and Jean Stearns have informed me that tap dancers sometimes spell out their ideas with syllables, in the West African manner, and I have observed similar instances among New York's Afro-Cuban dancers. Perhaps the absorption of this tradition has sharpened the exceptional mambos of James Evans, one of the finest Negro dancers of New York:

> Over the years Evans has worked out a "semaphoric" mambo that is his own, a means of metrically conversing with his hands. Unlike the handwork in certain Polynesian dances, Evans' is only occasionally pictorial; it is his aim to capture and describe percussion, not specific images, and the extent to which he succeeds is perhaps best summarized by [Hoyt Warner] who once shouted to him "You *caught* that riff."[6]

Warner, a young white mathematician and amateur of mambo, meant that the music indicated a sudden repeated phrase and that Evans had convincingly translated the iteration into motion.

Instead of emphasizing the expression of West African dance (and its derivatives) in terms of taps and rattles, clapping and stamping, it would seem far more penetrating to say that it is West African dancing itself that is percussive. The vigor and the attack of the

---

insights into similar practices in other parts of the world. For example, in South India, as among Yoruba, syllables ending in nasalization are sustained. And both Yoruba and Colonial North Americans seem to choose the consonant *k* (*que*, actually, in the orthography of the latter instance) to represent heavy beats. Compare, also, the Akan phrase "tiri tiri *kon*" with the American Colonial "ratama*que.*"

[5] I am especially beholden to Perk Foss for assisting in many ways the field documentation of Yoruba dancing at Ajilete in April, 1966.

[6] Robert Farris Thompson, "Portrait of the Pachanga," *Saturday Review,* October 28, 1961, p. 54.

idiom can be so subtly elaborated as when Ohori Yoruba open and close their shoulder blades in time to a mental gong.

Multiple meter, the second trait, is a well-documented element of West African music. The phrase means the simultaneous execution of several time signatures, not unlike the sounding of the ¾ of the waltz and the ¼ of jazz at the same time,[7] survivals of which enliven the Negro barrios of the Americas. Polymeter in the West African manner turns up in the urban music of the Spanish-speaking segments of the United States. A pleasing example has been recorded by Mongo Santamaria, wherein two types of drum establish parallel lines of ¼ time with machine-gun celerity while another type of drum lays down a ⅝ at a slow tempo.[8]

Multiple meter qualifies much West African dancing as a mirror image. A useful theoretical introduction to the problem was established in 1948 by Richard Alan Waterman:

> The dance of the West African is an essay on the appreciation of musical rhythms. For the performance of a good dancer the drums furnish the inspiration, in response to which the thread of each rhythmic element contributing to the thunderous whole of the percussion *gestalt* is followed in movement without separation from its polyrhythmic context.[9]

Waterman describes a maximum instance. The dancer picks up each rhythm of the polymetric whole with different parts of his body; when he does so, he directly mirrors the metric mosaic. But it is important to note that in many instances West Africans find it convenient to dance to only one rhythm, or to shift from two basic pulsations in their footwork to three (as in a kind of Ewe virtuoso dancing), or to follow three mental pulsations while the gong player actually strikes four. In other words, there are minimum instances of multimetric dancing to oppose against the full expression described by Waterman.

In this context, the notion of balance is not only a canon of West

[7]Richard Alan Waterman, "African Influence on the Music of the Americas" in *Acculturation in the Americas,* ed. Sol Tax (Chicago: University of Chicago Press, 1952). This article is a landmark in the literature of Africanist ethnomusicology.

[8]Some Afro-Cuban musicians maintain that the secret of their music is an opposition of two pulsations against three. This understates, in my opinion, a rich tradition of multiple meter.

[9]Richard Alan Waterman, "Hot Rhythm in Negro Music," *Journal of the American Musicological Society,* Spring, 1948, p. 4.

African dancing but an aesthetic acid test: The weak dancer soon loses his metric bearings in the welter of competing countermeters and is, so to speak, knocked off balance, as if a loser in a bout of Indian wrestling. Multiple meter is, in brief, a communal examination of percussive individuality.

Bertonoff defines multimetric dancing as bodily orchestration:

> The Ewe dances are the most fervent among all the Ghanaian tribes, for in them the body moves as though it were orchestrated. The various limbs and members, head, shoulders, and legs are all moving simultaneously but each in a rhythm of its own. The main movement is carried out at dizzying speed by the elbows. The motion resembles that of the wings of an injured bird, yet it is as light and easy as the swaying of a fish's fins.[10]

I suspect dancers from different African societies choose different parts of the body for emphasis within the polymetric whole. We know that the rhythmic emphasis of West African music shifts back and forth from meter to meter, and the parts of the dancer's body that reflect these shifts may also constitute major determinants of local styles.

On the northwest "verge" of Ghana, at Lawra, Bertonoff documented a second manifestation of multiple meter. The movement was actually the seated "dance" of the musician playing a xylophone:

> He held a stick in each hand, and the rhythm of the left hand was opposed to that of the right. His head was moving in a third rhythm between the strokes. It seemed to me that the soles of his feet were also on the move and giving the rhythm and counterrhythm an interpretation of their own. During the dance the feet interpret the rhythm according to which the other parts of the body are moving.[11]

The last observation is interesting. Implied is a notion of the dancer monitoring the rhythmic *donnée* of the music with his feet while with other parts of his body he duplicates or comments upon the polymeters of the music. The metric "given" of the music in West Africa is normally the accents of a gong. Significantly, A. M. Jones, who has also briefly studied Ewe dancing, finds that in the *Adzida* club dance ("very popular in Eweland") the foot and hand movements are staggered, though the feet are in phase with the gong. It should be noted, however, that Jones's careful notation shows the

[10]Deborah Bertonoff, *Dance Towards The Earth* (Tel Aviv: Alytiros, 1963), p. 46.
[11]Bertonoff, pp. 189-190.

bell pattern in $1\frac{2}{8}$ time, the feet in $\frac{3}{4}$; thus, even though the dancer follows the organizing meter of the music with his feet, he has executed a statement at metrical variance from it.

The notion of the feet interpreting the foundation beat of gongs finds an interesting corroboration among the Tiv of central Nigeria. Laura Bohannan reports a confrontation with informants who insisted that she dance at a wedding to prove her solidarity with the relevant family: "'Teach me then,' I retorted. Duly, she and the other senior women began my instruction: my hands and my feet were to keep time with the gongs, my hips with the first drum, my back and shoulders with the second."[12] Whenever Mrs. Bohannan subsided into an "absent-minded shuffle," indignant old women promptly poked her in the ribs and commanded "Dance." Thus, in at least one Tiv society, the articulation of multiple meter seems to amount to protocol.

Cult and secular dancing among the Negroes of Cuba evinces some multimetric dancing. Rumbaists, for example, sometimes introduce a passage of $\frac{6}{8}$ elbow-work at a fast tempo in opposition to the basic $\frac{3}{4}$ or $\frac{4}{4}$ pulsations marked by their footwork. Señor Julito Collazo, an excellent dancer of an entire range of Cuban cult dances, told me that "there have been many times when I was dancing rumba with or against the $\frac{3}{4}$ of the music when I varied my steps by adding passages of Cuban-Ibibio style in $\frac{6}{8}$ time." Whenever this happened, his steps were immediately at variance with the basic beat.

The third trait is apart playing and dancing. And perhaps the best way to gain an insight into the dissection of experience that affects Western life may be to study the physical movements of the musicians of a classic symphony orchestra. The violin section is seated in ordered rows; and when the violinists are observed in profile, their silhouettes, a repeated pattern of human figures seated stiffly erect, form a kind of step-fret series. At the sign of the conductor's baton, more than a score of violinists take up their instruments and, holding them against their chins, bow-and-finger them in unison; as they do so, their restricted action hovers like a nimbus over the more-or-less motionless body. Action has been restricted, essentially, to the right arm and to the fingers and wrist of the left hand, although the body may sway somewhat.

[12]Laura Bohannan, *Return to Laughter* (Garden City, New York: Doubleday and Co., 1964), p. 123.

In dramatic contrast to this remarkable compression of motion, West African musicians move the whole trunk and head, whether seated or standing, in response to the music. West African musicians dance their own music. They play "apart" in the sense that each is often intent upon the production of his own contribution to a polymetric whole. The members of a drum choir of three do not strike the skins of their instruments in unison. At least one—normally the master drummer—creates pleasing clashes with the rhythmic structure of his helpers; he departs from their text, as it were, and improvises illuminations. "Apart playing" defines much of the production of music in West Africa whereas "synchronous" playing defines much of the music of the West. (But certainly not all: "Classic" compositions come to mind wherein the clarinets may do something different from the violins.) Africans unite music and dance but play apart; Europeans separate dance and music but play together. As A. M. Jones notes: "With Western music deliberate synchrony is the norm from which our music develops: that is why it is possible for one man with a baton to conduct a whole orchestra."[13] Playing apart, on the other hand, grants the West African space in which to maintain his own private or traditional meter and to express his own full corporeal involvement in what he is doing.

A close inspection of dance modes in West Africa will reveal that "apart dancing" is as important a part of choreographic custom as "apart playing." It is one of the more striking traits of sub-Saharan dance,[14] and it is one of the few dance constituents that European outsiders consistently identified in verbal descriptions. F. de Kersaint-Gilly noted in 1922: "In Negro Africa—I have spent time among Bakota and among various societies of West Africa—man and woman never put their arms around each other while dancing, as we generally do in France."[15]

Apart dancing is not correlated with the apart playing of instruments in the sense of absence of body contact. The unity which the

---

[13]A. M. Jones, *Studies in African Music* (London: Oxford University Press, 1959), I, p. 193.

[14]The phrase "apart dancing" is my own. Marshall Stearns phrases the mode another way: "solo dancing—the universal way of dancing in Africa." See Marshall and Jean Stearns, "Profile of the Lindy," *Show*, October, 1963, p. 112.

[15]F. de Kersaint-Gilly, "Notes sur la danse en pays noir," *Bulletin du comité d'études historiques et scientifiques de L'Afrique occidentale française*, January-March, 1922, p. 80.

musicians and dancers share seems, rather, to constitute a constellation of solo and chorus performances. The master drummer (or drummers) plays alone, intent upon improvisation; the master dancer (or dancers), intent upon following or challenging these improvisations, also dances alone. And the drum chorus and the dancing chorus interact by repetitive patterns, which means that a certain amount of performing together balances the apartness. But the critical fact seems to be this: West Africans perform music and dance apart the better to ensure a dialog between movement and sound.

Dancers of the classic ballet do not touch either, as a rule, but these dancers are governed by a single metrical reference and, moreover, dance together in the sense that all their actions are governed by identical demands of pictorial legibility—which is to say that their *pliés* and *tours en l'air* must project crisply across row upon row of seated spectators. Considering the 'literary bias of the West, this tendency was inevitable. (Modern dance, in which apart playing and dancing are not uncommon, might be described as a dramatic break with this tendency, comparable with Cézanne's shift from representation to expression; but to what extent African influence and/or independent inventions shaped this revolution cannot be estimated in this article.) Africans seem to dance with full muscular actions so palpably syllabic that one can scarcely fail to comprehend the sense of linguistic community that pervades the whole. To dance with arms enlaced around the partner, in the manner of pre-jazz Western ballrooms, lessens the opportunity to converse. Even when Africans dance together, as in certain performing pairs of Abomey, they are actually operating apart to achieve a playing of hand movements against hips, something not possible were their hands locked in an embrace. Nor could their hands find individual metric inspiration were the members of the percussive choir similarly locked into a single metrical scheme. To recapitulate, West Africans and Afro-Americans dance apart and play apart to liberate their attention, as it were, for continuous conversation between motion and music, instead of specializing in purely musical or choreographic activity.

The fourth trait of West African music and dance is a special form of antiphony, wherein a caller alternates his lines with the regularly timed responses of a chorus; it is the formal structure of indigenous singing,[16] and it is known as call-and-response. The important fact is that the caller frequently overlaps or interrupts the chorus. Antiphony exists the world over, but nowhere else in the world does the overlapping of the phrases of leader and followers so consistently occur. Are there similar patterns in the dance? Yes. J. Van Wing summarized the dances of the important Bakongo peoples of what is now the Democratic Republic of Congo (Kinshasa): "There are always two bodies or two groups of bodies in movement: a solo dancer in front of a group, or an individual before another in a group, or an individual before another in a couple, or two groups placed in front of the other. They perform periodic movements that are like questions and responses."[17]

Similar patterns appear in the world of Spanish Harlem ballrooms, where Puerto Ricans improvise constantly varying steps — dancing apart while their partners maintain a recurrent movement. These men "interrupt" the movement of their women in a call-and-response manner, for they begin a new step or flourish considerably before their partners have finished the execution of their basic movements. In Ushi, an especially musical Ekiti Yoruba village, my wife and I observed a lead dancer improvise patterns that consistently began before a "chorus" had finished its "refrain," which consisted of swinging the ends of their head-ties in concerted rhythm, first to the right, then to the left, over their wrists.

The fifth trait, a nonmusical element, is the moral function of the songs of social allusion and the dances of derision. "In West Africa," Laura Boulton writes, "songs are frequently used as an important moral agent in the community. Songs of satire are very powerful because there is no punishment an African dreads more than being held up to the ridicule of his fellow men."[18] (A wealth of similar examples may be found in Alan P. Merriam's *Anthropology of Music.*) Although we are, of course, referring to *content* rather than to form or style — a different analytic level — we intend to illustrate briefly, in the conclusion, that a relationship between content and style is best displayed by singers' deliberately distorting their

[16]See Alan Merriam, album notes, *Africa South of the Sahara,* Ethnic Folkways FE 4503.

[17]J. Van Wing, "Les Danses Bakongo," *Congo: Revue générale de la colonie belge,* July, 1937, p. 122.

[18]Laura Boulton, album notes, *African Music,* Ethnic Folkways 8852.

voices when singing in traditions noted for moral allusion and inquisition.

The dance of derision, the choreographic correlate of the song of allusion, is a striking trait of much West African dancing. Even in Zululand, outside the purview of West Africa, derision dances are found and have been described by Kaigh as "dances of domestic oddities":

> They dance after any event, white or black, which takes their fancy. I have seen danced imitations of myself and party too veracious to be flattering, or even comfortable. After I had lost a steeplechase by being thrown from the horse my boys danced the accident so faithfully that I came away a sadder, if not a wiser clown. The boy who took the part of me was most embarrassingly accurate as to detail.[19]

Pride and pretension are as much a target of the African dancer as they are of the singer of allusion. Surprisingly, the connection between the arts in this regard has not, to my knowledge, been pointed out. The former colonial authorities of what is now the Republic of Zambia were aware of the potentialities of African derision dancing, or so Chapter 120, Section 7, of the former laws of that area implies: "No person may organize or take part in any dance which is calculated to hold up to ridicule or to bring into contempt any person, religion, or duly constituted authority."[20] This apparent characteristic was noted in 1825 by Captain Hugh Clapperton, who witnessed a dance, evidently danced at his expense, at Old Ọyọ, the ancient imperial capital of the Yoruba Peoples.[21]

Dances of derision in the Negro world are legion. Camille Poupeye mentions them in the Bamako area of Mali and calls them "satires in action."[22] and S. F. Nadel has described one instance at Bida in northern Nigeria. I have observed over the last ten years Puerto Rican dancers mock fatuous or eccentric dancing with cruelly accurate movements in New York City. The dance of derision brings

---

[19] Frederick Kaigh, *Witchcraft and Magic of Africa* (London: Richard Lesley and Co., 1947), p. 26.

[20] Quoted in J. Clyde Mitchell, *The Kalela Dance* (Manchester: Rhodes-Livingston Papers, 1956), p. 12, note 5.

[21] Captain Hugh Clapperton, *Journal of a Second Expedition into the Interior of Africa* (London: John Murray, 1829), p. 55.

[22] Camille Poupeye, *Danses dramatiques en théâtres exotiques* (Brussels: Le Cahiers du Journal des Poètes, 1941), p. 109.

home the fact that Africans and Afro-Americans are interested not only in force and the affirmation of fertility in their controlled energetic dancing, but also with ethics and right living. The man who misbehaves may not only have to "face the music," as in the "signifying songs" of the old-time New Orleans Negroes, but he may also have to face the movement.

To summarize these points with the help of a Yoruba critic: One cultivator—criticizing a dance by members of a society which performs during the installation of the king of the Anago town of Ipokia and during the funerals of its members—said: "This dance is aesthetically pleasing [*ijó nā wù mi dādā*] because the legs and all parts of the body are equal [*nítorípé ẹsẹ̀ tó ngbe àti gbogbo ara dógba*]." The key word is *dógba*, which means in Yoruba "is symmetrical." The native connoisseur of artistic motion had put his finger on one of the most important canons of West African dance—balance.

The point of one form of Ibo dancing in Nigeria, for example, is to infuse the upper torso and the head with violent vibrations without losing an overall sense of stability. In this case, equilibrium is shown by the relatively motionless extension of the open palms in front of the dancer, almost at arm's length, each palm at an equal distance from the body. And, moreover, despite the ferocity of the "shimmying" of the upper frame, the shuffling feet of the dancer indulge gravity and thus convey balance. When West Africans shuffle—and most of them do in their traditional dancing (although there are dances galore in which dancers, especially men, break the bonds of gravity with special leaps and other gravity-resistant motions)—their bodies are usually bent forward, toward the stabilizing earth. They maintain balance. And balance is cool.

A further case in point: A gifted Egbado Yoruba dancer maintains the whole time she dances a "bound motion" in her head, thus balancing a delicate terracotta sculpture on her head without danger, while simultaneously subjecting her torso and arms to the most confounding expressions of raw energy and force. It is not difficult to find similar instances of control in other African dances. Thundergod devotees, for instance, sometimes dance with a burning fire in a container coolly balanced on the top of their heads. Coolness in the sense of control and symmetry seems a metaphor of the spiritual. And this is not to mention the manifold secular manifestations of this basic tendency—for example, Africans traveling while balancing even ink wells and sheets of paper on their heads or African wrestlers defeating their opponents not by "pinning" them to the ground in the Western manner, but by knocking them off balance.

From this cultural background a philosophy of music and dance seems to emerge. In the case of the dominance of a percussive concept, one is talking about the vigorous involvement of the whole body (the performances of the aged continue to provoke the amazement of Western observers). The vibrations may be subtle but they are diffused throughout the body. This trait might be compared with Yoruba ephebism or the deliberately youthful depiction of the human frame in sculpture.[23]

Old age is rare in West African sculpture. Its depiction seems restricted to situations of satire, psychological warfare, and moral vengeance. The dignity of the Yoruba dancer's facial expression might be profitably compared with the phebistic (youthful) flawless seal of most Yoruba sculpture. In both cases, in any event, indigenous critics of art may characterize the dignity of the respective expressions as "cool." When Tiv (in northern Nigeria) dance satirically, as in the *Ngogh*"[24] dance making fun of swollen bodies, the flawless seal shatters and faces become twisted with exaggeration and grimaces. But in the aggregate, West Africans dance with a mixture of vigor and decorum.

Multiple meter essentially uses dancers as further voices in a polymetric choir. The conversation is additive, cool in its expressions of community. The balance struck between the meters and the bodily orchestration seems to communicate a soothing wholeness rather than a "hot" specialization. The implications of dialog in apart performing have been discussed. Call-and-response is a means of putting innovation and tradition, invention and imitation, into amicable relationships with one another. In that sense it, too, is cool. Finally, the dance of derision sometimes breaks these rules in order to mime the disorder of those who would break the rules of society.[25] Yoruba moral inquisitors do not really dance; they loom. Their shapes, their cries, their motions are unearthly, meant to startle, meant—quite literally—to frighten the hell out of people.

[23]See Robert Farris Thompson, "Yoruba Artistic Criticism," paper read at the Conference on the Artist in Traditional African Society, Lake Tahoe, May, 1965.

[24]I acknowledge with many thanks a personal communication, dated February 1, 1966, from Charles Keil, who, writing from the field, informed me of the *Ngogh* dance and other items of Tiv traditional choreographies.

[25]In a future volume, I shall intensively analyze the problem of the anti-aesthetic in African art, dance, and music.

The dance of derision attests that although most West African dances exist as concrete metaphors of right living, some Africans do cheat, steal, and kill. Terrible events occur in West Africa not because the inhabitants lack moral control (their dances make this clear), but because thus far no society on earth has ever completely satisfied or embodied a definition of ideal behavior.[26]

When Christians go to war (instead of turning the other cheek), they have the effrontery to do so within a system of ethics that imparts the promise of redemption. But when an African, finding his security threatened, kills his neighbor, depressingly large segments of the Western world believe that he does so instinctively, without any moral check whatsoever. But an increasing familiarity with the ideal of the cool, documented by the nonverbal "texts" of the dance, will reveal a fact of moral equality. Should Westerners, white and black alike, forsake comfort and estimate the meaning of the words that are made flesh in the dances of the Guinea Coast, they might find our double standards intolerable. They might even detect logical inconsistencies when they observe that the murder of Greek by Turk, of Turk by Greek, on Cyprus is described as an "historical conflict," but that the murder of Ibo by Hausa, and Hausa by Ibo, in Nigeria is described with horror as a "reversion to savagery."

The time-resistant dances of the cool form a kind of prayer: May humanity be shielded from the consequences of arrogance and the penalties of impatience.

---

[26] It is convenient for some Westerners to note this basic fact only outside their culture. Thus, in the *New York Times* of October 9, 1966, we read, p. 10E: "Asia, where nations preach morality and respect force."

Willis Richardson: Pioneer Playwright

by Bernard L. Peterson, Jr.

At a period in our history when attention is being focused on the accomplishments of numerous Black American dramatists who have paved the way for the present Black theatre renaissance of the 1970s, I would like to call attention to the life and work of the first to make a significant contribution to both the quantity and the quality of serious Black American drama. This is not to detract from the outstanding contributions of the early Black musical writers, such as Bob Cole, Will Marion Cook, Leubrie Hill, Aubrey Lyles, Flournoy Miller, Alex Rogers, the Tutt/Whitney Brothers, and numerous others. Nor do I wish to ignore the handful of serious plays written by such early Black playwrights as Ira Aldridge, William Wells Brown, Mary Burrill, Joseph Cotter, W. E. B. DuBois, William Easton, Angelina Grimke, or Alice Dunbar-Nelson, to name only a few.

However, as Darwin Turner, the eminent Black theatre essayist, anthologist and critic has said, "Willis Richardson...was not the first Afro-American to write a play, but he was the first significantly productive Afro-American playwright."[1] His dramatic output includes two anthologies of Black plays, which contain the works of other playwrights as well as his own; a collection of children's plays; and 48 individual plays, 20 of which have been published, and most of the rest deposited in either the Schomburg Center for Research in Black Culture or the Hatch-Billops Archives, both in New York

"Willis Richardson: Pioneer Playwright," revised and updated by the author, Bernard L. Peterson. Original version published in *Black World,* Vol. XXIV, No. 6 (April 1975). Copyright © April 1975 by *Black World.* Reprinted by permission of Johnson Publishing Company and Bernard L. Peterson, Jr.

[1]Darwin T. Turner, *Black Drama in America: An Anthology* (Greenwich, Ct.: Fawcett Publications, 1971), p. 25.

City. Several typescripts (one of which is not duplicated in either of the above collections) are located in the Moorland-Spingarn Research Center at Howard University in Washington, D.C. At least two scripts are in the Performing Arts Research Center in New York. Not only did Richardson write and publish a larger number of plays than did any other Black playwright up to and during the 1920s, but even today he remains one of the most prolific Black playwrights that America has produced.

Richardson is perhaps best known as the first Black playwright to have a serious (non-musical) play produced on Broadway, with the presentation in 1923 of his one-act folk.drama, *The Chip Woman's Fortune.* This significant fact is stamped on many people's minds, as Darwin Turner has observed, because of "The unfortunate tendency of many people to evaluate the achievements of Afro-Americans according to their successes within the white community...."[2]

Less well known are Richardson's contributions to the Black community and to Black theatre in particular. In the years following World War I, when the only plays of Black life deemed worthy of serious production were written by white playwrights, such as Ridgely Torrence, Eugene O'Neill and Paul Green, Black theatre groups were desperately searching for plays by Black writers. Richardson was the first to fulfill this need by providing these groups—the Ethiopian Art Theatre in Chicago, the Howard Players in Washington, D.C., the Gilpin Players in Cleveland, and numerous other college, community and school groups—with their first "authentic" Black plays.[3]

Although some of Richardson's plays were influenced by the folk tradition of Ridgely Torrence and Paul Green, many others were unique in their glorification of the Black hero long before the world was to affirm that "Black is Beautiful." Richardson was one of the first Black playwrights to write romantic plays of Black history, dramatizing the lives of such heroes as Crispus Attucks, the first martyr of the American Revolution; Alexander Dumas père, the French mulatto novelist and playwright; Simon, the Cyrenian, who carried the cross for Christ to Calvary; Menelik, Emperor of Abyssinia; and Massinissa, King of East Numidia.

[2]*Ibid.*

[3]The term "Black play" is used throughout this article to refer only to "a play of Black life by a Black playwright." The term "Negro" is used mainly for historical purposes, and should be read simply as a synonym for "Black people."

To appropriate to my own purposes an observation which Carter G. Woodson once wrote concerning the new Black playwrights whose works were included in one of Richardson's anthologies, and which I now apply as an accolade to Richardson alone: He had "the vision of the Negro in the new day." He undertook "to dramatize every phase of his life and history." His "conception of this task... shows no restriction to any particular period or place. The Negro is presented as a maker of civilization in Africa, a contributor to progress in Europe, and a factor in the development of Greater America." Richardson "has discovered that [the Negro] has something to dramatize, and in spite of mocking onlookers, he has the courage to undertake the task."[4]

But Richardson's plays were not confined to historical romances glorifying Black kings and heroes. Most of his plays were attempts at realistic treatment of Black life (both contemporary and historical) on such a variety of themes as manhood and bravery; suffering under white tyranny, oppression, and injustice; the problems of the urban family; joblessness and unemployment; the social strivings of the middle class; Black exploitation of other Blacks, and many other relevant subjects. His characters covered the widest possible range, including devout churchgoers, bootblacks, school teachers, bootleggers, washer-women, jailbirds, slaves and peasants.

Willis Richardson was born in Wilmington, N.C., November 5, 1889, the son of Willis Wilder and Agnes (Harper) Richardson.[5] As he wrote of himself in *Crisis* magazine, "I...lived there until the riot of 1898, after which my parents came to Washington [D.C.] where I obtained whatever school education I have in the secondary [i.e., elementary] and high schools."[6] He attended elementary schools from 1899 to 1906. Then he entered Dunbar High School, where one of his English teachers, Mary Burrill, herself a playwright, greatly encouraged his interest in drama.[7] After graduating from high school in 1910, he entered government service as a clerk

---

[4]Carter G. Woodson, "Introduction" to *Negro History in Thirteen Plays,* edited by Willis Richardson and May Miller (Washington, D.C.: The Associated Publishers, 1935), v.

[5]*Who's Who in Colored America,* 6th ed. (1941-1944), p. 435.

[6]Introduction to *The Broken Banjo* by Willis Richardson, *Crisis,* 31 (February 1926), p. 167.

[7]Fannie Ella Frazier Hicklin, "The American Negro Playwright" (Ph.D. dissertation, The University of Wisconsin, 1965; microfilm copy by University Microfilms, Ann Arbor, Michigan), p. 150.

at the U.S. Bureau of Engraving and Printing in Washington, D.C., where he remained until his retirement in 1954.[8] On September 3, 1914, he married Mary Ellen Jones. Their three children, Jean Paula, Shirley Antonella, and Noel Justine, were born in 1916, 1918, and 1920 respectively.[9]

In another *Crisis* article he wrote: "About 1916, I saw a performance of Angelina Grimke's *Rachel* and by that was influenced to study the technique of the drama."[10] Although Richardson admired Miss Grimke's play, he felt that it was not exactly the kind of "Negro play" that he himself wanted to write. As he stated in "The Hope of a Negro Drama," published in 1919:

> When I say Negro plays, I do not mean merely plays with Negro characters. ... Miss Grimke's *Rachel* is nearer the idea; still even this, with its Negro characters, is not exactly the thing I mean. It is called a propaganda play, and a great portion of it shows the manner in which Negroes are treated by white people in the United States. ... Still there is another kind of play; the kind that shows the soul of a people; and the soul of this people is truly worth showing.[11]

From 1916 to 1918, Richardson took correspondence courses in poetry and drama, and when he considered himself sufficiently prepared, he began to write plays, submitting them mainly to *Crisis,* where his work came to the attention of editor W. E. B. DuBois. Between 1920 and 1921, Dr. DuBois published four of Richardson's children's plays in *The Brownies' Book,* a magazine for children also edited by DuBois.[12]

In November 1920, his first adult one-act play, *The Deacon's Awakening,* was published in *Crisis.* It was also produced with little success in St. Paul, Minn., in 1921. Although its characters are ostensibly Black, this play is primarily concerned with women's voting rights (an important issue of that period), and today would seem

[8]*Ibid.,* p. 149.

[9]*Who's Who in Colored America,* p. 435.

[10]"Poetry and Drama," *Crisis,* 34 (July 1927), p. 158.

[11]Willis Richardson, "The Hope of a Negro Drama," *Crisis,* 19 (November 1919), p. 338-39.

[12]Introduction to *The Broken Banjo,* p. 167. The titles and dates of only two of these plays have been determined: *The Children's Treasure* in the June 1921 issue, and *The Dragon's Tooth* in the October 1921 issue. Other children's plays are included in his collection, *The King's Dilemma and Other Plays for Children* (New York: Exposition Press, 1956).

somewhat outdated, despite the current interest in "women's lib." It is the story of a church deacon who plans to bring all would-be women voters before the Church Board for disciplinary action, until he learns that his own wife and daughter are active members of the Voting Society.

Between 1921 and 1923, Richardson tried without success to get his plays produced at Howard University. He took them to the Librarian at Howard (who was then Edward Christopher Williams, author of a number of articles in *The Messenger* and *Crisis*), and he put him in touch with Alain Locke and Montgomery Gregory, who were in charge of the Howard Players. As Richardson stated in a 1972 interview, "They liked my writing and wanted to put on a play of mine, but you see the President of Howard University was a white man at that time and they couldn't get his consent."[13]

In the meantime, Richardson succeeded in getting two of his one-act plays published in pamphlet form. Both appear to be typical "darky farces" of the type that were popular among whites during the Twenties and Thirties. *Alimony Rastus* was published by the Willis N. Bugbee Company in Syracuse, N. Y., and apparently concerns the matrimonial affairs of Rastus and Mandy. *A Ghost of the Past,* the second play, whose title is the only clue to its content, was published by the Paine Publishing Company in Dayton, Ohio. Both plays were published during the 1920s, although their publishing dates are not known.[14] However, neither play seems to be representative of the large body of Richardson's published work, and perhaps these two plays are best forgotten.

It was in 1922 that the great break came for Richardson that was to bring him into the national spotlight. The Ethiopian Art Players were being organized in Chicago, and they wanted to produce a Black play, but didn't know any Black playwrights. They wrote to Dr. DuBois at the *Crisis* headquarters, and he put them in touch with Richardson, with the result that they produced his one-act play, *The Chip Woman's Fortune.*[15] This play is historically important as the first serious work by a Black playwright to be presented on Broadway. Black playwrights had previously been represented

---

[13]James V. Hatch and Ted Shine, *Black Theatre, U.S.A.* (New York: The Free Press, a division of Macmillan, 1974), p. 233.

[14]*Index to One-Act Plays*, 1924-1931, pp. 34, 93. It should be noted that Richardson denies having written these two plays and does not include them among his dramatic works.

[15]*Black Theatre, U.S.A.*, p. 233.

on the Great White Way by musical comedies and revues, but never before by a serious drama, albeit a one-act play. It was produced on a triple bill with Oscar Wilde's *Salome* and a jazz interpretation of Shakespeare's *The Comedy of Errors* (although apparently the third play was not presented on all programs). It opened in Chicago on January 29, 1923; in Washington, D.C., on April 23, 1923; at the Lafayette Theatre in Harlem on May 7, 1923; and on Broadway at the Frazee Theatre for one week on May 15, 1923. As Richardson reported in the 1972 interview:

> ...The reviews were so good they sold lots of tickets. Then at the end of the week the manager made a big mistake. People bought tickets for these...plays but when they came the next week, he put on another play and the people objected so much that they had to give them their money back. The manager left New York and went somewhere and left all the players stranded....[16]

In the form presented on Broadway, *The Chip Woman's Fortune* is a folk drama in one act about a store porter who is about to lose his job in a small Southern community because of non-payment on a record player. He attempts to get money from an old woman rooming with his family, who ekes out a living by picking up chips of wood and bits of coal in the street, because he believes that she has a small fortune hidden away. But the chip woman plans to give her life savings to her son who has just been released from prison. When the son arrives, he is grateful for the care that the family has given his mother and saves the situation by providing the money to pay off the debt. *The New York Times* drama critic John Corbin, in his review of the play, praised the author's realistic treatment of the characters:

> *The Chip Woman's Fortune*...is an unaffected and wholly convincing transcript of everyday character. No one is glorified or otherwise tricked out to please; no one is blackened to serve as a "dramatic" contrast. I am referring, of course, to points of essential character, not to that matter of walnut stain.[17]

The Chip Woman's Fortune was first published in *Fifty More Contemporary One Act Plays,* edited by Frank Shay (New York: Appleton, 1928). It has been republished in two recent anthologies: *Anthology of the American Negro in the Theatre,* edited by Lindsay

[16]*Ibid.*
[17]*The New York Times,* May 16, 1923, p. 22.

Patterson (New York: The Publishers Company, 1967) and *Black Drama in America: An Anthology,* edited by Darwin T. Turner (Greenwich, Conn.: Fawcett Publications, 1971).

Following his Broadway triumph, Howard University agreed to put on one of Richardson's plays, and according to the playwright, "this was the first play by one of our people that was staged there."[18] Except for a production of a play by one of Howard University's own students,[19] Richardson's one-act play, *Mortgaged,* was the first play by a Black playwright to be produced by the Howard Players. It was presented on March 29, 1924. *Mortgaged* is about two brothers, representative of two types of middle-class (or educated) Blacks: one devoted to making money by exploiting his own people; the other seeking to uplift the race by making a contribution in his field of scientific research. Following its Howard University premiere, *Mortgaged* was again produced by Dunbar High School and entered in a drama tournament in Plainfield, N.J., in May 1925. As Richardson reported in *Crisis* Magazine,

> The rare thing about this occasion was that out of eight or ten clubs, [only] one Negro club produced a Negro play by a Negro author. The play, which I consider one of my poorest, gained fourth place among some of the best American one-actors.[20]

Mortgaged was produced by numerous other colleges and schools during the 1930s, following its publication in *Readings from Negro Authors,* edited by Otelia Cromwell, Lorenzo Dow Turner, and Eva B. Tykes (New York: Harcourt, Brace, 1931).

Reuben Silver, historian of the Karamu Theatre in Cleveland, Ohio, reported that Willis Richardson's *Compromise* was produced by the Gilpin Players at the Karamu Theatre on February 25, 1925, and was their first play by a Black playwright, although not their first "Negro play." In referring to this significant event in the history of the Gilpin Players, Silver wrote:

> Willis Richardson's play *Compromise* was included in Locke's *The New Negro,* although he was not one of Locke's many literary discoveries. ... He was a "voice in the wilderness," "urging the reten-

[18]*Black Theatre, U.S.A.,* p. 233.
[19]*The Death Dance,* a play of African life, written by Thelma Duncan, one of Howard University's students, was produced by the Howard Players on April 7, 1923. Miss Duncan studied playwriting at Howard under Montgomery Gregory.
[20]Introduction to *The Broken Banjo,* p. 167.

tion of the Negro heritage through the arts." ... Richardson believed that it was essential to capture this Negro material—whether for folklore, poems, plays—or it would be lost. ... In addition to the psychological value of sharing their viewpoint, Richardson reinforced those Gilpin Players who championed the Negro drama. His *Compromise* was the second Negro play done by them, in February 1926, one year after *Granny Maumee* [by white playwright Ridgely Torrence]. It was done "with glowing pride and confidence. Ground thus gained was solid ground, and the Gilpins never turned back."[21]

In *Compromise,* a folk play in one act, a Black family suffers four tragedies at the hands of their white neighbors, for which no justice can be obtained. The drama depicts compromises which Blacks once had to make in their relationships with whites in the Deep South. Following its production by the Gilpin Players, it was again produced by the Krigwa Players in New York, May 3, 1926, and subsequently by the Howard Players on April 8, 1936. The play was first published in Alain Locke's *The New Negro* (New York: Boni, 1925) and republished in *Crisis,* July 1927.

Richardson was awarded first prize in the *Crisis* (Magazine) Contest Awards of 1925 for his one-act folk tragedy, *The Broken Banjo,* which was produced by the Krigwa Players in New York on August 1, 1925. *The Broken Banjo* concerns a man who loves his banjo more than anyone or anything else. He is fond of his wife, although he neglects her, but hates his parasitic brother-in-law and cousin and orders them to stay away from his home. Having once secretly killed a man for breaking his banjo, he is finally turned in to the police by his angry brother-in-law who was a witness to the murder. Eugene O'Neill, one of the judges in the *Crisis* Awards, wrote concerning the winning entry: "I am glad to hear the judges all agreed on *The Broken Banjo* and that the play was so successfully staged. Willis Richardson should certainly continue working in his field."[22]

Again in 1926, Richardson received honorable mention in the *Opportunity* (Magazine) Contest Awards for his one-act play, *Fall of the Conjurer,* which still remains unpublished and unproduced. In October 1926, he won first prize in the *Crisis* Contest Awards for his three-act play, *The Bootblack Lover,* which concerns a bootblack who manages to win the girl he loves, in spite of the fact that he is

[21]Reuben Silver, "A History of the Karamu Theatre of Karamu House, 1915-1960" (Ph.D. dissertation, The Ohio State University, 1961; microfilm copy by University Microfilms, Ann Arbor, Michigan), pp. 126-27.

[22]"Krigwa," *Crisis,* 30 (October 1926), p. 278.

looked down upon by almost everyone because of the nature of his occupation. Typescripts of this play are located both in the Hatch-Billops Archives and the Moorland-Spingarn Research Center. Also in the Moorland-Springarn collection are two additional typescripts, both dated around 1926. The first is *The Chasm,* written in collaboration with Edward Christopher Williams, mentioned earlier as the Librarian at Howard University who helped Richardson to get his first plays produced. The second is *The New Generation,* a one-act play for which no description has been located.

In December 1926, one of Richardson's one-acters, *Rooms for Rent,* was produced by the Negro Art Players in New York. It is a domestic comedy about a Black unmarried woman living in a rooming house, who becomes the subject of malicious gossip by the other occupants. A typescript of this play is deposited in the Schomburg Center for Research in New York.

Including *The Bootblack Lover,* discussed above, Richardson has written six three-act plays, not one of which has been produced or published. In 1926, he wrote in *Crisis:* "My disappointment is that up to the present time, none of my three-act plays has had an opportunity to be made visible."[23] One of his three-act plays is a full-length version of his earlier Broadway one-act play, *The Chip Woman's Fortune;* the longer version was completed in 1927. Of this play, he wrote in *Crisis:* "I have been asked many times which of my plays I like best and I have always been uncertain which one to name, but now that I have just finished it, I think I prefer the three-act version of *The Chip Woman's Fortune.*"[24]

Of his remaining three-act plays, *The Wine Seller* is a domestic comedy, also completed in 1927, which concerns the problems faced by a family of bootleggers during the prohibition era. *Family Discord* is a domestic drama concerning a Black youth who shocks his family by bringing home a "white" bride, only to discover later that she is really Black. A fifth three-act play is a full-length version of *The Broken Banjo,* completed by the author in 1965. The sixth play is *The Amateur Prostitute,* a social comedy in three acts, which concerns the attempts of a scheming mother to force the son of a prosperous Black family to marry her daughter. Typescripts of all four plays are located in the Hatch-Billops Archives. *The Amateur Prostitute* is also in the Schomburg Center for Research.

[23]Introduction to *The Broken Banjo,* p. 167.
[24]"Poetry and Drama," p. 158.

In April 1927, two of Richardson's plays were published in *Carolina Magazine,* a literary publication of the University of North Carolina at Chapel Hill. *The Idle Head,* a drama in one act, dramatizes the plight of a rebellious youth in the Deep South who wishes to find a job and help his struggling mother, a washerwoman. But he cannot find work because he will not play the role of an Uncle Tom. The young man is eventually arrested for stealing a valuable pin, which a white woman forgot to remove from her laundry before sending it to his mother for washing. The second play, a one-act historical drama, *Flight of the Natives,* was produced by the Krigwa Players in Washington, D.C., on May 7, 1927. It concerns the escape of a number of slaves and their leader from a southern plantation, despite the treachery of a slave informer and the brutality of an oppressive master. Both *The Idle Head* and *Flight of the Natives* were republished in 1974 in *Black Theatre, U.S.A.,* edited by James V. Hatch and Ted Shine (New York: The Free Press, a division of Macmillan). In 1929, his one-act play, *The Peacock's Feathers,* was produced by the Krigwa Players in Washington, D.C., on January 11. It is a domestic satire about snobbery among middle-class Blacks. Typescripts are located in all three collections—Schomburg, Moorland-Spingarn, and Hatch-Billops. A script is also in the Performing Arts Research Center in New York.

In 1930, Richardson edited his first anthology, *Plays and Pageants From the Life of the Negro* (Washington, D.C.: The Associated Publishers). This anthology consists of eight plays and four pageants by Thelma Duncan, Maud Cuney-Hare, John Matheus, May Miller and others. Richardson himself is represented by three plays: *The King's Dilemma, The House of Sham,* and *The Black Horseman. The King's Dilemma,* written in 1926, is a children's play in one act. It concerns a white prince in the last kingdom of the world's domain, who chooses a Black boy for his companion and will not play without him, in defiance of his father. The King then resorts to drastic means to break up the companionship. It was first produced in the Washington, D.C., public schools and won the Public School Prize, May 21, 1926. *The House of Sham,* a drama in one act, was written in 1929. It centers around the petty social strivings and extravagant lifestyle of a middle-class Black family who thought they were well-off until the father, threatened with exposure, reveals that he has been putting up a false front by fraudulent business practices. The play was produced by many high schools during the 1920s. It was republished in *American Literature by Negro Authors*, edited by Herman Dreer (New York: The Macmillan Co., 1960). *The Black Horseman*, an historical drama in one act, was also written in 1929. It glorifies the image of the Black hero by dramatizing a period in Africa's history when kings ruled magnificent kingdoms, and when there was great rivalry between Carthage and Rome to gain power in Africa. Through the character of the play's hero, Massinissa, King of East Numidia, Richardson sought to epitomize the intrinsic virtues of the Black race: dignity, bravery, and nobility. *The Black Horseman* was first produced by the Playground Athletic League in Baltimore, Md., October 12, 1931.

In 1935, Richardson published his second anthology, *Negro History in Thirteen Plays*, co-edited with playwright May Miller (Washington, D.C.: The Associated Publishers). Richardson is represented by five Black history plays: *Antonio Maceo, Attucks the Martyr, The Elder Dumas, Near Cavalry,* and *In Menelik's Court. Antonio Maceo,* an historical tragedy in one act, concerns the betrayal of the Cuban hero and patriot who led a rebellion against Spain. The General's wife avenges her husband's death by killing his personal physician, who permitted the Spanish assassins to enter the general's headquarters. *Attucks, the Martyr,* an historical drama in one act, dramatizes the heroism of Crispus Attucks, the escaped slave who was the first man to be killed in the American Revolution. The play shows Attucks as fearless and determined to express his opposition to the British, although he knows that it may cost him his life. *The Elder Dumas,* an historical drama in one act, is a surprisingly unsympathetic portrait of Alexandre Dumas père, the prolific mulatto French novelist and playwright. Dumas is accused of excessive commercialism, of writing plays and novels so fast that he is unable to do his best work, of polishing and painting and sending out the work of others under his own name, and of being oversensitive to criticism. This is Richardson's only play in which an eminent Black figure is subjected to more criticism than praise. *Near Calvary,* a Biblical play in one act, dramatizes the bravery of Simon, the man who carried the cross for Jesus, as seen through the eyes of his relatives who also face danger as suspected followers of Christ. This play was broadcast over "Voice of America," July 7, 1936. *In Menelik's Court,* an historical play in one act, is a drama of love and intrigue, with its setting in the palace of Menelik, Emperor of Abyssinia (Ethiopia) in 1898. The Italians, who have been unsuccessfully fighting to gain a foothold in Abyssinia, plan to abduct the Emperor's foster daughter in order to force the Emperor to come to terms with them. The Abyssinian Captain of the Guard, who is in love with the princess, successfully thwarts the plot, captures the Italian abductors and, at the climax of the play, kneels to ask the Emperor for his daughter's hand in marriage.

Little was heard from Richardson during the 1940s, except for a production of one of his one-act plays, *Miss or Mrs.*, by the Bureau of Engraving Dramatic Club in Washington, D.C., May 5, 1941. This production is of some significance, since the author worked in this Federal bureau and presumably was associated with the production. The play concerns the devious attempts by a group of self-appointed busybodies to determine the marital status of one of the teachers in a school system where only single women are employed. *Miss or Mrs.* has not yet been published. A typescript is located in the Hatch-Billops Archives in New York. Also in the Hatch-Billops Archives is a typescript of *Hope of the Lonely,* a one-act folk drama, which first came to light during the 1940s when it was listed as one of the manuscripts in the theatre collection of Karamu House in Cleveland. Set in Georgia during the 1920s, it concerns the attempts of a sharecropper and his family to accumulate enough money to move "up North." *Hope of the Lonely* is still unproduced and unpublished.

Richardson remained silent until 1956, when he issued his third and final collection, *The King's Dilemma and Other Plays for Children* (New York: Exposition Press). This collection includes *The Dragon's Tooth, The Gypsy's Finger Ring, The King's Dilemma, Man of Magic, Near Calvary,* and *The New Santa Claus. The King's Dilemma* and *Near Calvary* were included in previous collections, and have already been discussed. *The Dragon's Tooth,* originally published in *The Brownie's Book,* Oct. 1921, is a fairy tale in which some children try to win a leadership prize by stealing a dragon's tooth on which is inscribed the secret of the future. *The Gypsy's Finger Ring,* also a fairy tale, concerns an encounter with a gypsy, in which some children are permitted to see into the future. *Man of Magic* is about a character of a new race of the future, who is neither Black nor white. *The New Santa Claus* is a Christmas play involving a Santa of a different type than children are usually led to expect.

Typescripts of eleven additional undated one-act plays are deposited in the Schomburg Center for Research in New York: *Bold*

Lover, a domestic drama in which a daughter of a middle-class Black family wishes to marry a man who is unacceptable to her parents; *The Dark Haven,* a folk melodrama in which a Black man gets the best of an enemy; *The Curse of the Shell Road Witch,* a folk drama about superstition and religion among rural Blacks; *Imp of the Devil,* a domestic drama about an incorrigible child; *Joy Rider,* a domestic drama in which the son of a well-to-do family marries his brother-in-law's mistress; *The Man Who Married a Young Wife,* a domestic comedy in which an old man tricks a young woman into marrying him by pretending to be rich; *The Nude Siren,* a domestic comedy about the secret activities of a rather self-righteous "prude"; *A Pillar of the Church,* a domestic play in which a daughter is not allowed to complete her education because of the objections of an overly-religious father; *The Visiting Lady,* a social comedy about a neighborhood gossip who goes from door to door with her latest news; and two plays for which no descriptions have been located: *The Brown Boy* and *The Jail Bird.*

Two additional typescripts are deposited in the Hatch-Billops Archives in New York: *A Stranger From Beyond* is a folk drama about a mysterious stranger who saves a dying mother and disappears into the night. *Victims,* a folk tragedy (subtitled *The Deep Regret*), concerns a woman who borrows some money on the strength of a job that fails to materialize. A taped interview of Richardson is also located in the Hatch-Billops Archives, with copies in the Schomburg Center for Research and in the Cohen Library of the City College of New York. This interview, made in 1972, is part of the Hatch-Billops Oral History Collection of Black Theatre Artists, recorded by James V. Hatch and his assistants at the City College of New York.

Willis Richardson is one of Black Theatre's genuine pioneers; and, like all pioneers, he was considerably ahead of his time. Too far ahead, in fact, to personally realize all of the benefits which his prolific output would seem to have merited. It is my sincere hope that interest in his work will soon be revived. His "hope for a Negro theatre" has long been realized; it is now time to fulfill his lifelong dream of having his unpublished and unproduced plays "made visible." Richardson has tried to show us "the soul of a people, and the soul of [his] people is truly worth showing."

Shuffle Along:
Keynote of the Harlem Renaissance

by Helen Armstead Johnson

A period of undeniable excitement and artistic development in the history of Afro-American culture and the American theater was that of the 1920's when the Negro musical comedy first appeared. This new theater form was a concrete reflection of the "New Negro's" determination to reject outwardly imposed restrictions upon black creativity. In *The Big Sea*, Langston Hughes says that,

> The 1920's were the years of Manhattan's black renaissance. It began with *Shuffle Along* (1921), *Runnin' Wild* (1923), and the Charleston. But it was the musical review *Shuffle Along* that gave a scintillating send-off to that Negro vogue in Manhattan, which reached its peak just before the crash of 1929, the crash that sent Negroes, white folks, and all rolling down the hill toward the Works Progress Administrations.[1]

Following a passage in which he notes significant plays he has seen, Hughes makes this observation:

> But I remember *Shuffle Along* best of all. It gave just the proper push —a pre-Charleston kick—to that Negro vogue of the 20's that spread to books, African sculpture, music, and dancing.[2]

In *Black Manhattan*, James Weldon Johnson refers to *Shuffle Along* as an "epoch making" musical comedy. Writing in the

"*Shuffle Along:* Keynote of the Harlem Renaissance" by Helen Armstead Johnson. From *Speech Journal*, Vol. 8 (1970), pp. 25-29. Reprinted by permission of SCSC and the author.

[1]Langston Hughes, *The Big Sea* (New York: Alfred A. Knopf, 1940), p. 223.
[2]*Ibid.*, p. 224.

Chicago *Herold & Examiner,* November 17, 1922, Ashton Stevens, known as an unusually caustic critic, said of the Black musical:

> The plot is a rebuke to the plotlessness of white musicals. But there is even more music than plot, even more music than in Irving Berlin's most musical *Music Box Review.* ... If that hard-to-spell word, "rhythm" had not been invented, it would spring into the dictionary at Mr. Webster's first hearing of Mr. Eubie Blake's bandsmen. ... Rhythm is the life of this show.

And of Miller and Lyles's comedy: "The show is as clean as a hound's dentistry." In 1925 Jessie Byrd Fauset wrote that,

> ... a comedy made up of such ingredients as the music of Sissle and Blake, the quaint, irresistible humors of Miller and Lyles, the quintessence of jazzdom in the Charleston, the superlativeness of Miss Mill's happy abandon could know no equal. It would be the line by which all other comedy would have to be measured.[3]

Miss Fauset's memory failed her on one major point, however: The Charleston was not introduced until two years later, 1923, in another show, *Runnin' Wild,* starring Miller and Lyles, with a score by James P. Johnson and Cecil McPherson.

Montgomery Gregory, in an essay which appears in Alain Locke's *The New Negro* noted that,

> Historically these musical shows are a significant element in the groping of the Negro for dramatic expression, and who knows but that they may be the genesis for an important development of our drama in the future?[4]

And Locke himself in *The Negro and the American Stage* quotes the great German director, Max Reinhardt, with reference to *Liza, Runnin' Wild,* and *Shuffle Along:*

> It is intriguing, very intriguing,... these Negro shows that I have seen. But remember, not as achievements, not as things in themselves artistic, but in their possibilities. They are most modern, most American, most expressionistic. They are highly original in spite of obvious triteness, and artistic in spite of superficial crudeness. To me

[3]Lindsay Patterson, ed., *Anthology of the American Negro in the Theatre* (New York: Publishers Company, Inc., 1967), p. 34.

[4]Montgomery Gregory, "The Drama of Negro Life," *The New Negro,* ed. Alain Locke (New York, 1925), p. 156.

they reveal possibilities of technique in drama, and if I should ever try to do anything American, I would build it on these things.[5]

With such a place in the history of theater in America, Aubrey Lyles, Flournoy Miller, Eubie Blake and Noble Sissle deserve the kind of in-depth treatment which they have never been given. For this reason, after a review of people and events of significance before the keynote production of *Shuffle Along* in 1921, the major part of this paper will be devoted to it and to the men whose art it is.

One of the strongest breaks with the minstrel tradition came in 1898, when Bob Cole and Billy Johnson wrote *A Trip to Coontown*, which they described as a musical farce. Its historic significance is that it is known as the first show to be written, produced, and managed on the commercial stage by black people. It was built upon a structured script in which a thread of continuity was perceptible. Its title, of course, reveals that it was not a total departure from the entrenched darky show. In 1898, too, Will Marion Cook wrote *Clorindy, the Origin of the Cakewalk,* for which Paul Laurence Dunbar wrote the lyrics. Cook tells us that the morning after he and Dunbar had spent the night writing *Clorindy*, he was at the piano trying to play what he called his "most Negroid song," "Who Dat Say Chicken in Dis Crowd?": "My mother...came into the parlor, tears streaming from her eyes, and said: 'Oh, Will! Will! I've sent you all over the world to study and become a great musician, and you return such a nigger!' My mother was a graduate of Oberlin in the class of 1865 and thought that a Negro composer should write just like a white man."[6] The following year, 1899, additional progress was made when *Sons of Ham* was on the boards at the Grand Opera House in New York. This was a joint effort of Bert Williams and George Walker, who were incomparable partners until Walker died in 1909, during a run of *Bandana Land*, another of their musical shows.

One of the European musical forms extremely popular among white theater patrons was the operetta. In their early efforts to break away from the degrading, self-mocking images of minstrelsy, black lyricists and composers began to develop black operettas, hoping that they would be acceptable to white audiences. Only then could black artists play the top theaters. Inasmuch as white operettas were

[5]Alain Locke, "The Negro and the American Stage," *Theatre Arts Monthly,* Vol. X (February 1926), pp. 114-15.

[6]Patterson, *Anthology,* pp. 51-52.

invariably about royalty, black composers wrote operettas about black royalty. Thus *Abyssinia,* with a book by Jessie Shipp, was about King Menelik. One of the literally true songs was "It's Hard to Find a King Like Me." Earlier, from 1902 to 1905, Williams and Walker had starred in an operetta called *In Dahomey,* with lyrics by Paul Laurence Dunbar and music by Will Marion Cook. It is said to be the first American play on the London stage and the first American command performance. It was presented in the garden at Buckingham Palace for the birthday of the Prince of Wales.

During the same year Bob Cole and J. Rosamond Johnson, brother of James Weldon Johnson, wrote *The Red Moon,* first starring Abbey Mitchell, wife of Will Marion Cook, and later starring Anna Pankey. The story line of *The Red Moon* was that an American Indian princess had gone to Howard University to study; she met a Negro, fell in love, and decided to marry. Her brother, upon hearing the news, came rushing from the reservation to stop the marriage but, of course, all operettas ended happily. To white America, however, an American Indian princess was still a savage, to say nothing of the Negro, and the parallel which was apparent to Cole and Johnson was not apparent to their audience. Thus the production was another in a long line of financial failures. Without white audience approval, black writers simply could not book their shows into the first class theaters, where they could charge admission high enough to break even.

By 1911 such musical shows as those of Williams and Walker, and Cole and Johnson had come to an end. Bob Cole's death resulted from unbearable frustration; he literally walked into the water to his death. He and George Walker were both early victims of the white man's control of the theatre. But, together with their partners, their pioneer efforts to abandon darky shows were significant. They opened the way for the musical comedy and the era of the "New Negro" of the twenties.

The keynote of that era was sounded by *Shuffle Along.* We shall consider biographical data, the forming of the partnerships, matters of production, the comedy itself, and the lasting contributions of its writers to the American theater.

Eubie Blake was born on February 7, 1883, in Baltimore, Maryland. His parents were former slaves who were legally married after slavery. His father, John Sumner Blake, who named himself Sumner after his favorite general, had belonged to the Fredenburg family in Middlesex, Virginia, and his mother, Emily Johnstone Blake, came from Mathews County, Virginia. Eubie was the youngest of ten brothers and sisters whom he never saw; they all died in infancy. He himself, as a result of rickets, did not walk until he was three years old. He was eighty-seven years old in February, 1970. He describes his father as a "braggadocio," a man who made all of nine dollars a week as a longshoreman when it did not rain. Eubie Blake began his professional life secretly by playing in a whore-house known as Aggie Shelton's. His deeply religious mother learned to live comfortably with the fact that the money for the house which her son bought for her was made in such an "immoral" way. She tried extremely hard to wipe out the memories of slavery, but the father bore marks of the lashes across his back and was less reluctant to talk. One of his graphic stories was a description of stud, that is, breeding human beings like animals. About three days before being put in stud, the male slaves were fed meat and other proteins, after which six of them and twelve female ones spent about three days in the barn.

Eubie Blake's formal education was interrupted in the eighth grade and not resumed until he was sixty years old, at which time he studied at New York University with Rudolph Schramm, completing a four year course in two and one-half years. By this time his reputation as a composer and ragtime pianist had long been established.

Noble Sissle was born in Indianapolis, Indiana, July 10, 1889, where his mother was a teacher and his father a Methodist Episcopal preacher. He attended both DePauw and Butler Universities before becoming part of Jim Reese Europe's famous 369th Infantry band during the first World War. His mother's mother had been born in slavery. Because of her inability to support her baby just after freedom, she gave her to a close friend. Slavery was not really over when freedom was declared. His grandmother remembered slaves running down the road, throwing up their hands, and shouting, "Free at last, free at last! Thank God A'Mighty we're free at last!" The realities of sudden freedom, however, forced many slaves to return to their masters for food and pennies if anything, for their labor, and the masters of the devastated plantations were often equally impoverished, comparatively speaking. Thus slavery continued on the basis of mutual need, and Sissle's grandmother was of this period. The act of giving her daughter away was a survival technique for her child.

Sissle's grandfather came from the Cecil plantation in Kentucky. He resented the origin of his name so intensely that he changed it to Sissle. Noble says about this that, "He gave me one of the finest stage names, because I have never heard of another." Once when his orchestra was playing in Lexington, Kentucky, a white man who had been watching him intently eased up to him during a break and in quiet undertones asked, "Why don't you spell your name right?" and disappeared. Sissle's grandfather was the son of the master. In reflecting upon the effect of the white man upon black morality, Sissle says, "It's a wonder we had any sense at all so far as morals are concerned." Reflecting still further upon the high degree of morality among Negroes, he says, "Slaves didn't allow all that mess in those tribes in Africa."

Of considerable interest to us is the first meeting between Noble Sissle and Eubie Blake. In 1915 Sissle went to Baltimore to play at River View Park, where he and Blake were introduced by Joe Porter, leader of a sextet. The name Sissle rang a bell with Blake, who tells what happened. "I said, 'Sissle, Sissle. You write words, don't you?' He said, 'Yes,' I said, 'Well, I'm looking for a writer.' And he said, 'Well, I'm looking for a composer.' And we shook hands. That was fifty-three years ago [as of December, 1968]. And that's the only contract we ever ever had."

Miller and Lyles had been students at Fisk University, where they wrote and performed in a number of shows. In Chicago, in a theater owned by Robert Mott, they wrote and produced a show called *The Mayor of Dixie*, which became the book for *Shuffle Along*, with Dixie changed to Fairville. Miller and Lyles had been to London by the time they met Sissle and Blake, and were already seasoned and polished performers. All four of these men were practically driven out of vaudeville by the same thing. They would be billed as the No. 2 act, which paid second lowest money. They were so good, though, that in both cases they would be moved up next to closing, the top spot, but they were still paid second spot money. In the top spot they were followed only by animals, who could not complain that they were too hard to follow.

Langston Hughes described *Shuffle Along* as a show written by Negroes for a Negro audience. This is an unqualified error in fact.

Nevertheless, Doris Abramson has perpetuated it verbatim in her book *The Negro in the American Theater, 1929-1959.* The facts are that Sissle and Blake and Miller and Lyles met at the annual convention of the NAACP in Philadelphia, in 1920, where all of them had performed in a benefit at the Keith Theater. Miller and Lyles were black-face comedians who wrote all of their own material, and it was of such quality that they could play what were known as the "high class" theaters. Sissle and Blake had played society music, unlike many Negro musicians who had been confined to the blues circuit and to melodrama and burlesque theaters. After seeing the Sissle and Blake act, Miller came over to Sissle and said, "You know one thing, you two fellows are the missing link in a Negro show getting to Broadway." To which Sissle responded: "Yes, what do you mean?" Miller's explanation was that twice, while playing the Lafayette Theater in Harlem, they had brought theater managers from downtown to see their shows. The reaction of these managers was that, "Your comedy's clean and funny and everything, but there's not one number that we can whistle when we come out." Such a number would advertise a show more than anything else, and it was Miller and Lyles who said that Sissle and Blake wrote such music. *Shuffle Along* was written for Broadway. It opened at the Cort Theater on Sixty-third Street, after road tests for white audience reaction, and ran for nearly a year and a half.

In addition to Sissle, who wrote the lyrics, sang, and acted, and Blake, who wrote the music and conducted the orchestra, the other major performers in the first cast were Lottie Gee, the star, and Gertrude Saunders, the ingenue. Josephine Baker was accepted for the chorus and then turned down by Miller at the end of the audition when he found that she was only fifteen years old. A clever enough girl, she slipped into the road company in Boston, creating such a sensation that the roadshow company was booked into Brooklyn for a week, running simultaneously with the Manhattan one, so that the writers could see who the sensational girl was. By this time Josephine Baker was sixteen and able to join the New York cast. Since he had recommended her to Miller originally, Sissle had some part in Miss Baker's first movements in the direction of fame. Gertrude Saunders was replaced by Florence Mills, who was then appearing with The Tennessee Ten, a vaudeville act. It was Sissle's first wife, Harriet Toy Sissle, who suggested that he consider Florence, which is to say that he had something to do, too, with the rise of another star, one whom Eubie Blake thinks has had no superior.

Shuffle Along was first performed in Trenton, New Jersey, on its way to a trial run at the Howard Theater in Washington, D.C., on Palm Sunday, 1921. The one night performance was to help finance the Washington trip, but a drenching rain made it a rather inauspicious first night: the total take was ninety dollars. Cort was not willing to invest money in costumes and sets, since he doubted, about as much as any other white theater owner, that the show would draw the downstairs crowd. When the balcony was full the owner made his rent; when the orchestra was full, he made his profit. The Schuberts, as potential brokers, did not trust the audience reaction in a Negro theater, because the whites who were there were not sure whether they were laughing at the Negroes laughing, or laughing because the show was really funny. All of this accounts for the fact that the show was road tested in such places as Reading, Pennsylvania, before white audiences, and for the fact that the costumes used were left over from a "Negro" show written for a white audience by Eddie Leonard, a white comedian. The road test revealed that Negroes and whites laughed in the same places: however, the Negroes laughed harder.

In brief, *Shuffle Along* is the first sophisticated Afro-American love story. More than this, it is the first truly American show. It was not a darky show, and it was not, as Langston Hughes said, a review. It had a complete book. It looked at political corruption, which is certainly an American theme. Two partners, Sam Peck and Speed Jenkins, operated a grocery store. Tom Sharper, played by Sissle, represented the "smart boys downtown" who wanted to get control of the political situation in the town of Fairville by putting into office a mayor whom they could control. The hero was Harry Walton. In essence, the comedy dealt with a three-way mayoralty race. Part of the rich comedy was supplied by the two partners, each stealing from the same cash register to finance his own campaign. Sam Peck was a 5'4" man married to a towering, buxom woman, who was his campaign manager. Jenkins was under particular pressure, because Sharper kept pressing him for more money with which to buy votes. He also stood to lose his wife if he did not win, which explains "Love Will Find a Way" as the theme song at the top of the show. The melody was written on a train when Blake was going from

Passaic, New Jersey, to New York to meet Sissle. Years earlier, Lewellyn Wilson, a black symphony orchestra conductor in Baltimore, had taught him not to compose at the piano.

Another song, "Bandana Days," is described as reflecting the admiration of these sons of slaves for their mothers who had somehow managed to survive. Part of the truth is that costumes with bandana handkerchiefs were left over from the Eddie Leonard show. The song illustrates the roots of rhythm in America. Every show, of course, had its soft shoe number, and in this one it was "Honeysuckle Time." The title song, "Shuffle Along," was a spirited number in the second act: "If you lose, don't·start singing the blues; just shuffle along."

During this period in the American theater, a lot of shows used one title on the road and another if they wanted to come to New York, so that they could change the show a bit and keep it alive, even if it had not been very successful on the road. The original idea with this show was to call it *Shuffle Along* on the road and *Mayor of Fairville* in New York, but it caught on so well that no one wanted to change the title. Although successful black operettas had been on Broadway at the turn of the century, *Shuffle Along,* with a run of 504 performances, arrived there in 1921 as the Negro musical comedy which was to influence generations of all musical comedy that followed it.

The most famous number in the whole show was "I'm Just Wild About Harry." After Harry Truman used it as his campaign song, Sissle and Blake presented the original manuscript to the Truman Library in Independence, Missouri. They are still collecting substantial royalties from this song written forty-nine years ago.

We have really only begun to look at this period and some of the great names which illuminate it: Bert Williams and George Walker; Will Marion Cook and Paul Laurence Dunbar; Bob Cole and J. Rosamond Johnson; Flournoy Miller and Aubrey Lyles; Florence Mills; Josephine Baker, Noble Sissle and Eubie Blake. They are part of the heritage of the American theater. In an almost singular way, *Shuffle Alonw* influenced the whole of the Harlem Renaissance and the "New Negro" of the 1920s. It was the father of the most popular form of American theater today, the musical. It created a purely American idiom and treated an American theme: political corruption. It humanized Negroes, permitting them to fall in love.

It literally chased the coon up the tree. It introduced the chorus line of beautiful girls who actually danced, thereby influencing Ziegfeld whose girls only pranced and looked "like a melody." It opened up first-class theaters and drew downstairs audiences to black shows for the first time. Moreover, it put fame within the reach of the greatest female stars of any time or race, and we are still singing, even on commercials, "I'm Just Wild About Harry." Most of all, it inspired countless others. No wonder Langston Hughes remembered *Shuffle Along* best of all.

Langston Hughes as Playwright

by Darwin T. Turner

Throughout his professional writing career of forty-six years, Langston Hughes maintained keen interest in theater. He published his first play, *The Gold Piece*, in 1921. In 1935, he had his first Broadway show—*Mulatto*, which established a record by remaining in production on Broadway longer than any other play which had been written by a Negro. During the thirties and early forties, he founded three Negro dramatic groups—the Suitcase Theater in Harlem, the Negro Art Theater in Los Angeles, and the Skyloft Players in Chicago. As late as 1963, Hughes was still polishing *Emperor of Haiti*, which had been produced as *Drums of Haiti* twenty-seven years earlier.

Langston Hughes took pride in his achievements in the theater. In addition to the record-setting *Mulatto* and *Simply Heavenly*, which appeared on Broadway in 1957, he wrote seven other plays which were produced professionally. He also wrote musicals, a movie script, radio drama, a passion play, and the lyrics for the musical version of Elmer Rice's *Street Scene*. Nevertheless, despite his extensive efforts, Hughes never became outstanding as a dramatist. The reasons for his failure are evident in a close examination of his works.

Produced in 1935, but written in 1930, *Mulatto* is an emotionally engaging drama, marred by melodrama, propaganda, and crudities common to inexperienced playwrights. Developed from a short story, "Father and Son," *Mulatto* dramatizes the conflict between Colonel Norwood, a wealthy white man, and Robert, his "yard

"Langston Hughes as Playwright" by Darwin T. Turner. From *Langston Hughes, Black Genius: A Critical Evaluation*, ed. Therman B. O'Daniel for the College Language Association (New York: William Morrow & Company, Inc., 1971), pp. 81-95. Reprinted by permission of the College Language Association and the author.

child." Since he was seven years old, Robert has hated his father for refusing to recognize their relationship, of which he himself had been proud. During his summer's vacation from college, Robert has strained tension to a breaking point by defying the mores of his father and of the Georgia town in which they live. Finally, on the scheduled day of Bert's return to college, the tension snaps. Incensed to learn that Bert has defied a white woman, has sped past a white man, and has entered the front door of the house regularly, Norwood threatens to kill him. Bert, instead, kills his father and flees; but, chased by a posse, he returns to the house, where he kills himself.

Much of the power of the play derives from the subject itself. A traditional subject in drama, father-son conflict inevitably generates excitement and frequently produces memorable characters and confrontations: Polonius and Laertes, Theseus and Hippolytus are only a few. In this instance, the excitement was intensified for American audiences by the first professional dramatization of a conflict between a mulatto and his father.

The play gains strength also from Hughes's characterizations of Bert and Cora. Although he is obviously modeled on the proud and noble slaves of Negro literary tradition, Bert is an interesting character. His contempt for other Negroes, his stubborn insistence that he be recognized as a man, and his arrogant defiance of custom symptomize a fatal *hubris*. In his deliberate provocation of trouble, a manifestation of what seems almost a suicidal complex, he anticipates James Baldwin's protagonist in *Blues for Mr. Charlie*, written a generation later.

Cora too seems a familiar figure from American stories about the antebellum days. At first, she is merely the docile servant who, for many years, has lived with the master, nurtured him, and borne his children without concern for herself and without complaint. After Norwood's death, however, Cora assumes more significant dimensions. Revealing that love had caused her to excuse Norwood's faults and cling to him, she now repudiates him because his death threatens her son, who is even more precious to her. Unfortunately, as Hughes has written the scene, a reader is uncertain whether Cora is insane or is, for the first time, rationally aware of the manner in which she has been abused by Norwood. Regardless of the reason for her transformation, Cora, like all of Hughes's other heroines, appears more carefully delineated and more admirable than the male figures who dominate her life.

Even Colonel Norwood is interesting as a character. Although Hughes, writing protest drama, stereotyped him from racial bigots of his own day and slave masters of the previous century, Norwood gains reality in his final confrontation with Bert. Transcending racial identity, he becomes, like Hughes's own father, a man in conflict with his son. When Norwood cannot pull the trigger of his gun to kill Bert, Bert strangles him. Although Bert could only wonder why Norwood did not fire, a reader suspects, romantically perhaps, that, at the critical moment, Norwood realized that Bert was actually his flesh and blood, not merely a "yard child" whom he could ignore.

Despite the subject and the interesting characterizations of Bert and Cora, the play is weak artistically in plot structure, language, and thought. From the moment of Norwood's death, the action moves with the rapidity and inexorability of Greek tragedy. Prior to the death, however, it too frequently seems painfully slow and digressive. For example, Bert's sister Sally appears in Act I, talks, and then leaves for college. Rather than contributing to the plot or background, she merely distracts the reader, who puzzles about the reason for her existence. One can almost argue artistic justification for the play's producer, who revised the play to cause Sally to miss her train in the first act and be raped in the third. Even though the producer was motivated by the commercial possibilities of sensationalism, he at least provided dramatic reason for Sally's presence and carried to their logical conclusion hints which Hughes planted casually and forgot.

Hughes forgot some other matters in the drama. From the opening scene onward, he reiterated the fact that Norwood does not permit Negroes to use the front door. Negro servants who haul a huge trunk down the front hall steps are required to carry it out the back door. When Norwood learns that Bert frequently enters through the front door, he threatens to break Bert's neck. Nevertheless, only a few moments after Norwood has voiced his threat, a Negro servant helps his master enter through the front door and leaves through the same portal. Nothing in the stage directions indicates that Norwood pays any attention to this dark transgression of his hallowed sill.

Because Hughes was a talented poet, it is difficult to understand his apparent insensitivity to language and to effective usage in *Mulatto.* His faults are various. "Kid" and "old man" seem inappropriate slang for rural Georgia of the early 1930's. Even more incongruous is the use of "papa." Norwood slapped seven-year-old Bert for calling him "papa." One wonders how the word came into Bert's vocabulary since no one else in the play uses it. Cora uses "daddy" and "pappy." Bert's brother says, "Pa." Norwood says, "Pappy." Even Bert himself fails to use the counterpart when addressing his mother. He calls her "Ma."

Other words are questionable. It is doubtful that a Southerner would use "lynching" to describe an activity in which he participated. It is improbable that Norwood would emphasize his own immorality by calling his son a bastard. It is unnecessary for the overseer to inform the audience that he will form a posse from *white* men.

Quibbling about words may seem petty criticism of a writer. Nevertheless, one assumes that a poet, more than other writers perhaps, would exercise care in selecting words. Occasionally but too infrequently, Hughes demonstrated ability to use language effectively when he chose to. The most appealing scene in the play is that in which Cora, in a monologue, recalls her early relationship with Norwood. The speech rings true in every respect. It is colloquial, faithfully representative of the dialect of Southern Negroes, and poetic. Hughes also demonstrated incisive use of language in the ironic moment at which a Negro servant, disregarding Norwood's five Negro children, agrees with a white undertaker's assertion that Norwood had no relatives.

Part of Hughes's difficulty with language resulted from his desire to be certain that spectators understood the full implications of the characters' statements. In order to assure himself that no one would miss the point, Hughes sometimes overstated it. For example, Norwood, explaining his financial security, says that he has "a few thousand put away." A wealthy man who is not boasting would probably say merely that he has a few *dollars* put away. But Hughes wanted the spectator to realize Norwood's wealth. Similarly, Higgins, a white man, says, "All this postwar propaganda on the radio about freedom and democracy—why the niggers think it's meant for them." Psychologically, the statement is false. A bigot would not verbalize his awareness of a difference between the condition of the Negro and America's promise to its citizens. In fact, he probably would not be aware of any difference. But Hughes, using a white man as mouthpiece, wanted to emphasize the discrepancy in the minds of his audience.

Finally, in *Mulatto,* Hughes slipped into improbable contradictions which sometimes are amusing. For instance, to emphasize the sacredness of the Colonel's library, Cora says that even she has never been permitted to enter it in thirty years. Surely someone, however, cleaned the room at least once during that time. Certainly, Colonel Norwood was not a man to clean and dust a room; certainly also, the individual who most probably would be assigned the task would be Cora, the most trusted servant.

Not amusing, but even more improbable, is the picture of life in the Norwood house. Except for allusions to contemporary personalities and inventions, one might assume that the story was set in the antebellum South. For instance, there is never any mention of paying the servants. Surely, however, most working Negroes in Georgia in 1930 at least touched the money they earned even if they immediately handed it on to a creditor.

Little Ham, written during the thirties, is set in the Harlem Renaissance of the twenties. Webster Smalley, in the preface of *Five Plays by Langston Hughes,* has described it as a folk comedy. To a Negro reader, however, it is a slow-moving, frequently dull, artificial attempt to present within a single play all of the exotic elements which distinguish life in Harlem from life in the rest of America. Here, jumbled together like the animals in a box of animal crackers, are shoe shiners, beauticians, numbers runners, homosexuals, West Indians, followers of Father Divine, gangsters, middle-class Negroes. They cut, shoot, drink, make love, gossip, play numbers, flirt, but rarely utter a significant thought.

The slight and confused story, better suited for musical comedy where it might be obscured by attractive songs and dances, recounts the adventures of Hamlet Hitchcock Jones, a "sporty" ladies' man. When Little Ham, who flirts with all women, meets fat Tiny Lee, a beauty parlor owner, his conversation ends in a promise to escort her to a Charleston contest the following evening. Soon afterwards, he purchases a stolen coat for his new girlfriend, wins $645 playing the numbers and is given a job as a numbers runner. When he visits Tiny at her shop, he is surprised to find Mattie Bea, his married girlfriend, who, expecting to accompany him, bought the contest tickets which Ham has given to Tiny and who believes that Ham will give her the stolen coat which he has already given to Tiny. When she discovers the true situation, she attacks Tiny; but Ham is arrested by the police, who assume that he is beating her. Later, Gilbert, Tiny's former boyfriend, visits her apartment to take her to the Charleston contest. His efforts are interrupted by the arrival of Ham, who has secured his release from jail by charming a female judge. To forestall trouble, Tiny hides Gilbert in a closet and locks him in. Still later, at the dance, Mattie Bea and Gilbert, both arriving late, threaten to continue their quarrels with Tiny and Ham. Coincidentally, however, it is revealed that Mattie Bea and Gilbert are husband and wife. Finding themselves together for a change, they become reconciled, and all the couples participate in a frenzied Charleston contest, which is won by Ham and Tiny.

A play with such insignificant action needs to be redeemed by characterization, language, humor, or thought. *Little Ham,* unfortunately, is weak in each of these.

The language probably is the most effective element of the play. In the Harlem dialect and slang, with which he was familiar, Hughes wrote more freely and more accurately than in *Mulatto.* The language constitutes a significant source for the humor of the play. Hughes wrote effective quips: "She is just a used blade, and I got a new razor"; "I don't duel, I duke"; "love is taking 'til you can't give no mo." Hughes also drew comedy from the strangeness of the Harlem dialect—"she-self," "perzactly"—and from such malapropisms as "reverted" (instead of "converted") and "prostitution" (instead of "prostration").

Like Zora Neale Hurston he assumed that non-Negro audiences would be amused by the colorful language of Negroes, especially the language of invective. This is effectively illustrated by Tiny's tirade directed towards Mattie Bea:

> *Tiny.* I'm a real good mama that can shake your peaches down. ... I hear you cluckin' hen, but your nest must be far away. Don't try to lay no eggs in here.

Unfortunately, however, some of the expressions already had been overworked by the time Hughes wrote the play. Now they seem hackneyed: "I'm from Alabam, but I don't give a damn"; "God don't love ugly."

Hughes based his comedy almost as much on slapstick actions

and situations, such as that in which Gilbert, locked inside a closet, quarrels with and shoots at Ham, who is outside. Hughes found humor in low comedy, such as the ridicule of the effeminate movements and cowardice of a homosexual and Tiny's accidental burning of the head of a middle-class woman who is her client. In general, the comedy is heavy rather than subtle.

The characterization too is heavy and stereotyped. Ham is a wisecracking, fast-talking ladies' man. Tiny is fat, pleasant, and undistinguished. The other characters are such obvious types that Hughes frequently did not even name them. They are listed merely as "West Indian," "Staid Lady," "Youth," "Shabby Man," etc.

The action is heavily foreshadowed and overly dependent upon chance and coincidence. For example, the complicated love triangles of Tiny and Ham are eased by the improbable coincidence that their former lovers are married to each other. Motivation is puzzling. For example, although love is reputed to work marvels, a critical reader might wonder what attracts Ham to Tiny. Is he enchanted by her money, or is he conquered by her dominance? Without the necessary explanation, the incongruous pairing seems comic rather than sentimental.

Although serious ideas do not intrude upon the apparently continuous gaiety of the Harlemites, shadows of a troubled world appear at the edge of the gay and the comic. Such a shadow is the pathetic joy of the Shabby Man, who has secured a job for the first time in two years. Such a shadow appears in the wish-fantasies and self-delusions of the numbers players who, praying for the one wonderful windfall, overlook the vast sums which they are dribbling away by daily dimes and quarters. Shadowy too are social protests: a janitor's complaint about long hours, the silence of Madam Lucille and Ham when police, without a warrant, search the shoeshine parlor for evidence of gambling.

Don't You Want To Be Free?, also written in the thirties, is a poetic drama—or, more appropriately, a pageant—which traces the history of the American Negro from the original enslavement to the Depression. The scenes are predictable—a slave auction, a slave rebellion which ends in massacre. Nevertheless, effective narration provides pride for Negro spectators by recounting Negroes who struggled for freedom—Nat Turner, Denmark Vesey, Harriet Tubman, Sojourner Truth. Furthermore, Hughes effectively underscored the emotion by using lyrics and melodies of spirituals and the blues. A product of the thirties, however, the pageant overemphasizes a call for a uniting of the workers of the world. In language and in thought, the play was the most artistic which Hughes had written, but its obvious aiming at a Negro audience made it unsuitable for commercial production on Broadway.

The Sun Do Move (1942) echoes, expands, individualizes, and dramatizes the thought which was narrated in *Don't You Want To Be Free?* After two Negro porters strip to reassume their identity as Africans, the play begins with the auction of two young Africans, Rock and Mary. After a period of time Rock is sold before he has time to see the birth of his child. On the new plantation, he becomes friends with Frog and resists the advances of Bellinda, who has been chosen as his new mate. When they attempt to escape, Frog is killed and Rock is recaptured. Meanwhile, on the other plantation, Mary, Rock's wife, has reared their son. When Little Rock attempts to protect his mother from her mistress's brutality, he is sent to another plantation, where he dies. Escaping again, Rock this time reaches Mary and, with her, flees to the North, where assisted by Quakers, they become free.

Despite structural weaknesses caused by cinematic flashes from scenes of Rock to those of Mary or Little Rock and despite Hughes's characteristic interpolations of irrelevant low comedy, the play is much more forceful and dramatically interesting than the earlier one. The dispassionate historicity of the pageant is emotionalized by Hughes's focus upon Mary and Rock, struggling to live as human beings rather than chattel.

Simply Heavenly (1957), designed for the commercial theater, reached Broadway in a state weaker than [Hughes's] *Simple Takes a Wife,* the book upon which the play was based. The major sufferer in the adaptation is Jesse B. Semple himself. In the tales and dialogues of the Simple books, Jess assumes the dimensions of a folk hero. Even though he drinks, cavorts with women, has difficulty paying rent, talks ungrammatically and excessively, his foibles never detract from his dignity; for, like the Greek gods and the heroes of various myths, he is larger than life. It may be appropriate even to say that he, like Joseph Conrad's Kurtz, is remembered primarily as a voice, in this instance a voice which utters common sense even when the speaker seems emotional and illogical. Reduced to actable dimensions, however, Simple, losing his grandeur, shrinks into a more sincere, more conservative, and more thoughtful Ham. In the play, he peeks beneath his legs to watch Joyce, his fiancée, change clothes; he turns somersaults; he is thrown from a car to land on his "sit-downer"; he is propped comically in a hospital bed with his legs in traction; sentimentally and pathetically, he tries to reform and to win Joyce. In short, Simple's reality as the embodied spirit of the Negro working class is reduced to the Harlem barfly; the Chaplinesque Comic Hero shrinks to a farcical fall guy in the pattern of Stan Laurel and Lou Costello.

The second major injury resulting from the transformation from the book to the play is suffered by the material itself. Even though incidents occur in the book, they generally serve merely as acceptable devices to generate Simple's philosophizing. Consequently, what matters is not what happens but what reaction it stimulates from Simple. For a Broadway musical, however, it was necessary to emphasize action and to minimize Simple's reflections. As a result, undue attention is given to Simple's unsuccessful efforts to seduce Joyce, to the Watermelon Man's pursuit of Mamie, and to the domestic difficulties of Bodidilly and Arcie.

Judged merely in its own terms, however, without reference to the Simple material which it distorts and cheapens, *Simply Heavenly* is vastly superior to *Little Ham*. Simple is more likable than Ham. Joyce and Zarita are less grotesque than Tiny, whose type reappears in Mamie, a secondary lead.

Similarly, the ideas of *Simply Heavenly* have significance missing from *Little Ham,* where Harlemites seemed to concern themselves only with numbers, gossip, parties, sex, and killing. In fact, the differences in *Simply Heavenly* underscore the fact that *Little Ham* was intended as a commercial exploitation of Harlem's exoticism rather than as a presentation of its actuality. In *Simply Heavenly,* the people occupy the same socioeconomic level as those in *Little Ham;* they take interest in numbers, gossip, parties, and sex; but they also think and talk about racial problems, economic problems, and domestic problems.

Hughes reacted sensitively to the allegation that he had stereotyped the characters of his earlier books and plays. When a middle-class man says that the denizens of Paddy's Bar are stereotypes, Mamie, defender of the race, answers furiously:

Why, it's getting so colored folks can't do nothing no more without some other Negro calling you a stereotype. Stereotype, hah! If you like a little gin, you're a stereotype. You got to drink Scotch. If you wear a red dress, you're a stereotype. You got to wear beige or chartreuse. Lord have mercy, honey, do-don't like no blackeyed peas and rice! Then you're a down-home Negro for true—which I is—and proud of it! I didn't come here to Harlem to get away from my people. I come here because there's more of 'em. I loves my race. I loves my people. Stereotype!

Nevertheless, it is true that Hughes generally created stereotypes. Even in *Simply Heavenly,* Hughes clung to gross, time-honored models. Joyce is a loving but prim heroine, who probably will become a shrew. A good-hearted, fun-loving girl, who wears her morals loosely, Zarita is from a tradition as old as literature itself.

Both comedy and language seem improved in *Simply Heavenly.* In addition to writing better quips, Hughes, writing lyrics for songs, was able to display his poetic talent more persuasively than in earlier plays. Using the contemporary idiom of Harlem, he created a free and natural dialogue, sometimes rising to colloquial eloquence, as in Simple's recollection of his aunt's efforts to reform him.

Despite the improvement, Hughes continued to relish sentimentality and farce which too frequently detract from the reality of the characters. For example, it is difficult to believe Boyd's honesty when he describes Simple's crying at night.

During the sixties, Hughes worked on his two best plays—*Emperor of Haiti* and *Tambourines to Glory. Emperor of Haiti* was a generation old. Hughes first presented it as *Drums of Haiti* (1936), rewrote it as *Troubled Island,* an opera, revised it further, and completed his final revisions in 1963, shortly before he presented a script to the Schomburg Collection in Harlem.

Emperor of Haiti is the story of Jean Jacques Dessalines' progress from slave to emperor to corpse. Beginning during the Haitian blacks' rebellion against their French masters and treating historical fact freely, the play focuses on the economic and personal problems of Dessalines' rule as emperor. Economically, the kingdom suffers because Dessalines refuses to require labor from the liberated blacks. When he finally realizes the need, they turn against him. Personally, Dessalines fails in Hughes's play because, after becoming emperor, he rejects his uneducated wife, Azelea, who loves

him. In her place, he takes Claire Heureuse, a pawn of the mulattoes who seek to overthrow him. The play climaxes and ends when,
riding to crush a rebellion, Dessalines is killed in the trap set by
mulattoes. Melodramatically, Azelea, now a penniless street seller,
discovers his body and mourns his death while Claire flees with
her mulatto lover, and two passing Haitians fail to recognize their
emperor.

The play has artistic and historical flaws. As in much of Hughes's
drama, low comic relief is overworked while the plot lags. For instance, prior to the climactic arrival of Dessalines at the trap, street
sellers talk and joke interminably. Furthermore, history is distorted.
Although Toussaint is mentioned, the play suggests that Dessalines
is the only leader of the slaves' rebellion. Moreover, Dessalines'
character is given a moral bath. The libertinism which characterized Dessalines after his becoming emperor is reduced to his affair
with Claire Heureuse.

Nevertheless, the historical events provided Hughes with plot,
thought, and character superior to those which generally emerged
from his imagination. Although Azelea is perhaps idealized as a
devoted, self-sacrificing wife, Dessalines is well-drawn, even in
outline.

Hughes's final play, *Tambourines to Glory*, was adapted from his
novel of the same name. It is a modernized morality play and, as
such, is surprisingly good. To make money, Laura Reed, a gay girl
like Zarita, persuades staid, religious Essie Johnson to join her in
establishing a church. They are assisted and protected by Big-Eyed
Buddy Lomax, who actually is the Devil. Gradually Laura slips
further and further into sin as Buddy's mistress. She swells membership by giving tips on numbers; she sells tap water as holy water.
Vainly, she tries to thwart Buddy's pursuit of Gloria, a singer, and
Marietta, Essie's teen-aged niece. Finally, fearing him, Laura stabs
Buddy. Essie is arrested but released when Laura confesses. Laura
is charged with manslaughter.

There is more development in this plot than in any Hughes had
written previously; and, although the action is tinged with melodrama, it is free from the irrelevant comedy and improbable coincidence which characterize most of Hughes's work. The characters
are not new, but they are smoothly delineated—perhaps because
Hughes's frequent recreation of the same types enabled him to know

them fully. As has been explained, Laura is modeled after Zarita, and Essie is a quieter, more mature, less attractive Joyce.

More than in any work since *Don't You Want To Be Free?* Hughes used poetry to develop thought. Instead of being entertaining diversions, as in *Simply Heavenly,* the lyrics of the songs explain the motivation and personalities of the characters. For example, Laura sings her love for Buddy; Buddy sings the blues characterizing life in Harlem; Marietta sings her purity.

Perhaps the chief reason for Hughes's success is that the musical morality play permitted him to display his major talents without straining the credulity of the audience. Stereotyped characters and heavy underlining of ideas are accepted in morality plays, and colloquial poetry and broad comedy have a place in musicals.

As Webster Smalley has pointed out, Langston Hughes must be credited with establishing several all-Negro professional dramatic groups. In doing so, he contributed significantly to the development of American drama. In his own work, however, even though he continued to write and to be produced through two generations, he never developed the artistry of a first-rate playwright. Least successful when he catered to the predictable taste of Broadway audiences, he was most artistic when he wrote simply and lyrically of the history and aspirations of black people.

Three Black Playwrights:
Loften Mitchell, Ossie Davis,
Douglas Turner Ward

by C. W. E. Bigsby

I

The names of black playwrights such as Lorraine Hansberry,
James Baldwin and LeRoi Jones are reasonably well known to the
American theatre-goer and literary critic alike. Broadway success
and political militancy have conferred a fame which, though de-
served, was largely denied their predecessors. As Loften Mitchell
points out in his essay,[1] white recognition of the black playwright
has been more than a little belated. The reason for this has had less
to do with simple perversity than with the mainly poor quality of
Negro drama until comparatively recent times and the economic
exigencies of Broadway production which have successfully kept
the Negro writer and actor out of the limelight. Nevertheless it is a
fact that while writers like Jack Gelber, Arthur Kopit and Jack
Richardson gained a quick and largely undeserved reputation,
black playwrights seemed to exist only on the periphery of white
critical awareness. Today this situation is being in some degree
rectified as appreciative gestures are made in the direction of the
Negro Ensemble Company and the more powerful products of the
revolutionary black theatre. It remains true, however, that virtually

"Three Black Playwrights: Loften Mitchell, Ossie Davis, Douglas Turner Ward"
by C. W. E. Bigsby. From *The Black American Writer,* Vol. II, ed. C. W. E. Bigsby
(Deland, Florida: Everett/Edwards, Inc., 1969), pp. 137-55. Reprinted by permission of the author.

[1]["On the 'Emerging' Playwright," *The Black American Writer,* Vol. II, ed. C.
W. E. Bigsby (Deland, Florida: Everett/Edwards, Inc., 1969), pp. 129-36—ED.]

a whole generation of Negro playwrights has failed to secure the kind of critical attention which their work deserves. Writers like Loften Mitchell, Ossie Davis and Douglas Turner Ward have produced plays of considerable merit, winning Mitchell a Guggenheim Award and Ward two off-Broadway prizes. If they are not, for the most part, innovators nor to be compared to LeRoi Jones or Lorraine Hansberry at their best, they have played a significant role in moulding a theatre rooted in the black experience, while, with the exception of Mitchell's *A Land Beyond the River,* they have avoided the melodramatic implications of the racial situation which had undermined plays like Eugene O'Neill's *All God's Chillun Got Wings* and even Langston Hughes's *Mulatto.*

II

Although he had written sketches for a drama group while still in high school, Loften Mitchell, like Ossie Davis, really started his theatrical life as an actor with the Rose McClendon Players. It was a short-lived career. After receiving poor notices for his performance in Dennis Donaghue's *The Black Messiah* (1939) he relinquished his acting ambitions, and went first to Talladega College in Alabama and then into the navy. Having completed his naval service he moved to Columbia University where, under John Gassner, he began work on a history of the Negro in the American theatre which was subsequently published in 1967 under the title *Black Drama.* At the same time he returned to playwrighting, producing *The Bancroft Dynasty, Shame of a Nation, The Cellar* and *Land Beyond the River.*

Shame of a Nation, which took as its theme the case of the Trenton Six, was produced by the Harlem Showcase in the mid 40s and the same group was responsible for his first modest success when it produced *The Cellar* in November 1952. This was concerned with a Negro blues singer whose detective fiancé destroys what Mitchell calls a "fugitive from southern injustice." Paradoxically, given the play's title, the performance was staged in a loft theatre. Although performed only at weekends it nevertheless enjoyed a considerable run.

Despite the moderate popularity of this work it was another five years before Mitchell scored his greatest success with *A Land Be-yond the River* which opened at the Greenwich Mews Theatre in March 1957. Scheduled for a ten week run, it eventually continued, with a brief break, for a year. After its New York success it was sent on tour, one performance being given at Mitchell's old college at Talladega. In 1958 he was the recipient of a Guggenheim Award for creative writing in the drama.

A Land Beyond the River[2] tells the story of a small South Caro-lina community which played a part in the process that finally led to the Supreme Court desegregation decision of 1954. The Negroes of Clarendon County, led by the Rev. Dr. Joseph DeLaine, decided to press for buses to transport their children to remote rural schools. Thurgood Marshall, then head of the legal division of the NAACP, took up the case and encouraged them to extend their demands to include separate but equal schools. This in turn gave way to an on-slaught on the principle of segregation itself. The play takes the story up to the point at which the State Supreme Court had ruled in favour of the old separate but equal doctrine.

Mitchell's interest was stimulated when Ossie Davis used the material for a concert reading. With Davis's encouragement he met Dr. DeLaine and started work on the play. DeLaine himself had been forced to leave Clarendon County after his house had been burnt down and eventually he had been driven out of the south altogether. Those who stayed behind were subject to economic harassment. Thus the play which Mitchell now started writing quickly assumed the nature of a testament to their courage and a polemical denunciation of white injustice. Appropriately enough the work was subsequently sponsored by the Automobile Workers as a means of raising funds for the people of Clarendon County. From the proceeds a harvester was actually dispatched to those who had been suffering such hardships since the events which Mitchell details in his play.

As the play opens the black community is facing a minor crisis. The floor of the school house has collapsed. Suddenly their cam-paign to secure buses seems pitifully ironical since the school itself is demonstrably so inadequate. Nevertheless even this campaign has served to highlight the divisions within the Negro community and the real nature of the hostility between black and white.

---

[2]Loften Mitchell, *A Land Beyond the River* (Cody, Wyoming, 1963).

In so far as the Negro community is concerned, the conflict is embodied in the antagonism between Dr. Layne and a school principal, Philip Turnham, who is described as a "humorless, fair complexioned Negro." Turnham is an Uncle Tom. As one of the characters puts it, "he's colored all right, but sometimes he don't know it." (p. 22). Thus the debate is not really about schools but about the attitude which the Negro should adopt towards white authority. Turnham's family history is the history of the Negro middle class, which had originally grown-out of the caste divisions between the house slave off-spring of white slave-owners and the black children of the field slaves. Turnham's family had taken pride in its white blood and he himself identifies with the white world. Yet his sycophancy is reflected in some degree by the determined passivity which has characterized the black community up to this moment. Rather than combine against white injustice they have fought amongst themselves. They now realize that they are faced with a straight choice between passivity and activism.

While the white world, as represented by the school superintendent, Rev. Mr. Cloud, is prepared to discuss the possibility of securing transportation, as soon as the demands are increased and go, indeed, to the heart of the issue, all pretence of liberality is dropped. Dr. Layne is dismissed and intimidation, legal and illegal, is applied. Cloud is presented as a sanctimonious hypocrite. While seeing it as "our Christian duty" to "lead the colored people forward" (p. 18) he stops short of anything which might provoke any kind of opposition. He even has the effrontery to tell Layne that he does not "know what it is to be a Negro down here" (p. 19). Yet his dislike of Layne does not prevent him from cynically offering to bribe him with a principalship for both himself and his wife. The episode epitomizes Mitchell's analysis of black/white relations in the South. The black leader is first assured of white benevolence, then made the victim of persecution and finally, when he has demonstrated the reality of his leadership, he is bribed. Thus Layne's fight stands as the epitome of the whole fight for justice in the South.

Mitchell does create a white character who is bereft of prejudice. Dr. Willis has learnt by experience that irrational hatred and fear are finally self-defeating. He urges Layne and his wife to withdraw from the fight but does so because of his genuine regard for their well-being. The fact remains, however, that he feels no real commitment to their cause. He stands on the sidelines, offering moral support but unwilling to translate this into concrete action. Thus the white community is presented as consisting simply of pathologically violent tear-aways, hypocrites and ineffectuals. Whatever the justice of this assessment of small town white southerners the effect, in terms of the play, is to underscore the melodramatic tone of Mitchell's homily. For just as the whites are without exception either willfully perverse and destructive or simply weak and vacillating so the blacks, with the single exception of Turnham, are the epitome of courage, tenacity, wit and dogged determination. If they are tempted to settle for considerably less than total victory, this serves merely to underline their passionate commitment to life rather than to the techniques and strategies of social skirmishes. Mitchell is as much a Calvinist as are the whites who for so long had used religion as their justification. He is in danger of replacing one form of elitism with another. The elect are now black where formerly they were white.

Mitchell himself has admitted that *A Land Beyond the River* "is far from the well-made play" and that "sometimes the dramaturgy is coarse." He also claims, however, that "This is, in a sense, deliberate, for the emphasis of the work is on character illumination."[3] Despite his sensitive treatment of Joseph Layne's personal doubts and frustrations, his treatment of the other characters scarcely bears out his claim. He has said that he was glad of the opportunity to bring to the stage a group of "simple" human beings. The phrase, unfortunately, is more revealing than it should have been. They are "simple" not because they are pleasantly unsophisticated, bereft of the self-justifying formulas of the intellectual faced with a moral or social dilemma, but because they are one dimensional. *A Land Beyond the River* is a morality play in which vice and virtue are personified and the victory of the latter over the former an accepted assumption.

To serve the cause of Mitchell's didactic purpose characters tend to be reduced to essential components. Turnham is the Uncle Tom, Cloud, the hypocritical white man, Duff Waters, the convert won over from passivity to proud rebellion and Mrs. Simms, the wise old woman who knows a thing or two about life. The action itself, although based on actual events, is melodramatic in the extreme.

---

[3]Loften Mitchell, *Black Drama: The Story of the American Negro in the Theatre* (New York, 1967), p. 180.

Joseph Layne's house is burnt to the ground and his wife drops dead from a heart attack as the white fire brigade refuse to help.

Where characters are not simply elements in Mitchell's homily all too often their complexity is sacrificed to his symbolic purpose. A minor subplot, which involves the emancipation of Philip Turnham's daughter, Laura, remains shadowy and ineffectual. Laura had originally opposed the campaign for buses, sharing her father's fear of antagonising the white authorities. She had even taken this as far as precipitating a break with her lover, Ben Ellis, an attractive and intelligent young lawyer. Her conversion is potentially very significant as one of "Uncle Tom's children" is won over to the need for activism. Yet the entire episode lacks credibility, never becoming anything more than a symbolic redemption. Ellis is an undeveloped figure who appears only briefly at the beginning and end of the play. His skill and authority remain untested and when he presumes to act as Layne's conscience, insisting on the need to continue the fight, we have no reason to feel that this is anything more than bombast. We have seen Layne suffer for his cause; Ellis's exhortations remain only an intellectual commitment. Yet Mitchell clearly intends us to take Ellis as a valid and wise counsellor.

His involvement with Laura is similarly insubstantial and seems little more than a contrivance, useful for its symbolic overtones. Laura herself seems from the very beginning too much of a humanitarian ever to have accepted her father's reactionary views. Her break with him at the end of the play thus tends to seem an artificial climax owing more to the exigencies of the plot than to the apparent truth of her character and her relationship to her father.

It is no longer possible to view this play without an overpowering sense of irony. When it was written and first produced the fact of the Supreme Court desegregation decision of 1954 stood as an unstated reality against which the struggle could be viewed. It was a comment on the folly of those whites who opposed Negro agitation. The temporary set-backs of the Negro cause could be looked at in the light of the known achievement which would inevitably follow. The stage directions actually indicate that the stage should be dominated by the courthouse, with a flag flying from the top—a visual reminder of the ultimate success of their efforts and the attainability of justice.

By the late 60s the failure of the 1954 decision had become self-evident. The decay of the inner cities together with population movements now meant that for many areas, particularly in the

North, segregation was worse than it had been prior to the Supreme Court's decision. Anyone viewing the play now could not help but be affected by the irony. The play has become something of a period piece. At the same time of course the nature of the civil rights struggle itself has changed radically. Integration, the great goal of the 50s and early 60s, is now increasingly rejected as a strategy and a target. The assumption that Negroes should be assimilated by white society is dismissed as Caucasian arrogance. Hence, for a modern black audience the whole ethos of Mitchell's play is liable to seem increasingly alien as are the virtues of Joseph Layne, steadfastly working through the law and placing his faith in the integrity and effectiveness of democratic institutions. The fact that he now seems painfully naive is an expression not of Mitchell's sense of ambiguity but of the pace of social change. The passage of time has served both to reveal the weakness of his approach and to give an added his-torical dimension to the play itself.

Layne's determined pacifism is an accurate reflection of civil rights' strategy but it is not without its ambiguities. When he declares that "if a white man walked into this church and stuck a gun in my face, I'd have to go down on my knees and pray for him" (p. 60) one looks in vain for a sense of irony to deflate the pretentious tone. By the end of the play, with his wife dead and his home in ruins, his stoical acceptance seems, perhaps admirable, but also a little excessive. Nor is it totally devoid of a self-justifying pride. As he declares, "The Voice of God has roared in my ears, testing my faith—by letting them burn up my house, by letting them crucify my beloved wife—testing me as Job was tested" (p. 28). And yet one is never entirely convinced that this irony is a product of Mitchell's sensitive objectivity. Ambiguity seems rather to be a product of our changed perspective. To a modern audience there seems to be more than an element of the masochist in Layne. At times he seems little more than a would-be martyr. As he says at one stage "God Almighty, you're calling me to have the guts to let people kill me" (p. 60).

Yet while Mitchell occasionally permits his characters a self-indulgent rhetoric, the play is not without a saving humor which explains his bitterness at those critics who later hailed *Purlie Victorious* as a refreshing revival of humour in Negro drama. One character, for example, tries in vain to reconcile the South's determined advocacy of segregation with its liberal willingness to "integrate" his tax dollars. For all its faults, then, the play is both moving and powerful. Part of its effectiveness undeniably stems from the emotive nature of the central theme, but Mitchell's ability to capture the essence of the courage and somewhat facile optimism of the 50s shows his skill as a writer. If the simplistic approach to character and theme suggests his limitations as a playwright, it also says something about the nature of a period in the civil rights campaign which seems in many senses a whole world removed from the present.

Following the success of *A Land Beyond the River* Mitchell returned to his critical work, producing, among other things, an article on the Negro in the American theatre for the *Oxford Companion to the Theatre*. In the course of researching this article he met Bert Williams, the old Negro entertainer. *Star of the Morning*, the story of Bert Williams, was the result of this meeting. This was followed by *Ballad for Bimshire,* a musical which Mitchell wrote with Irving Burgess. It was, in Mitchell's own words, "a throwback to the days when Negroes wrote, produced, directed and managed their own shows."[4] Despite the support of largely Negro audiences the play had only a short run and closed in mid December, 1963. This in turn was followed by *Ballad of the Winter Soldiers* which Mitchell wrote with John O. Killens and which took as its subject what he called "freedom fighters throughout history." Finally, he again collaborated on a musical play when he and W. F. Lucas wrote *Ballad of a Blackbird* which is based on the life of Florence Mills who had starred in *Shuffle Along,* the famous Negro revue which had marked the beginning of the 20s Renaissance. The play owed its title to the name of the show in which she was appearing at the time of her death.

III

Ossie Davis, who came from Waycross, Georgia and was educated at Howard University, has contributed to the American theatre as actor, stage manager, promoter and playwright. On coming to New York he joined the Rose McClendon Players in the late 30s and was in the famous production of *On Strivers Row*. Later

[4]*Black Drama*, p. 197.

he joined the American Negro Theatre which, like the Rose Mc-
Clendon Players in its latter stages, tried to establish a purely Negro
repertory group performing, where possible, plays by Negro playwrights. Ironically, its greatest success was Philip Yordan's *Anna
Lucasta,* a play originally about a Polish Family and only adapted
to suit the ANT. When this transferred to Broadway Ossie Davis
went with it, as did his wife, actress Ruby Dee, and such other famous Negro actors as Canada Lee and Sidney Poitier. Davis continued his acting career, appearing in many plays, including
Lorraine Hansberry's *A Raisin in the Sun* (1959), Loften Mitchell's
Ballad for Bimshire (1963) and Howard Da Silva and Felix Leon's
The Zulu and the Zayda.

His first play was produced in 1952 at the Elks Community
Theatre. *Alice in Wonder* was one of three plays which appeared
under the same generic title, the other two being by Julian Mayfield. Davis's contribution was concerned with the pressures exerted on a Negro artist by a television company which wishes him
to testify before a Washington committee. Although it had only a
short run Davis was encouraged to expand it into a full-length play
and in its new form it opened as *The Big Deal* in 1953. Davis's
greatest success, however, came in 1961 with the Cort Theatre production of *Purlie Victorious*[5] in which he and his wife played the
two main roles, and which was subsequently made into a film under
the title *Gone are the Days.*

The Negro has always been the victim of those who would make
him into a stereotype. Davis's achievement in *Purlie Victorious* is
to take precisely those stereotypes and manipulate them for his own
purposes. The Uncle Tom, the Afro-American nationalist, the race
leader, the civil rights worker are all gently mocked but at the same
time they achieve a symbolic victory over the forces of white oppression. It is this subtle mixture of self-irony and biting satire
which gives the play its special tone and which makes of Purlie himself a picaresque hero capable of exposing the faults of black and
white alike. As Davis realized, only a Negro could dare to present
such stereotypes on stage in the 1960s. He himself pointed out that
things "which would be offensive in the hands of a white writer,

---

[5]Ossie Davis, *Purlie Victorious* (New York, n.d.).

might become, in the hands of a Negro writer a totally unexpected revelation of the true substance of Negro wit and humor."[6]

The play is set in South Georgia, in a community dominated by the scatologically named Ol' Cap'n Cotchipee, the white cotton boss. The black community crosses swords with him in its attempt to get him to part with five hundred dollars which they intend to use to buy the Big Bethel church. The money is a legacy payable to Cousin Bee who has inconvenienced them by dying. Rather than see the money lost Purlie Victorious Judson thoughtfully provides a substitute in the person of an ex-maid, Lutiebelle Gussie Mae Jenkins, whose name Purlie calls "an insult to the Negro people." Purlie is confident that the ploy will succeed since "white folks can't tell one of us from another." Unfortunately, although attractive, Lutiebelle is not really qualified to imitate the college-educated Cousin Bee. Thus, when asked to sign a receipt for the money which they have acquired she uses her own distinctive name.

Subtlety having failed, they turn to more direct methods and work through the Cap'n's liberal-minded son, Charlie, who, to the Cap'n's dismay, has recently shown a tendency to "get nonviolent." He steals the money and gives it to Purlie while securing the deeds to the church in Purlie's name rather than his father's. Shocked by this act of treachery by a true Caucasian, the Ol' Cap'n literally dies on his feet and is buried in the same position—out of respect.

Purlie Victorious presents a series of satirical portraits which *in toto* constitute a vivid parody of the racial situation. Lutiebelle is a gullible if amusing dupe, but despite the wild humor of the scene in which she tries desperately to imitate the educated Cousin Bee, Davis cannot resist making a serious point in his stage directions. He says of her that she is "like thousands of Negro girls...keenly in search for life and for love...but afraid to take the final leap: because no one has ever told her it is no longer necessary to be white in order to be virtuous, charming or beautiful" (pp. 6-7). But Lutiebelle is not only intimidated by the white world, she is also a gullible disciple to any leader with the right blend of personal attractiveness and glib conviction. Her admiration for Purlie has less to do

---

[6]Ossie Davis, "Purlie Told Me!" in *Harlem, U.S.A.*, ed. John Henrik Clarke, p. 155.

with his emotive appeals for freedom and justice than his personal magnetism which puts her in mind of marriage.

Purlie himself is the would-be Negro leader whose rhetoric outreaches his possibility for action. One of the highlights of the play, indeed, is its skillful deflation of demagogic language. The mixture of bombast, religious appeal and meaningless rhetorical devices is seen at its painful worst in the oration which Purlie delivers at the Cap'n's funeral and in which he calls upon his followers to "stifle the rifle of conflict, shatter the scatter of discord, smuggle the struggle, tickle the pickle, and grapple the apple of peace" (p. 81).

Purlie's heart is obviously in the right place. Wanting to show solidarity with the Montgomery bus boycotters but balked by the lack of buses he boycotts mules instead since they are the cotton patch equivalent. But while voicing the "correct" sentiments his very exuberance becomes an element in Davis's satiric method. When he hails Lutiebelle as "This Ibo prize—this Zulu Pearl—This long lost lily of the black Mandingo—Kikuyu maid, beneath whose brown embrace Hot sons of Africa are burning still" (p. 15), his inflated language serves to undermine the poetic assumptions of the "Negro Renaissance," for the lyrical references to Africa can scarcely survive the determined plebianism of Gussie Mae Jenkins. When he goes on to denounce her name as the mark of a "previous condition of servitude, a badge of inferiority" (p. 15), this commonplace of nationalist jargon is made to seem pitifully excessive. At the same time his resounding insistence on the need for race pride is met with Lutiebelle's unanswerable confession that, as a house maid, black pride is something of a luxury. His proud enumeration of the languages of Africa and his attempt to link his wide-eyed disciple to his fanciful "ten thousand Queens of Sheba" (p. 16) is thus inevitably deflated by the mundane reality of the cotton patch. Try as he will he cannot make reality match up to the ideas of racial glory to which he has pledged his allegiance. Posing at one moment as a professor of Negro Philosophy and another as a minister, he struggles to destroy the racial mores of the South with his own stock of black mythology. His eventual success, thanks to the cooperation of the Cap'n's white son, is thus a sign of his determination rather than his cunning but it is also an expression of Davis's personal conviction that Purlie's tenacity must eventually prove victorious, given the help of at least a section of the white community. Charlie, however, is the only available white ally. The incompetent sheriff and his deputy have a marked tendency to arrest and beat Negroes on sight, while the Cap'n clings tenaciously to an outdated vision of black/white relations. Since he is as determined as Purlie to reshape reality to fit his own philosophy he sees only what he wants to see. The black community has long since capitalized on this fact and Purlie is particularly skillful in playing on his need for flattery and reassurance, even persuading him that he has been elected Great White Father by his grateful darkies. Since the Cap'n, for his own peace of mind, has to believe that "the old-fashioned, solid, hard-earned, Uncle Tom type Negro" (p. 35) still exists, he is easily taken in by this.

The submissive Negro is, of course, not entirely a figment of the Cap'n's imagination, and Davis is at his best in his portrait of a man whose respect for the white man is so profound and unreasoning that he is mortified when he drops a cotton bale because "cotton is white" and "We must maintain respect" (p. 12). Gitlow, the appropriately named Uncle Tom, is gloriously obsequious, indulging only in the occasional irony. He is so pliable that he is accepted by the white' world as a spokesman for the black community, even being conferred with the ambiguous title "Deputy-for-the-Colored," surely a comment on the Negro spokesman whose real loyalty lies with his white masters.

Thus we have two examples of black leaders, the one appointed by the white community to reflect its own prejudices and the other self-appointed, determined to "preach freedom in the cotton patch" to those whose ambition is "Freedom—and a little something left over." The cotton patch thus contains the wider scene in microcosm and the battle over Cousin Bee's inheritance is a wild parody of another, more significant, struggle for justice. As Davis himself has said, *"Purlie Victorious* is, in essence, the adventures of Negro manhood in search of itself in a world for white folks only."[7]

Purlie Victorious is, I suppose, what Harold Cruse would call an integrationist drama in that it sees integration as a desirable objective and satirizes the old attitudes on the assumption that things are changing for the better in the South. Ol' Cap'n Cotchipee has had his day; the future lies with his son Charlie and if his name still contains a satirical comment on the white world (Mr. Charlie), there is no mistaking the integrity of his liberal motives. Thus, when he asks to be accepted as a member of the Big Bethel Church this is

[7]"Purlie Told Me!" p. 152.

a natural outcome of the play's action and a logical result of his dogged humanity. The central target of the play is clearly segregation. In the words of "Purlie's I.O.U." which prefaces the play, "our Theatre will say segregation is ridiculous because it makes perfectly wonderful people, white and black, do ridiculous things" (p. 4). Segregation produces not merely the white bigot but also the Uncle Tom, the Afro-American nationalist and the civil rights worker, and despite Davis's personal commitments he satirizes all their excesses with striking impartiality. Indeed, he has more than a sneaking admiration for the unashamed Uncle Tom, whose charm lies precisely in his determined passivity.

Predictably, there are those who have regretted the play's "integrationist" tone. Adam Miller, of the San Francisco Aldridge Players/West, points out that "Young white Cotchipee...becomes the first member of Big Bethel.... He is happy to join, they are happy to have him." To Miller's mind this shows that Davis is falling into the trap of "either catering to the good will of a white audience or of making statements irrelevant to the Negroes,"[8] This might seem a strange accusation to level at a man who had been a member of both the Rose McClendon Players and the ANT, yet Davis's involvement with Broadway and his equivocal attitude with regard to the black writer's responsibilities towards the Negro community, had cast doubt on his *bona fides.* After the success of *Purlie Victorious,* however, he made his position clear. He admitted that the play had itself brought about a complete change in his outlook. As he subsequently explained, "the act of writing became my long moment of truth; it took me five years to adjust my eyesight, to be able to look squarely at the world, and at myself, through Negro-colored glasses." He now came to feel that "my *manhood* was hidden within by Negroness,"[9] and in 1962 he announced that the Negro writer must learn to create for his own people and that he should write from "a black position."[10] It is difficult to appreciate precisely what this means in concrete terms. Is *Purlie Victorious* itself written from a "black position?" Davis himself has denied it, saying that since oppression, and the resistance of oppression, are universal themes, "If Purlie speaks at all he speaks to everybody—black and white."

[8] Adam David Miller, "It's a Long Way to St. Louis," *The Drama Review,* XII, IV (Summer, 1968), pp. 149-150.

[9] "Purlie Told Me!" pp. 152-153.

[10] *Op. cit.,* p. 156.

Certainly the play would appear to offer a comfortable feeling of well-being to a white audience. The setting is purely southern and bigotry is demonstrably on its last legs. The new generation seems generously prepared to embrace the black community even in its more bizarre manifestations. But this is a rather tendentious way of looking at a play whose purpose is not so much to analyse America's radical problem as to deflate the pretentions of black and white alike. Davis's commitment to black culture came after and not before the production of his play, and perhaps it is just as well since it relies so heavily for its effectiveness on his willingness to parody black zealots as well as white bigots. This is the source of much of the play's humor.

Even when an underlying seriousness threatens to break through, the context largely serves to undermine the bitterness. Thus, when Purlie exclaims that his mother had "died outdoors on a dirty sheet cause the hospital doors said—'For White Folks Only'" (p. 72), Davis is not trying to repeat the point of Albee's *The Death of Bessie Smith*. The claim is part of Purlie's desperate attempt to divert attention from his own cowardice. Nevertheless, the reference is not entirely de-fused. It hangs in the background, like an earlier reference to white brutality, as an oblique comment on the play's farcical tone and a reminder of the bitterness which lies only just beneath the surface.

The play was well reviewed but attracted poor audiences, and it was only the support of Negro theatregoers which guaranteed it a reasonable success. This fact played an important part in Davis's conversion. He now came to feel that "if we can, in fact, create for our own people; work for our own people; belong to our own people we will no longer be forced into artistic prostitution. . . . It is time for us. . . to rejoin the people from which we came. . . . Only then can we begin to take a truly independent position within the confines of American culture."[11]

IV

Douglas Turner Ward began his career as a writer but when the market showed signs of drying up he turned to acting. Under the

---

[11]*Ibid.*

name of Douglas Turner he understudied Robert Earl Jones in Jose Quintero's famous Circle-in-the-Square production of *The Iceman Cometh,* and later appeared in Mitchell's *A Land Beyond the River* and Lorraine Hansberry's *A Raisin in the Sun.*

In 1960, according to Loften Mitchell's account, attempts were made to raise money to finance a production of two one-act plays which Ward had written. The attempt was a failure and it was not until 1964 that actor/producer Robert Hooks acquired an option on the two plays and after further difficulty staged them in November, 1965. Philip Meister, who had desperately tried to find financial support five years before, now directed the plays. Douglas Turner Ward, under his stage name, himself worked as an actor in the production, as did Robert Hooks.

Even now there was more trouble in store. A subway strike reduced audiences considerably. Nevertheless, in spite of this catalogue of disasters, the plays enjoyed a fourteen-month run and in the spring of 1966 Douglas Turner Ward achieved the remarkable distinction of receiving an Obie award for his acting and a Vernon Rice award for his writing.

Both *Happy Ending* and *Day of Absence*[12] are in a sense plays for a black theatre not merely because they utilise Negro actors but because they derive much of their humour from the ironical reversal of stereotypes. Where white audiences had been amused by minstrel shows in which whites performed in blackface, Ward, in *Day of Absence,* reverses the process. The humour of both plays is largely at the expense of a white community which is seen as insipid and stupid, unconsciously manipulated by a Negro world which it holds in contempt. These are plays primarily for a black audience but which are by no means limited in their appeal to such an ethnic audience. Neither do they resort to the bitter and humorless denunciation of whites which has become a commonplace of the revolutionary black arts movement. As Ward has said, "I've always felt that those Black plays which seem to be so clenched-fist-and-teeth, almost shrill, in their attack against Whitey emerge out of the Black writer's knowledge that he's talking to white people who don't hear him, don't understand him. He's got to sock it—scream."[13] Despite the ambiguity created by the Negro Ensemble's initially white-

[12]Douglas Turner Ward, *Happy Ending, Day of Absence* (New York, 1966).

[13]Quoted in the Negro Ensemble Company's program for the World Theatre Season at the Aldwych Theatre, London, May 1969.

dominated audience it is clear that the subtle satire of Ward's own one-act plays owes more than a little to the nature of his audience. This is not black theatre for its own sake. The fact that the cast is a black one is itself the origin of many of the play's complex ironies.

Happy Ending, like its companion piece, is based on a simple anecdote. Ellie and Vi are Negro domestics who work for a rich and self-indulgent white couple, Mr. and Mrs. Harrison. At the beginning of the play they are in tears over the prospect of the imminent breakup of the Harrison marriage after the husband has caught his wife in the arms of her lover. When their nephew, Junie, a young black militant, sees the distress which their employers' trouble inspires, he is horrified. They seem to conform to precisely those stereotypes which he is anxious to forget. "Maybe *Gone with the Wind* was accurate! Maybe we jist can't help 'Mis Scarrrrrlet-ing' and 'Oh Lawdying' every time mistress gets a splinter in her pinky" (p. 12). The reason for his aunts' depression, however, has nothing to do with racial humility. They are simply distraught at the loss of their meal ticket. The Harrisons have long financed the entire household, paying for Junie's food and clothes, for the furniture and even for his mother's air-fare on her regular yearly visit. When Junie finally understands the real reason for .their dismay he becomes equally depressed and news that the Harrisons have become reconciled is greeted with enthusiasm by the whole household.

In *Happy Ending* Ward is creating an image of Negro/white relations. The whites seem to have the monopoly of wealth and power but are in fact manipulated and exploited by a cunning black community which, if it cannot secure justice directly, can at least drain off some of the surplus money as a result of its knowledge of the working of white society. As Ellie points out, "after cutting cane, picking rice and shucking corn befo' we could braid our hair in pigtails" we figure we just getting back what's owed us" (p. 18). But while they recognise that "waiting for the Harrisons to voluntarily *donate* their Christian charity is one sure way of landing head-first in the poor-house dungeon" (p. 17), they avoid the effusions of the black militants. In fact Ward satirises Junie's nationalist ardour. His rhetorical appeal to black pride is shown not only to be out of all proportion to the ostensible pretext but also to be built on a naive perception of the reality of black/white relations. His description of "Africa rising to its place in the sun wit' prime ministers and other dignitaries taking seats around the conference

table" and "us here fighting for our rights like never before, changing the whole image, dumping stereotypes behind us and replacing
'em wit' new images of dignity and dimension" is merely a prelude
to his attack on his aunts for "DROWNING themselves in tears
jist 'cause bos man is gonna kick bosslady out on her nose" (p. 12).
His black pride is also in contrast to his studied indolence as he lives
contentedly on relief and the charity which his aunts are able to
offer thanks to their white connections.

The ending is "happy" for everyone. The white community is
happy with its illusions of power and superiority while the black
community is content to foster those illusions so long as there is a
percentage in it for them. In the words of the toast which Junie offers
at the end of the play, "To the victors and the vanquished, top-dog
and bottom dog! Sometimes it's hard to tell which is which" (p. 22).

Yet beneath the humor the play might seem to endorse the status
quo and even to reinforce those stereotypes against which Junie had
rebelled. For Ward is drawing on the old tradition of the light-
fingered black house servant and the bemused and deceived white
master. It is scarcely surprising that Ward should have found himself under attack for his ambivalent attitude both in this play and in
Day of Absence. Thus Junie's comment that "if some gray cat was
peeping in on you, he'da sprinted home and wrote five Uncle Tom's
Cabins and ten Old Black Joes" (p. 13) is not entirely without its
ironical implications for a writer who seems to feel that the mutual
deceptions of a racial stand-off do indeed constitute a happy ending.

Day of Absence is what Douglas Turner Ward has called "a re-
verse minstrel show done in white-face" (p. 29). Again the basic idea
is an extremely simple one. All the black inhabitants of a southern
town simply vanish from the scene, leaving the whites to realize the
consquences of life without Negroes. By degrees the town grinds to
a halt as essential services collapse under the impact of this basic
assault on the economy.

The disappearance of the Negroes also serves to throw a new
light on the racial pretensions of some of the whites. Not only does
it expose the weaknesses of white society, it also reveals the pre-
carious nature of ethnic purity, for along with the domestics, the
chauffeurs and general menials, various prominent citizens, including the chairlady of the Daughters of the Confederate Rebellion,
simply disappear. The streets are then patrolled by distraught and

surprised relatives carrying signs reading "WHY DIDN'T YOU TELL US—YOUR DEFILED WIFE AND TWO ABSENT MONGRELS" (p. 45).

Ward also attempts a side-swipe at white welfare arrangements. In the person of the significantly named Mrs. Aide, he presents a savage satire of schemes whose ostensible aim is that of finding "meaningful work" for the "Nigras." These turn out to be no more meaningful than careers as "maids, cooks, butlers, and breast-feeders, cess-pool-diggers, wash-basin maintainers, shoe shine boys, and so on" (p. 48). Mrs. Aide's motto, "Work or Starve," is thus not altogether inappropriate either to the exaggerated world of this southern town "on a somnolent cracker morning" or even to the realities of southern ADC payments which are as bizarre as anything Ward could create.

The whites themselves are presented as simple incompetents or dedicated sycophants desperate to embrace the American dream even if this means simultaneously embracing "the boss' left rump." They rely on the black community for everything from rearing their children to serving their coffee, and in the construction of their mechanical Eden are prepared not only to exploit the Negroes but even to justify their actions by reference to a pliable religion. The Reverend Reb Pious appeals to them to fulfill their usual passive role, quoting in the process a fraudulent line from Booker T. Washington, whom he predictably calls "one of your greatest prophets." When they refuse to fall in line with their usual alacrity, an air of panic seizes the town and its mayor, appropriately named Henry R. E. Lee, appears on television in a frantic and unsuccessful attempt to lure back lost Negroes. Having tried persuasion and intimidation, he finally resorts to abject contrition, being thereafter beaten by a white mob for his pains. The play ends as the Negroes reappear. It is apparent, though, that things can never again function in the same old way. The whites have learnt that they are dependent on the blacks; the blacks have discovered the reality of their power.

The real strength of the play rests in its humor. The unabashed caricatures of the white world are obviously designed for Negro consumption, yet they are drawn with such vigor and presented with such panache that *Day of Absence* can be almost as effective with a white audience. The use of Negroes in white-face, a device repeated by Ray McIver in *God Is a Guess What,* permits Ward not merely to create a series of ironical comments on white pretentions but also to claim a freedom in revealing white contempt for Negroes which would have been impossible for a white writer. White abuse is thus adroitly turned back on itself.

Ward's theme in *Day of Absence* is basically that of *Happy Ending* and it is scarcely surprising to find Adam Miller attacking the play for its racial conservatism. In his own words, "In Douglas Turner Ward's *Day of Absence,* we see a black audience laughing at the whites in their helplessness at the loss of their Negroes for a day. Look, they say, the white folks need us. Ha, ha. One must ask if this is something Negroes need to be told. The image of the black woman who raises Miss Ann's children at the sacrifice of her own is one all too familiar to Negroes. What Negroes need to know is not that they are needed by whites but that they are needed by one another. They need to be shown by their playwrights how to reach out to each other across this need."[14] While this kind of dogmatism is a dubious basis for criticism and particularly so when leveled at a play whose comic purpose perhaps precludes such profound racial objectives, there is an undeniable undertone of self-justification which might indeed antagonise the ethnic separatist. More recently, however, Ward has made the real nature of his own commitment abundantly clear.

In August, 1966, he was approached by the *New York Times* and asked to write an article on the role of the Negro in the American theatre. In this article he called for the establishment of a black oriented theatre on the basis that, "If any hope, outside of chance individual fortune, exists for Negro playwrights as a group—or, for that matter, Negro actors and other theatre craftsmen—the most immediate, pressing, practical, absolutely minimally essential active first step is the development of a permanent Negro repertory company." This was to be a "theatre concentrating primarily on themes of Negro life, but also resilient enough to incorporate and interpret the best of world drama.[15] Together with Robert Hooks and Gerald Krone he had already participated in a modest venture along these lines. The Group Theatre Workshop had established a training program and a production group. Now, with the aid of a substantial grant from the Ford Foundation, he was instrumental in founding

[14]"It's a Long Way to St. Louis," p. 150.

[15]Douglas Turner Ward, "American Theatre: For Whites Only?" *New York Times,* Aug. 14, 1966, Section II, pp. D1, D3.

the Negro Ensemble Company of which he became artistic director. With this company apparently firmly established, perhaps we need no longer fear that writers of the calibre of Loften Mitchell, Ossie Davis and Douglas Turner Ward will go unnoticed by critics for whom the Negro playwright was formerly an unknown quantity.

Mom, Dad and God:
Values in Black Theater

by William Cook

I

Much has been made in recent literary and sociological studies of the matrifocal nature of the American Black family and the influence of the church on Black values. Meier and Rudwick in *From Plantation to Ghetto* offer one explanation of these phenomena:

> In a society where the man is regarded as responsible for the support of his family, Black men often felt inadequate. The results were frequent separations and many households where the mother or grandmother was the central figure..... The store front churches and cult groups, creating a life meaning out of meaninglessness, self-respect out of poverty, functioned for the slum-shocked urban Blacks in much the same way that Garvey did. The promise of self-esteem, rather than nationalism, was the significant ingredient of the Garvey movement.[1]

While the matrifocal family was a dominant structure among poor Blacks, it would be wise to question whether its major effect is pathological as so many reports inform us, or if it represents a creative response to the conditions in which Blacks find themselves. Like the matrifocal family, the church was created to fill a gap in the sociological and psychological life of Blacks; providing a setting in which they could release their political energies, satisfy their desire for power and position, affirm their sense of specialness and worth, and find refuge from the uncertainty and terror of their everyday lives.

"Mom, Dad and God: Values in Black Theater" by William Cook. Reprinted by permission of the author.

[1]August Meier and Elliot Rudwick, *From Plantation to Ghetto* (New York: Hill and Wang), pp. 220-231.

Drama is often concerned with examining social institutions and the relationships of individuals to and within these institutions. We turn therefore to the playwright and his vision of Black America in an attempt to understand the role of the family and the church in shaping Black lives.

This examination will differ from much of the analyses presented heretofore, for it is based on the belief that the politico/social position in which Black characters find themselves is not as crucial to an understanding of their lives as is the vital relationships between man and woman, parent and child. Diane Weathers states:

> What most of the plays from the sixties and early seventies had in common was that they were serious dramas dealing either with Black-White confrontations or describing how Black people maintain their humanity and dignity and cope with their situation in the midst of oppression.[2]

Barbara Ann Teer in the April 21, 1975 edition of *Encore* states that she

> ...has long felt that we've needed more visionaries who could go beyond the subjects of oppression and poverty. There are many different ways in which we can deal with Black experience. Many types of images can be used in order to make your experience anything you want.[3]

Because Black/White confrontation, oppression and poverty, and the resultant debilitating effect of both on the Black psyche have been so much a part of the contemporary stance, the purpose of this discussion will be to bypass these already well-traveled roads and to examine that aspect of Black drama which is too often ignored by critics of the art: the effect of the matrifocal family and the Black church on the young person engaged in the painful task of coming to some decision as to the meaning of life and his own role in the world.

Given the large number of plays that are relevant to such an examination, I have chosen to limit the present discussion to four plays that focus rather clearly on (i) family: the status of the mother and the father and their function in defining the values of their children; (ii) religion: the store front churches and religious cults;

---

[2]Diane Weathers in *Encore*, April 21, 1975.
[3]Barbara Ann Teer in *Encore*, April 21, 1975.

and finally, (iii) the transference of values from one generation to another. In addition, I have chosen plays published or presented in recent times and which therefore are readily available. They are Lorraine Hansberry's *A Raisin in the Sun* (1959), James Baldwin's *The Amen Corner* (1965), Ed Bullins' *In the Wine Time* (1968), and Joseph Walker's *The River Niger* (1973).

Lena Younger, materfamilias of Lorraine Hansberry's *A Raisin in the Sun*, has become something of an archetype of the Black matriarch—that powerful and commanding figure who inaugurates and imposes the life-style which she considers appropriate for the world she sees. A careful consideration of the play, however, might point to another function for Hansberry's mother. Since the play opens after the death of the father, it is easy to dismiss his role as dictator of values and at the same time to exaggerate the control which Lena exercises. Lena Younger's function in the play is not so much to create values and to impose her will on her children as it is to interpret for them Walter Senior's values and to mold them into the kind of people he would have them be. When she speaks of values, she refers not to values that are hers alone, but rather to values which she shared with her husband. This is apparent in her response to Walter Lee's ambitions and his subsequent disenchant-ment. Having faced defeat, he voices a philosophy of bitterness that is opposed to the life-view which Lena and her husband espoused. Walter Lee releases in his conversation with Murchison all the bile that has been building up inside him:

> And you—ain't you bitter, man? Ain't you just about had it yet? Don't you see no stars gleaming that you can't reach out and grab? ... Bitter? Man I'm a volcano. Bitter?[4]

Later he voices this same dark pessimism in response to his sister's criticism of him:

> There ain't no causes—there ain't nothing but taking in this world, and he who takes the most is smartest—and it don't make a damn bit of difference how.   (P. 425)

[4]In Lindsay Patterson, ed., *Black Theatre* (New York: New American Library, 1971), pp. 338-339. All subsequent quotations from *A Raisin in the Sun*, *The Amen Corner*, and *In the Wine Time* are from this book. Page references are incorporated into the text.

In countering this view with her attitude toward life, it is significant to note that Lena sees Walter Senior and not herself as the source and example of these values:

Oh Big Walter, is this the harvest of our days?   (P. 399)

The notion that values clarification for the family is a joint effort of the father and mother is clear in the following exchange with her daughter:

Beneatha. Wasn't it you who taught me to despise any man who would do that. Do what he's going to do?
Mama. Yes—I taught you that. Me and your Daddy. I taught you something else, too. ... I thought I taught you to love him. There is always something left to love. ... When do you think is the time to love somebody the most; when they done good and made things easy for everybody? Well then, you ain't through learning—because that ain't the time at all. It's when he's at his lowest and can't believe in himself cause the world done whipped him so.   (P. 427)

That these are not empty words is apparent in Lena's conduct, for she has seen her husband and now her son reach this "low ground of sorrow" and yet has not given way to bitterness or scorn. Qualities that were so evident in her life with her husband are the ones she attempts to instill in her children for, to her, they are enduring values; as relevant to the experience of Beneatha and Walter, Jr.— symbols of the new generation—as they were to her husband and her. Big Walter laid the foundations for this view of life when he sacrificed for his family, accepted defeat without becoming bitter or self-destructive, assumed responsibility for the welfare of his family and placed that welfare and love above any personal material gain he might have realized.

At the close of Act I, Lena states directly for the first time the proper direction for her son: he is to be the man his father was. Her words are those of a loving mother who wants her son to become a man in the fullest sense of that term. They are hardly the words of a woman desiring to control and castrate him:

I waiting to hear how you be your father's son. Be the man he was. ... And I'm waiting to hear you talk like him and say we a people who give children life, not who destroys them—I'm waiting to see you stand up and look like your daddy and say we done give up one baby

> to poverty and that we ain't going to give up nary another one. ... I'm
> waiting.   (P. 382)

Walter, blinded by the materialistic values of the society in which
he lives and deaf to anything but the voices that speak to him of his
own success in the "corporate" world, cannot be touched by such a
plea or inspired by such an example. He does not respond. "You're
a disgrace to your father's memory." By invoking the father's memory Lena has tried to guide her son in the way of manhood and has
failed to do so.

In the final act of the play, however, she repeats this attempt with
greater success. Walter has grown; he "come into his manhood."
When Walter faces Lindner in the closing scene of the play, Lena
challenges his decision to humble himself by placing his son before
him, thus forcing Walter to see himself as heir to a proud and strong
sense of family. He is the son of his father and can he now act in such
a way that he disgraces his heritage? Walter, finally remembering
and honoring this heritage, responds not as he has had planned but
as a man dedicated to continuing the work his father began:

> This is my son, who makes the sixth generation of our family in this
> country. ... We have decided to move into our house because my
> father—he earned it.   (P. 429)

Walter comes into his manhood when he chooses his father's values
and rejects the corrupted standards which he has learned from the
Murchisons and Willy Harrises of the world. He matures when he
decides that whether it profit him or no, he will live according to
those values and not submit to the grab-what-you-can mentality of
his world.

It is not surprising to any student of Black drama that the church
or, perhaps more accurately, religion, plays a role in shaping the
values for which Lena Younger is the medium. Her religion is a
source of strength when she feels that she lacks the power to deal
with life. Her prayer at the end of Act II is not an empty ritual but
rather a plea for strength to resist the bitterness and despair that
threaten to destroy her and her family:

> Oh God. ... Look down here—and show me the strength. Strength. ...
> Strength!   (P. 416)

Any careful reader and especially any actress interested in understanding how to play these lines will realize that the repetition of

the last word is not mere restatement. By the third utterance we should see a woman who has been strengthened, who has triumphed over the darkness that has engulfed her for so many years.

Act I closes with the evocation of the father as symbol of pride and familial love; Act II closes with the evocation of God as a source of strength and endurance. We have here the twin springs from which Lena draws her sustenance: her husband's way of life and her religious faith. For this reason, the closing moments of Act III are very telling. When Walter finally taps the well of pride and power that is his father's memory, when he becomes the man his father was, Lena is described as having "her eyes closed...rocking back and forth as though she were in church, with her head nodding the amen Yes." The transformation of the boy Walter into the man is complete, the restoration of the father as source of pride is accomplished, the integration of religious values with secular concerns has triumphed and Lena, high priestess and exegete, can say amen and rest.

II

Hansberry's Lena is concerned with keeping alive the values and example of her husband and with instilling these values in her children; Sister Margaret in James Baldwin's *The Amen Corner,* on the other hand, struggles to protect her son from the destruction which she believes awaits anyone foolish enough to emulate her husband. Lena Younger feels that she must recreate the father for her children. Margaret is dedicated to expelling any memory of her husband from her son's mind and, failing to do this, she is determined at least to debase that memory. Lena draws strength from religion and her conduct affirms the worth of a life of love and consideration for others. This is in direct contrast to Margaret, who corrupts religion and creates a church which is removed from the reality of life—a place in which one can hide from commitment to the struggle which full living entails. While Lena remembers life with her husband as a rewarding struggle by two people sustained by love and trust, Margaret looks back in guilt at her early experiences with her husband. She sees her youthful love and sexual desire for him as the result of evil, destructive forces in the world. Lena remembers a life of sharing; Margaret remembers being forced to struggle alone.

Luke (and the name of the husband in Baldwin's play is significant) is a bringer of light, a healer. In Hansberry's work there is no contradiction between the man himself and the memory evoked by his wife. Luke's appearance in Baldwin's play makes Margaret's distortions all too apparent. Consider the Luke Margaret has created in order to warn her son of the dangers of a worldly life. To Margaret, Luke illustrates the insanity that is inherent in a life devoted to pleasure and love. Note her response to Brother Boxer's analysis of her son David's fatherlessness:

> *Boxer.* I reckon you must have missed your daddy sometimes, didn't you son?
> *Sister Moore.* If he'd stayed around his daddy, I guarantee you David wouldn't be the fine, saved young man he is today, playing in church, would you, boy?
> *Boxer.* He better off without the kind of daddy who'd just run off and leave his wife and kid to get along the best they could.
> *Margaret* (to David). You hear him, don't you? He know—miss his daddy? The Lord, he give me strength to be mother and daddy both.
> (P. 540)

Luke is representative of the sensual life from which Margaret has retreated. It is a life which she not only denies herself, but one which she teaches her congregation to avoid. Celibacy is the road to holiness. Sister Moore, one of the most faithful members of Margaret's church, expresses this view most aptly in her testimony:

> I want to thank Him for keeping me pure and set apart from the lusts of the flesh, for protecting me—Hallelujah!—from all carnal temptation. When I come before my Maker, I'm going to come before Him *pure.* I'm going to say "Bless your name, Jesus, no man has ever touched me!"   (P. 432)

Margaret's solution for the ills of all women is very clear when she offers advice to Mrs. Jackson, the young mother of a sick child, and suggests that maybe the Lord wants her to leave her husband.

Having built a wall of lies around the memory of her husband Luke—lies about her relationship with him and his devotion to the family—Margaret finds it difficult to imagine a Christian life as anything less than denial of love and passion between a man and a woman. Having created the fiction of Luke the Destroyer, she must struggle to remove her husband from the apartment or, failing that, to prevent his talking too openly to her son. So much of her energy has gone into the creation of the fictional Luke, so many nights have been spent in reshaping her actual experience with him, that she finds it difficult to believe that he is not the character she has created:

> You ain't changed, have you? You still got the same carnal grin, that same carnal mind—you ain't changed a bit.   (P. 545)

Her values are so distorted and her fears of the resurrected Luke are so powerful that, hearing he is sick and needs care, she reacts by refusing to postpone a trip to Philadelphia. Ironically, she is going there to visit a fellow minister who is ill. She explains her decision to Sister Moore:

> The Lord made me leave that man in there a long time ago because he was a sinner. And the Lord ain't told me to stop doing my work because he's come the way all sinners come.   (P. 547)

Her fear is based not on any real damage that Luke has done her but on the conviction that the tragedies she has suffered and those that all Black people suffer are punishment for a life lived in happiness and shared love. God's plan is that his Black children should suffer in this world and that they resist the temptation to be happy in their bodies, for happiness in this world is a sure indication of suffering in the next. To enjoy each other, to glory in passion, is to invite divine punishment. The reality of her world is suffering, and to escape eternal suffering, she must forgo carnal pleasures and retreat from life. She ceased being the "funny, fast-talking, fiery little thing" which Luke had held in his arms. Or, more accurately, she convinced herself that the other woman was dead, "burned out...by the power of the Holy Ghost." Margaret left Luke's arms and crawled into the cold, unreal embrace of the church.

Luke, however, represents something other than safety. He hopes to convince his son and Margaret, his wife, that there is a value in living fully, in confronting all of one's desires and not denying the validity of experience. Man is not created to be safe, to nibble timidly at the edges of life:

> Son, don't try to get away from the things that hurt you—sometimes that's all you got. You got to learn to live with those things—and—use them. I've seen people—put themselves through terrible torture—and die—because they was afraid of being hurt.   (P. 554)

And he reiterates this attitude in talking to his wife about his son:

> I don't care what kind of life he lives—as long as it's HIS life—not mine, not his mama's, but his own. I ain't going to let you make him safe.   (P. 569)

This view—that man should live fully and celebrate his life, even the tragedy of his life—is a frequent theme of Baldwin. His short story "Sonny's Blues" also deals with a character who accepts his life in all its agony and creates music from the darkness in which he lives. We find this attitude reflected not only in Baldwin. There is more than an echo here of Lena's reasons for letting Walter Lee take charge of the money, even though she knows there is good reason to believe that he will squander it foolishly. She sees his failure, accepts it finally, and still persists in her determination to grant him the right to "come into his manhood."

Unlike Lena, Margaret fears living freely, and is also tragically incapable of risking love. For her, both roads are lined with snares and she has determined not to risk but rather to retreat in the face of obstacles. Her final awareness—and this comes later than that of her son and is in part a result of his action—is not that the church and religion are wrong, but that she has distorted the meaning of both; not that loving is dangerous and hence foolish, but that it makes possible a warmth and happiness that more than make up for the risk and pain; not that she and all other Black people must hide from life, but that life is to be lived as fully as possible.

Baldwin finds in a true exercise of religion a source of strength and in the father a sense of direction and a source of healing. This latter function is evident in his choice of a name for the father in the play. He is Luke the physician; ironically, a physician who is dying. His son David, the musician, must leave the safety of his flock and confront the Goliath that awaits him in the world outside the congregation.

III

Hansberry's father is an absent member, a memory kept alive by his wife; Baldwin's appears to challenge the distortions of his memory which threaten the lives of his wife and son. Unlike these two, Cliff, the father-figure in Bullins' *In the Wine Time*, is very much a presence from the opening scenes of the play to the end. The difference in Bullins' view of the Black family is most evident in two areas: first, his characters neither fear sex nor feel the religious inhibitions that mark the people in Hansberry's and Baldwin's world; and secondly, his characters celebrate the life of the ghetto streets. The celebration here is not the product of buoyant optimism but rather a stoic acceptance of life's limitations—limitations that drive his people to a desperate grasping after the few pleasures life affords.

Like Walter, Sr., and Luke, Cliff is a man who has suffered defeat. From that defeat he has come to some rather firm conclusions on how life is to be lived. Although he still retains the dream of the Navy and the transcendence it represents, he has resigned himself to a future with the Derby Street Donkeys. He drinks wine because "everybody else drinks somethin' around here" and because he needs to stay high to blot out his sense of failure. Throughout the play, he struggles to instill in his nephew Ray (and to recreate in himself) the dream he knows is now beyond reach: escape from Derby Street to the tropical islands and exotic foreign ports that the Navy has come to represent for him.

Lou, Ray's surrogate mother, functions quite differently from the other women. Although she opposes Cliff and attempts to deny the validity of his dream, we cannot for a moment see in her the formidable opponent that Sister Margaret is. Lou's protests are not founded on any deep conviction—the Lou that Bullins creates is not capable of deep conviction—but rather, her attempts to counter Cliff's views are rote responses from the residue of some unnamed "proper upbringing" and are based on a value system she has hardly examined. They strike a strangely discordant note when uttered in the setting of Derby Street and are consistently contradicted by her actions and her retreat in the face of Cliff's attacks. She begins scolding him for cussing and ends up cussing herself; she laments his drinking and then joins him; she challenges the myth he has created from his hitch in the Navy but the challenge fizzles out:

> *Lou.* You wasn't shit, Cliff...you know that, don't you?...Pour me a drink, Ray...and give your no 'count step-uncle one, too. .... I hardly know where I'm at some of the times when I start in drinking after I come home from work...but it sho' do relax me...the devil's in Cliff,

> I know that, to do what he's doin' to us...and I ain't helpin' things much. Listen to what I say, Ray, not to the Devil.
>
> (pp. 606-607)

Cliff's rage is directed against a world and a god which have refused to let him live as a human being. That he has not surrendered to it or hidden himself completely in dreams is evident in his later refutation of Lou's criticism of his attitude toward that world and its God:

> I'm goin' ta get me a part of that world or stare your God in the eye and scream why. I am not a beast...an animal to be used for the plows of the world. But if I am, then I'll act like one, I'll be one and turn this fucken world of dreams, lies and fairy tales into a jungle or a desert. And I don't give much of a happy fuck which. There's a world out there, woman. Just beyond that lamppost...just across "The Avenue" and it'll be mine and Ray's.   (pp. 610-611)

He shouts his defiance and his determination at Lou, but she is not convinced, for she is certain that Ray must not be like Cliff. So strong is Cliff's control of her, however, and so feeble the support she can draw from her own convictions that she is powerless to prevent her husband from having his way. He uses both his superior physical strength and her sexual desire for him to silence her feeble protests.

If Cliff has a dream of a Navy Eden and Lou a vague memory of a "respectable" world, Ray also has created in "the Girl" an image that runs counter to the squalor and degradation by which he is surrounded. His relationship to her is that of worshipper and virgin goddess, not man and woman—the antithesis of the relationships he sees around him. To Cliff, Lou, Bama, Red, Bunny and Doris, sex is a furious coupling, an attempt to snatch a few moments of joy and passion from the deadening grip of Derby life, a battleground from which both combatants emerge torn and bleeding. In rejecting this attitude, Ray creates in his dream girl a creature who lacks the violence and passion which he sees. But this dream figure is too pure and unsubstantial to defeat the harsh reality of Derby Street. Her destruction is accomplished when Ray is finally initiated into the violence that exists in the world of the play, a violence that permits no fragile thing to stand, that permits nothing clean to remain so for long.

Ray has accepted Cliff's version of the possibilities that lie out-side Derby Street. He believes with Cliff that he can reach out and grasp that other world. He is not limited by who he has been or by what he has experienced:

> Ray...just learn this one thing in life...when the time comes...be a man...however you've lived up till then...throw it out of your mind. (p. 628)

And Ray, trying to be a man, kills Red. With this action, he is come of age:

> *Ray.* She's gone...she's gone.
> *Doris.* Who's gone, Ray? Who?
> *Ray.* She is...my girl...my girl on "the avenue!"
> *Doris.* She'll be back.
> *Ray.* No, she's not. She won't be back. (p. 633)

The gift of the father, his sacrifice of himself for his children, his bequeathing to them a value system which will take them through life, is rendered hopeless by the reader's refusal to believe. Even though Cliff takes the blame for Red's death, hoping that in so doing he will free Ray to pursue life away from Derby Street, we are not convinced that Ray will ever reap the rewards of the gift, for Bullins has so powerfully communicated to us the fatal air that surrounds his characters that Cliff's last words ring hollow:

> It's your world, Ray...it's yours, boy...go on out there and claim it. (p. 634)

We emerge from Bullins' world knowing in no uncertain terms that while it is not Ray's world, no amount of sacrifice can make possible the vague dreams of purity and passion that float always beyond the reach of Bullins' characters. Given the destruction that waits outside the door, Cliff's inability to provide any real means of coping with it, and Lou's ineffectiveness, Ray is lost to the world beyond Derby Street. Nor can he find in the religion that Bullins personifies in unattractive characters like Miss Minny and Beatrice any hope for inspiration. The irony of their conversation at the end of the play and Beatrice's final amen is not lost on the perceptive viewer:

Beatrice. The Lord bless you tonight.
Miss Minny. He will dear...'cause he works in mysterious ways.
Beatrice. Amen.   (p. 406)

IV

Joseph Walker's *The River Niger* also deals with the preserva-
tion of values inherent in the Black experience. The play provides
a vision of (i) a family coming to terms with failure and the social
and political forces involved; and (ii) the role played by mother and
father in the maturing of their offspring.

Mattie is partly responsible for her husband's failure to achieve
his dreams. Like Bullins' Lou, she fears the risk inherent in pur-
suing those dreams. Like Hansberry's Mama Younger, she is a
powerful figure who is sure of her own values. But the differences in
the male-female roles in Walker's play and those assigned by the
other dramatists and the difference in plot structure itself far out-
weigh the similarities. Walker's father-figure is not an absentee
parent; he is an active force from the beginning to the end of the
play. His relationship with his wife is a passionate one, and it is a
relationship of equals. The child, Jeff, because of the example of
his parents, does not fear his own sexuality. Likewise Ann, the
woman to whom he is engaged, experiences none of the fears and
repressions that haunt the characters of the earlier plays. Rather
than escape into the narcotizing atmosphere of religion, these characters work their way to a confrontation with the world, and in this
confrontation they are worthy adversaries of everything they struggle against. They do not abandon their dreams. Rather, they
demand the right to make those dreams real.

If in other works we have been concerned with the legacy children receive from their parents, it is necessary that we examine
the ways in which Jeff of Walker's play differs from Walter, David,
and Ray. From his father Johnny, Jeff learns to love. Witness the
exchange with his fiancée and notice how uninhibited and open
their relationship is:

> *Jeff.* Ann, my love, the most glorious bitch I ever done run across, let's
> get married. Let's get married and screw right at the ceremony. Mon-
> day we'll get the license. There's a three-day wait—Tuesday, Wed-

nesday, and Thursday—Friday we'll get high off this bad-ass smoke
I been saving and fly on to the preacher.
Ann. Are you serious?
Jeff. Indubitably.
Ann. Oh, Jeff, why so sudden?
Jeff. Honey, with the way these niggers is acting up 'round here, I
figure I better get me some hep.
Ann. Jeff, I—
Jeff. I know you love me to pieces, and I don't blame you one bit.
Ann. You conceited—
Jeff. The problem is, I don't really love you. (Pause.) I glory for you,
baby. Besides, you got the bossest dogs I ever seen.[5]

It is significant that in his proposal of marriage, he is looking for
"some hep," a woman who has the strength to stand, to assist, not
one who will lean on him.

Not only has he learned to love freely, but because of the kind
of parents he had, Jeff has learned to bear pain and to look to those
parents and their example as a source of strength:

I was nursing in Quebec when they brought him into the hospital.
He had fractured his ankle skiing. Everytime it started paining him,
he'd laugh—Said his dad had taught him to do that.   (p. 44)

He has learned to distinguish between the bogus and the real, to
fight real enemies and not deceive himself as to his own strength
or that of his adversary. When he is asked to join an organization
bent on self-destruction in the name of some ill-defined revolutionary goal, he demurs:

The one advantage I have over you, Mo, is my daddy taught me to
see through bullshit, to believe that I don't need bullshit to be somebody.   (pp. 99-100)

Ironically, it is this very heritage which causes his first real clash
with his father; for Johnny, having come through a series of frustrations, has forgotten the values he once knew and which he so
clearly inculcated in his son. Johnny's desire that his son have a
distinguished career in the Air Force, like Cliff's Navy career for
Ray, Walter's dream of becoming a business tycoon, and Sister
Margaret's desire that David become a saint of the church, are

[5]Joseph Walker, *The River Niger* (New York: Hill and Wang, 1973), pp. 101-162.
Subsequent references are incorporated into the text.

goals determined with little thought for the person who is to pursue them or of the realities of the world in which they must be pursued. Johnny believes the Air Force is the final victory over the forces that threaten his son, but the son has not chosen aerial navigation as a career. Jeff avoids the blind alley of someone else's expectation because of his independence and honest self-appraisal, qualities that have been instilled in him by his father. He explains why he left the Air Force:

> On my last flight exam—a night celestial—I wound up eighty miles into Mexico, according to my computations, while everybody else's figures put us at Harlingen Air Force Base, Texas. ... They sent me before a board of senior officers. You see, this was the second time I'd failed my night celestial flying exam. ... I told the board, "Let go my toe!" And they replied, "What?" You know, the way white people do when they don't believe their ears. So I screamed at the top of my voice, "Let go my nigger toe so I can stand up and be a man."   (pp. 128-129)

Much of the discussion to this point has centered on the father and son but, unlike the other women we have seen, Mattie is an equal partner in this marriage and as much a source of understanding and wisdom as her husband. He is not a person to be feared, a child to be coddled, or an adversary against whom she must arm herself to do battle. That he has failed, she accepts. That she is in part responsible for this, she does not deny. That given the power and joy of their love, his failure and her guilt are unimportant, she makes very clear. Her conversation with her son's fiancée clearly demonstrates her refusal to practice self-deception. She watches her mother slyly drink herself into a stupor, but will not admit she knows about this surreptitious tippling. Hers are not the words of a woman who refuses to face truth in all its baldness nor are they the words of a woman who seeks pity and understanding:

> I got nobody to blame but myself. Treasures in heaven!—shit. A good man is a treasure. ... Johnny ran a powerful race with a jockey on his back who weighed a ton. So now he's tired. Do you hear me? Tired—and he's put himself out to pasture—with his fifth a day; and I say good for Johnny.   (p. 76)

Although she loves and admires her husband, she does not attempt to force her son to follow his example. The values she communicates are those of independence and love but, more importantly, they are her own. Unlike the other mothers, she does not lean on her husband for support. Nor does she invoke his life as a positive or negative pattern for her son, for either would serve only to blind him to his own way. Her relationship with her husband is uniquely theirs and not a pattern for others. Her refusal to make it a pattern is based on a sense of what is best for her son and not on shame or regret for what her life has been, for nowhere in the play do we see her despair over what has been. Realistic yes; despairing, never. And it is this realism that is so much a part of her eloquent testimony to her love for Johnny, a testimony based on an acceptance of herself with all her errors and faults as well as an acceptance of her husband, warts and all:

Johnny. I coulda done it, Mattie. God knows, I coulda done it!
Mattie. I know, baby. I put it on you. I stopped you, and I'm sorry. I'm sorry. Will you forgive me, sweet baby? Please forgive me! I was selfish, Johnny. I've been so goddam happy! All I ever cared about was seeing you walk, stumble, or stagger through that door. I only complained because I felt I should say something—but I never meant it, Johnny. I never meant a word. You couldn't have given me nothing more, baby. I'da just keeled over and died from too much happiness, just keeled over and died. (pp. 152-153)

With him she faces the final crisis in the play as they attempt to find a way to rescue their children (for by now they claim their son, his fiancée and friends as their own) from destruction. Johnny makes one request of her in this last scene, never doubting that she is strong enough to fulfill it and willing to do so:

I got to get our children straight before I go—Now be my superbitch. My battlefield! My battlefield! (p. 174)

He has found the battlefield he sought, has seen the action that his manhood requires and Mattie, an equal partner all their lives, does not weaken:

Shut up! and tell it like Johnny told ya. He ain't gonna die for nothing, 'cause you ain't gonna let him! Jeff—open that door, son! Tell 'em to come on in here! And you better not fuck up, (p. 177)

This is the distance, then, that the men and women have traveled; from dead or absent father to living and potent force; from mother hiding behind illusions and dreams to woman confronting the world in all its harshness; from a religion of suffering and escape to a religion of poetry:

> Poetry is religion, the alpha and the omega, the cement of the universe...God himself. God himself is pure distilled poetry.

(p. 122)

From a fear of commitment that is reflected in a fear of sex to a passionate and joyous mating of man and woman; from children twisted and destroyed by a burden of ugly memories to young people freed by glorious example and sacrifice.

Gilbert Moses, director of *The Wiz,* provides an apt conclusion:

> The days are over in which many people in theater become hung up on the notion of positive as opposed to negative Black images on stage and screen. Black characters weren't real people; they were symbols. Even when playwrights tried to make their heroes more than symbols representing all Black men or all Black women, critics, and the public in general, resisted.[6]

It is high time we stopped resisting and let the men and women live and speak to us.

---

[6]Gilbert Moses in *Encore,* April 21, 1975.

Structural Elements
in Ed Bullins' Plays

by Samuel A. Hay

A playwright learns quite early in his career to pay no attention to critics. Applied to the Black playwright and the non-Black critic, this axiom gains in importance. For we should not expect people not of our own culture and heritage to respond in the same way that we do to our arts and letters. Therefore, I suspect that Ed Bullins summarily dismissed the non-Black critics' comments about his play, *The Duplex* (1971). But these critics, with their national media outlets, are to be reckoned with. Taking their cues from Walter Kerr of *The New York Times,* the critics mold public (and this includes Black) opinion. Their influence, however, is not the issue here; it is the arrogance and inconsistency of their arguments. These arguments, as Addison Gayle, Jr., has pointed out, almost always focus on dramatic structure: "Form is the most important criterion of the work of art when Black literature is evaluated; whereas form, almost non-existent in Dostoyevsky's *Crime and Punishment,* and totally chaotic in Kafka's *The Trial,* must take second place to the supremacy of thought and message."[1]

In his review of *Duplex,* Kerr opens with structure: "Mr. Bullins sees the Black experience in a certain light. Whether [or not] it is lived in a Southern California duplex..., it is without present shape or clear future. Oppression has denied it a structure, casting its peo-

"Structural Elements in Ed Bullins' Plays" by Samuel A. Hay. From *Black World,* Vol. XXIII, No. 6 (April 1974), pp. 20-26. Copyright © April 1974 by *Black World.* Reprinted by permission of Johnson Publishing Company and Samuel Hay.

[1]"Cultural Strangulation: Black Literature and the White Aesthetic" in *The Black Aesthetic,* ed. Addison Gayle, Jr. (Garden City, N.Y.: Doubleday & Co., Inc., 1971), pp. 39-46.

ple loose on a dirty tide of drugs, drink, all-night card games, self-flagellation, hysterical religiosity."[2] He continues: "Plays can be written in all shapes; the shape need only be appropriate to the experience being reflected. But what shape shapes shapelessness? How do you reach out for all that is true, or all that is felt, and gather it into a net that will hold? Hold in the playhouse, hold together its own good parts?" Good questions. Let us briefly analyze both the structure of *Duplex* and Kerr's arguments about its lack of structure to see if *Kerr* reaches "out for all that is true, or all that is felt, and gathers it into a net that will hold."

Set during the early Sixties in a duplex in Southern California, *The Duplex* tells the story of Velma Best's search for self-completeness, for a love that transcends sex. To understand better the Search for Self-Completeness (not "emotion," as Kerr asserts),[3] we might turn to an incident in the Amos Tutuola novel, *The Palm-Wine Drinkard:* A Nigerian lady, searching for Completeness, pursues a "beautiful 'complete' gentleman." Warned repeatedly not to interest herself in this stranger to the village, she nevertheless decides that he completes her being. She sees him one day in the marketplace and decides to follow—into the Forest. She sees him "return the hired parts of his body to the owners," until the complete gentleman is reduced to a head. She senses danger but follows still, until she is captured by the gentleman and his community of the Skulls. Only after several disarming experiences is she rescued by the Drinkard.

In his *Symposium,* Plato has Aristophanes explain the origins of this search for Self-completeness: Man was once a strong being (globular in shape) "with rounded back and sides, four arms and four legs, and two faces, both the same, on a cylindrical neck, and one headed, with one face on one side and one the other, and four ears, and two lots of privates, and all the other parts to match." Angry at these powerful beings for trying "to scale the heights of heaven and set upon the gods," Zeus "cut them all in half." The bi-

---

[2]Unless otherwise noted, Kerr's comments are from "Mr. Bullins Is Himself at Fault," *The New York Times,* 19 March 1972 Sec. D, p. 1.

[3]Bernard F. Dukore argues that *Duplex* raises no issues: "By the time the play's single intermission came, I was not only unconcerned as to how things would turn out, I was unsure what was to turn out, since no issues had been raised, and uninterested in any of the characters, since Bullins showed only their surface. With no reason to return to my seat, I left." Rev., *Educational Theater Journal,* 24, No. 3 (1972), 318-320.

section "left each half with a desperate yearning for the other, and they ran together and flung their arms around each other's necks, and asked for nothing better than to be rolled into one."⁴

In his plays, Bullins (a leading playwright of the Drama of Self-celebration)⁵ continually portrays this Search: Jack and Clara in *Clara's Ole Man* (1959), Cliff and Lou Dawson in *In the Wine Time* (1966), Steve and Grace in *It Has No Choice* (1966), and Steve and Liz in *New England Winter* (1967). In *Duplex,* Bullins elects to make the Search the controlling idea. Velma's husband, O. D., makes "ah ca-reerah ah stayin' in the streets"; he comes home "to change his clothes and eat and then try and get me [Velma] in bed." Consequently, Velma turns her Search toward Steve Benson, "the guy from upstairs": "Steve, be mah friend. Please be mah friend." But Steve is interested primarily in getting his college degree, his one-way ticket from the confines of the duplex. After considerable vacillation about his feelings for Velma, Steve discovers that he loves Velma, faults and all:

> Nobody knows the love and beauty I find in holding my woman in my arms....My woman...a poor little scared black girl that's even dumber than I'm supposed to be. Nobody knows that I don't care if she has kids...children who will hate me forever if I get her like I plan. Nor will anybody know that she'll never know me...really know me...this black man...with this mind....They'll never understand the thoughts that flash through my head and scorch the back of my eyes...these eyes that see her being beaten and raped, these eyes that see the flames of the hell that we all live in...live our black lives in here...in our cool dark little lives...getting ready to become something we ain't now or will ever be...really.   (III, 2)

But Steve's discovery is too late: Velma decides that Steve's vacillation (the stripping to the Skull) proves that he is not her "other half," that she must save her mismatched marriage to O. D., who decides that *his* "other half" is another woman. Several other fruitless searches in and around the duplex elaborate the main action: searches by Mama and Pops, Lola and Tootsie, and Wanda and Marco.

When analyzing a play for dramatic structure, the critic must focus upon the basic unit of the structure, the scene (not used here

⁴Michael Joyce, trans. in *Plato: Collected Dialogues,* ed. Edith Hamilton and Huntington Cairns (Princeton: Princeton Univ. Press, 1969), pp. 526-574.

⁵See my "African-American Drama, 1950-1970" in *Negro History Bulletin* 36, No. 1 (1973), 5-8.

to mean place of action or formal division of an Act, but the portion of the play in which the stage is occupied by an unchanging group of players). Within this unit, structure involves the selection and arrangement of exposition (recounting of the past), action (forward movement), and preparation (hint of things to come). In the larger unity of the entire play, structure means the selection and arrangement of scenes. Combined, these units should evidence the dramatist's singleness of purpose and clarity of vision, or central idea. Identifying these structural elements in most mainstream drama is an easy enough task. But when a dramatist tampers with the formula, or makes the formula subordinate to theme, mainstream critics often lose their bearings (especially if the critic opposes the theme of the play). Like John Coltrane in his late period, Bullins not only tampers with the formula for structure, but, in some cases, he completely disregards it.

Marked by a flowing conversational style, *Duplex* relies on two structural devices to create mood and to transport its unifying idea: (a) unplanned and casual action, and (b) frequently disconnected dialogue. Also, there is very little developed action in the play. (Action "is not here thought of as mere physical activity, but as what the characters do: fight, fall in love, make or evade making decisions, voice their secret thoughts, or harangue either other characters or the audience."[6]) The characters continually drink, play cut-throat pinochle, signify, dance, and screw. O.D. and his watchdog Crook enter periodically to knock a few heads together—to interrupt, in other words, this systematic combination of exposition and casual action. As the characters party, we receive considerable information about their pasts, their hopes, and their fears. The search for structure, then, must focus not on the development of action, but on the development of the theme, the recurrence of hopes for Self-completeness. These hopes are gradually exposed as illusions and are later shattered. Bullins' structural pattern is dissatisfaction with reality, flight into fantasy (or envisioned reality), and a return to an adjusted reality.

An earlier theatrical example of this structural style can be found in the Russian playwright Chekhov, whose simplified plot fabric and apparently unsystematic combination of facts and actions caused his plays to be termed "drama of mood." That action is undeveloped

[6]H. Darkes Albright, *et al. Principles of Theatre Arts* (Boston: Houghton Mifflin Co., 1968), p. 15.

or static in mainstream drama (and particularly in Chekhov's *Cherry Orchard*) does not bother Kerr: "I don't think I have ever attended a production in which the naturalistic flow of events was so matter-of-fact that there was no event at all, only the indisputable comings and goings of the of-course people, the people who of course live there, always have."[7] He concludes that the play deserves the success it achieves. On the other hand, Bullins' naturalistic flow of events drowns his drama: "An idle sally, a friendly insult, an incidental character from nowhere are all recorded and re-recorded as though the fact that Mr. Bullins had *heard* them somewhere were sufficient justification for our hearing them now. Aimless recall drowns the drama that is trying so very hard to assert itself." One wonders if Kerr understands that too often whether the naturalistic flow of events heightens or drowns a drama depends most often on the viewer's understanding and appreciation of the events. In other words, that Kerr understands and appreciates Chekhov's depicted life-styles, but does not understand and appreciate (perhaps, even detests) Bullins' depicted life-styles probably explains Kerr's contrasting attitudes.

Kerr also dislikes Bullins' second structural device, desultory conversation. The characters frequently do not listen or respond to each other. Each spins his own yarn to others, who are far more interested in spinning their own:

> *Velma.* You know...this is the only real home I've had.
> *Mamma.* When I met Pops he thought he'd stand up on his rear legs... yes, indeed he did...
> *Velma.* First time I ever sunk roots this deep.
> *Sukie.* I had an ole nigger man once. Thought he was bad.
> *Mamma.* Called himself "Dawg" then...leastwise that's what his no-count friends used to call him...not so long ago neither.
> *Velma.* Even when I was back home...that wasn't like home...really. That was just my mamma and daddy's place. I just lived there.
> *Sukie.* I told that man, "Nigger! If you ever look at me funny, you gonna be sorry...you gonna be sorry for the day you was born." Yeah... that's what I told that nigger.   (III, 4)

Contrary to Kerr's suggestion that disconnected conversation impairs the play, the desultory dialogue highlights the casual action and points to the desperation of the Search for Self-completeness.

[7]*Thirty Plays Hath November* (N.Y.: Simon & Schuster, 1970), p. 154.

The remarks are charged not only with the particular meaning for the character who is speaking, but with a special meaning that illumines the Search of the others present. Again, we can turn to Chekhov (to *The Three Sisters,* about which Kerr raves) to see an extensive use of the desultory conversation device. Chebutykin reads from a newspaper: "Tsitsikar. Smallpox is raging here." Neither Tsitsikar nor smallpox bears any relation whatsoever to Chebutykin, or to any other person, or to anything that will happen on the stage. A newspaper report happens to catch his eye. He reads it through and it has no direct bearing on anything that is being said around him. Subsequently, it is left without any echo.

In *Duplex,* Bullins also leaves several subjects unechoed. Such occurrences in *Three Sisters* do not worry Kerr: "If [Chekhov] lets [his characters] loose and keeps them close to the truth, they will take care of themselves, making their own comedy as they rush or drift or skitter from mood to mood."[8] Bullins', however, is another story: "In his anxiety to record honestly and fully his sense of the sound of Blackness, [Bullins] is at this stage in his career wildly unselective. He is willing to let the most desultory of conversations go on into infinity so long as he feels he is telling the truth." "If acceptable in Chekhov, why not in Bullins?" is the question that immediately comes to mind. The answer, perhaps, is that Kerr is unwilling to accept Bullins' "truth."

Bullins selects and arranges his scenes so that they resemble the Search itself: looking, finding, testing, detesting, re-searching. Each character's Search "is examined at length," as Kerr points out. His complaint that the characters are "independent entities," that they "spin off into space without having made vital connection" is the very strength of the play, is in fact the successful meshing of form and content.

Finally, Kerr asserts that *Duplex* "doesn't close down to a core or reach a sum that could be called a conclusion" (the restoration of a semblance of equilibrium): "If no clear future can be envisioned for the most intelligent or the most savage of a play's characters, how do you bring it to an end? Where, short of infinity, do you stop?" This question, more so than any of his other pontifications, is evidence of Kerr's innate hostility towards and complete misunderstanding of *Duplex.* Near the end, Steve finally fights O. D. for Velma: Seeing O. D., "Steve walks toward him. O. D.'s face is blank, but at the last

[8]*Ibid.,* p. 158.

moment he smiles slightly, before Steve punches him squarely in the face with all his might." But O. D. recovers, slams Steve against the wall, butts him, grabs him like a rag doll, and strangles him. When O. D. finally lets him loose, Steve struggles upstairs and threatens: "Next time! Man, next time. ..., I'll do it the right way." But there will be no next time. His friend, Tootsie, reminds him: "Man...that woman's wit her ole man....Can't you understand that?" We know that Steve's and Velma's future is to live and to learn to accept their altered reality. The play and the Search end and begin anew with Steve's friends arriving and yelling: "Hey, ev'vabody! Grab yo cards, whiskey 'n' women. It's party time!"

Kerr's inability or refusal to accept Bullins' successful use of certain structural innovations—the same ones that he raves about in non-Black drama—points to something else behind his arguments about structure. Typical of non-Black critics, Kerr is not really all that concerned about the shape of Black drama, but about the shape of the ideas, attitudes, and practices. His artistic judgments about Black drama cannot be trusted. In fact, in a commentary on murder mysteries, Kerr once warned: "I have been brought up on purposeful treachery. I have learned to be treacherous myself; and it's too late to make a trusting (or trusted, I might add) man of me now."[9]

[9]*Ibid.*, p. 20.

The Delicate World of Reprobation:
A Note on the Black Revolutionary Theatre

by Michael W. Kaufman

> The relation between form and content (the latter is to be understood not simply as the "theme," but as a living complex of moods and ideas which seek artistic expression) is determined by the fact that a new form is discovered, proclaimed, and developed under the pressure of an inner need, of a collective psychologic demand, which, like all human psychology, has its roots in society.

I

With this pronouncement Leon Trotsky,[1] the very archetype of a revolutionary, elucidated the shifting collective impulses that shape and reshape imaginative literature. Trotsky's interpretation of the way literary forms organically correspond to social-psychologic demands illuminates with remarkable clarity the growing body of drama that thus far constitutes the Black Revolutionary Theatre.[2] In the past decade several black playwrights have attempted to dramatize the "inner need" of their people in order to shape the

"The Delicate World of Reprobation: A Note on the Black Revolutionary Theatre" by Michael W. Kaufman. From *Educational Theatre Journal,* Vol. XXIII, No. 4 (December 1971), pp. 446-59. Reprinted by permission of the American Theatre Association, Inc. and the author.

[1] *Literature and Revolution* (Ann Arbor: University of Michigan Press, 1966), p. 233.

[2] The movement began in the Spring of 1964 when the Black Arts Repertoire School opened in New York. Larry Neal, "The Black Arts Movement," *The Drama Review,* 12 (Summer 1968), 32-33, describes the Arts movement as "the aesthetic and spiritual sister of the Black Power concept," and provides a brief account of its history.

drama of their lives, and have coincidentally reshaped the life of their drama. More than anything else the demands for authentic black self-expression dictate the form of this drama, and the success of that cultural definition distinguishes the achievement of the Black Revolutionary Theatre.

The significance of this idea of a theatre will be more intelligible to anyone who has read even a little of the *Kerner Commission Report.* Whether we like it or not, these dramatists take as their unassailable premise "that there are in fact and in spirit two Americas —one black, one white."[3] Their plays are energized by attempts to give the lie to pat assumptions concerning the hegemony of human experience, designed to repudiate Arthur Miller's claim that the only valid social drama teaches us "how much the same we are."[4] Now, instead of falsifying their hopes by trying to bring them into line with the elusive promises of the American dream, instead of trying to swim in what Julian Mayfield has called "the mainstream of American literature,"[5] these writers have rejected that society— "that great-power face that the world knows and the Negro knows better"[6] —and the literary forms it nourishes. This awareness of the futility of appealing to America's ruling majority has resulted in the emergence of a new black political drama which repudiates reformist movements and the protest literature they foster, and ac-

[3]Neal, p. 29. Nowhere, I think, is the importance of understanding the social and political premises of this theatre more in need than in the outraged critical reaction to Black Revolutionary drama. C. W. E. Bigsby, in his recent study of contemporary American drama (*Confrontation and Commitment* [Columbia: University of Missouri Press, 1967], p. 115), expresses the salient attitude concerning these plays when he complains that "the Negro playwrights of the sixties have tended all too frequently to embrace the moral absolutism of thirty years ago. Relying on the stereotype and facing social injustice with anger they have tended to create not valid drama but fantasies of revenge." My use here of Bigsby is cautionary for his principal objection that these black dramatists "obsessed by the reality of racial barriers…stress not the uniformity of human fate but the divisions of society" (pp. 115-116) describes the illusions of white, liberal Americans better than it reflects Black Revolutionary drama. It is a judgment based on a fundamental misconception of the governing assumptions of this theatre, misconceived precisely because it demands of these plays the forms, conventions, and attitudes that black dramatists want above all to reject.

[4]"On Social Plays," in *A View from the Bridge* (London: Cresset, 1957), p. 8.

[5]"Into the Mainstream and Oblivion," in *Dark Symphony: Negro Literature in America,* ed. James A. Emanuel and Theodore L. Gross (New York: The Free Press, 1968), p. 559.

[6]Mayfield, p. 558.

cepts instead a racial separatism and a drama written exclusively for blacks, calculated to promote a cohesive unity among their audiences. By reflecting the black man's vision of reality these dramatists have accepted the political and psychological challenges of attending "directly to the needs and aspirations of Black America," dedicating themselves "to define the world in their terms."[7]

How does the black dramatist define the world in his own terms, how does he instigate "a cultural revolution in art and ideas"? One pertinent answer may be glimpsed in the recent attempt to create "new history, new symbols, new legends," the necessary constituents for a reinvigorated culture. LeRoi Jones's *Black Mass,* Charles Fuller's *The Rise* the life and work of Marcus Garvey), Ben Caldwell's *The King of Soul* (the death of Otis Redding), and at least two plays concerning the life and death of Malcolm X (N. R. Davidson's *El Hajj Malik* and Jones's *The Death of Malcolm X*) indicate some of the ways these playwrights have sought to establish indigenous mythic and historical heroes as the nucleus of a positive black cultural tradition. These historical or legendary redactions stress at once the immoral evil of white society and the beauty and spiritual superiority of blacks, and the imaginative scope moves beyond the narrow limits of a minority striking a national or international resonance, heralding the emergence of the third world. "All points of reference will emerge from within the nation," writes K. William Kgositsile. "So will our heroes, literary and national—Dedan Kimathi, Malcolm, DuBois, Nkrumah, Nyerere, Babu, Touré, Fanon, and many more living and being born every day, pulsating with visions of a world worth killing and dying for."[8]

[7] Neal, p. 29.

[8] "Towards our Theatre: A Definitive Act," in *Black Expression,* ed. Addison Gayle, Jr. (New York: Weybright and Talley, 1969), pp. 147-148. Ben Caldwell's play *The King of Soul* is an excellent example of the way black playwrights imaginatively reorder history. In Caldwell's play white society is embodied in the devil who makes a contract with Otis Redding promising him fame and fortune in exchange for his soul. But the Faust myth is inverted. When the time comes for the agreed payment Otis refuses, and his lawyer declares the contract "not only illegal but immoral." However the devil, now in the guise of an airplane mechanic, sabotages the craft which sends Otis to his death. Although the play ennobles Otis and exposes the diabolic purposes of the whites, Caldwell's point pushes beyond the melodramatic portraiture of a martyred hero, by elucidating a less fantastic aspect of his death—why white society wants Otis dead:

"1st man:

He' makin' more money for them now that he's dead cause now they

But when Ed Bullins says that in ten years "our art will be completely different from White Anglo-Saxon Western art,"[9] he has in mind a more profound theatrical revolution than merely dramatizing black mythic figures. For having recognized the need to develop a cultural authentication quite apart from the values and mores of the "racist West," it follows that these dramatists must reject the imposed Western dramatic traditions which in forcefully symbolic ways represent only legacies of an oppressive, brutalizing, alien culture. The logic is simple if difficult to put into practice, for like Genet's Blacks these revolutionary dramatists must in effect find "new gestures for love." Only by repudiating Western dramatic precedents, by demolishing inherited dramatic conventions either by parody, travesty, mock heroics, or disregard, can the black dramatist claim his radical alternative "to the sterility of the American theatre."[10] "We don't want to have a higher form of white art in black face," Bullins insists. "We are working toward something entirely different and new that encompasses the soul and spirit of Black people."[11] If these dramatists can create their own authentic idiom, if they can find radically new forms congruent with their content, they will have achieved a dramatic definition of self precisely because they no longer need define their Negritude in relation to white culture.

"The revolutionary theatre should force change, it should be change."[12] LeRoi Jones's aphorism crystallizes both the fundamental aim and the underlying strategy of Black Revolutionary Theatre. These dramatists seek to precipitate a new order of existence, a

---

don't have to pay him! That's part of their game! ... Otis was moving in the direction to get more of it — of ALL of it! ... Now to the white man its hard enough to take a nigger makin' some money, but when a nigger wants all the money — when he starts goin for himself — competing with the white man — 'He's got to go!'"

Here fiction begins to merge with historical reality and what happened to Otis Redding becomes a symbolic example of the historical exploitation of all black men.

[9]Marvin X, "Interview with Ed Bullins," *New Plays from the Black Theatre* (New York: Bantam Books, Inc., 1969), p. xii.

[10]Neal, p. 33. LeRoi Jones, "The Revolutionary Theatre," *Liberator*, 5 (July 1965), 4, makes the same point in these terms: "But the Revolutionary Theatre, even if it is Western must be anti-Western. It must show horrible coming attractions of the crumbling of the West."

[11]"Interview with Ed Bullins," p. xxi.

[12]"The Revolutionary Theatre," p. 4.

social change partly reflected by their radically different dramatic idiom. The rhetoric of this theatre is consciously intended to excite an audience to act decisively and to transform their lives and the society that oppresses them. In one important sense the *raison d'etre* of this theatre is to dramatize black point-of-view, the black as "victim and chronicler" living in a "no-man's land, a black country, almost completely invisible to White America."[13] The plays are concrete illustrations of the living actuality of being black and pose for their audience the radical alternative which in the unambiguous words of the title of one of Jones's plays is "arm yourself or harm yourself." But to force such changes theatrically the plays themselves must be images of change, their medium mirroring their message. By presenting images of blacks in new roles, by incorporating the rhythms of music and reflecting the special character of black experience, by stressing direct and persuasive communication and the attendant emotional participation, and by disdaining the rigorously ordered structure and traditional verisimilitude associated with the well-made theatre, these plays are change simply by being unlike anything seen on the stage before.

The primary purpose of this essay is to suggest that in order for white readers to respond more imaginatively to a theatre written especially for blacks, we must resist the temptation to judge these plays narrowly according to our own critical terms and social visions and make the necessary effort to understand the special world the black dramatists strive to create. The challenge that Black Revolutionary Theatre confronts the white reader with is in fact a concrete example of the crisis in theatre aesthetics of which William Oliver has written so incisively.[14] Oliver puts the problem this way: "We must avoid standards that define drama by means of technical or conventional strictures which do not make reference to both the rhetorical purposes of communication and to the sensuo-hypnotic communion of ecstatic arousal."[15]

With these general remarks in mind I propose to contrast two plays, LeRoi Jones's *The Slave* and Jimmy Garrett's *And We Own the Night,* both written by black dramatists and both evidently about racial revolution. My choice of *The Slave* is deliberate, for by se-

[13]LeRoi Jones, "The Myth of a Negro Literature," *Saturday Review,* 20 Apr. 1963, pp. 20-21.

[14]"Theatre Aesthetics in Crisis," *Educational Theatre Journal,* 21 (Mar. 1969), 20.

[15]*Ibid.,* p. 21.

lecting one of Jones's early plays written before he went "uptown" where he realized his commitment to radical community theatre I want to emphasize a crucial point about revolutionary theatre: that although *The Slave* is ostensibly about revolution it is neither ideologically nor formally a revolutionary play. The moral complexity of its action, the tragic contradictions expressed by its central protagonist, the probative relativism of its vision stand in striking contrast with the Black Revolutionary Theatre's self-conscious emphasis on techniques and values that clearly affirm a course of political action and offer unambiguous moral judgments and self-clarification to their audiences.

Both *The Slave* and *And We Own The Night*[16] are concerned with the emerging black identity, developed as they are around protagonists in the process of discovering and affirming selfhood through their experiences and confrontations with white society. Both plays share the common environment of revolution visually emphasized by dead or dying bodies and aurally enforced by screaming bullets and deafening explosions. And, both plays end with the implicit assumption of victory over the common enemy—white society—seeking through the theatrical experience to expose the audience to new orders of meaning. Yet each play has its own distinctive shape and, as I will argue, a decidedly different impact on the viewer.

Near the end of *The Dutchman*, Jones's protagonist, Clay Williams, describes how for centuries black rage has either been repressed or deflected into the musical expressions of a Bessie Smith or a Charlie Parker: "A whole people of neurotics, struggling to keep from being sane" (p. 35). In an important sense Clay's memorable speech expresses the pervasive theme in Jones's work. Although the Negro's suppression of his hatred must lead eventually to neurosis, and only the free expression of that murderous rage is requisite for the black's sanity, this health is precisely what Clay himself has failed to achieve since he hid his "pumping black heart" beneath his three button suit, and his spiritual suicide results in his actual murder. But Walker Vessels, the protagonist of *The Slave*, has acted upon Clay's insight and has put the symbol of black sanity into action. With his revolutionary theories already in operation when the play begins, Walker prepares for the irreversible break with his

[16]*Dutchman and The Slave* (New York: Apollo, 1964). All quotations from Jones's play are from this edition. Garrett's play appeared in *The Drama Review*, 12 (Summer 1968), 62-69. All subsequent references will be incorporated into the text.

own past represented by his former white wife, Grace, and the liberal, intellectual Easley. As the play begins Walker appears ready to emerge triumphantly as the mythical black revolutionary hero. But the appearance of such a figure never quite materializes; instead Jones produces a different perspective on the revolution, a complex intellectual dimension that plumbs profound conflicts between Walker's public and private selves and brings to the surface disturbing moral paradoxes inherent within the dialectic of oppressed and oppressor.

This over-all pattern of complexity crystallizes not only in the play's action and themes, but in the single figures as well. Bradford Easley, the white intellectual, might serve as example. It is obvious that Jones attempts to reduce Easley to the embodied symbol of white cultural decadence, particularly its liberal element. Easley is described as "broad...with thinning hair," and his impotence, to which Walker continually refers, is further emphasized by his childless marriage and his defenseless acceptance of Walker's physical aggression. Surrounded by a multitude of books and paintings, constant visual reminders of his academic pretensions, Jones equates Easley's liberal idealism with his ineffectual indictments, imprecations, and threats, easy lipservice that lacks the substance of action.

Yet despite all the obvious implications of the professor of humanities who himself lacks the force of his convictions, it is Easley's intellectual perception that throws into sharp relief the remarkable tensions within Walker and within the play's perspective on revolution. His remark that Walker's poetry, like his revolutionary histrionics, is nothing more than "ritual drama" insidiously invoked to induce blacks to spill their blood, not only describes accurately the successful revolutionary play, but more significantly reveals how far Walker is from complacently accepting this idea. Soon after, when Easley asks Walker if the new regime can possibly be better than the old, if the haves exchanging places with the have-nots "will ...change the essential function of the world?" we are reminded of Walker's earlier admission that the revolution "will only change, ha, the complexion of tyranny."

This brief description introduces us to Jones's complexity. By attempting to create strawmen against whom the black mythological revolutionary flexes his physical and spiritual muscles, Jones has only succeeded in bringing to the surface the ambivalent pressures and terrible dilemmas attendant upon revolutionary action. In effect, he reminds us that in the world of men black and white are never as simple as they seem. Walker himself is a perplexed and perplexing character carrying within him the ambiguities of his revolutionary role. His solipsistic obsession, and the dehumanizing abstractions he has forced himself to accept are most clearly formulated by Grace:

> But because somehow I've become your enemy, I suddenly no longer qualify. Forget you're their mother, Grace. Walker has decided that you're no longer to perform that function. ... I'm *not* in your head, Walker. ... We are all flesh and blood and deserve to live...even unabstracted by what you think we ought to be in the general scheme of things.   (pp. 67-68)

Besides these focal colloquies which complicate greatly the moral scheme of the play, the possibly debasing and dehumanizing effects of such revolutionary commitment are revealed on several other occasions. For brevity's sake I shall enumerate only a few to give an idea of how this pattern of moral complexity permeates the play. Grace's observation, "I don't even think you know who you are anymore," is not entirely incorrect, for Walker has returned to his past precisely to seek his lost identity. Moreover, her suggestion that he only discovered what he was when he "sold out the last of [his] loves and emotions,...until [he] killed [his] last old friend," induces Walker's breakdown and his confession that he has lost his "soul, or heart, or warmth." Finally, in what is perhaps his most illuminating revelation of the anguished moral upheaval of his life, Walker confesses that rather than leading the revolution against white society, he would prefer their intellectual company, even Easley's academic debates.

These confessions are far more than a recognition of the hardships and loneliness a great leader must face; they reveal strikingly the ambivalent feelings and ambiguous moral position of a complex individual. To Grace, Walker admits that "with no other advisor except my own ego" he has "promoted a bloody situation where white and black people are killing each other" (p. 66). Nor does he dare disagree with Easley's judgment that any revolution conceived only to give other folks a chance to play the oppressor is an "ugly idea." In fact the full force of this ghastly recognition impels Walker to hide his head in his hands in order to evade momentarily the actuality of the truth. But that actuality is inescapable, for Walker knows that the poet and the revolutionary are mortal enemies, that he has "killed for all times any creative impulse…by the depravity of my murderous deeds."

Indeed, a systematic and detailed study of *The Slave* would reveal numerous and significant ways in which Jones dilutes and qualifies the revolutionary thrust of the play. The detailed exposition which serves to develop the important private relationships among the characters and to provide crucial information about their past also allows their personal destinies and specific conflicts to overshadow the political events and racial confrontation. In fact, by actually putting Grace and Easley on stage, by allowing them their hopes and fears, by reminding us of the children upstairs, and by depicting them as helpless victims of the revolutionary wrath, Jones not only humanizes the symbolic enemy, he has forfeited much of the audience's sympathy for Walker.

It is most importantly the play's structure that focuses at once the complexity of Jones's treatment of the revolution and, paradoxically, the play's inadequacy as revolutionary drama. The play opens with the appearance of an "old field slave" who serves as prologue for the action to follow. It is clear that Jones employs the familiar symbol of Negro servility and oppression, the archetype or stereotype of white imagination, in order to convert this image into something more positive and complex. As the prologue warns: "Whatever I am or seem…to you, then let that rest. But figure still, that you might not be right. … You might be lying…to save yourself." The notion of deceit dominates the prologue: not only the hypocrisy of the white world which invents roles for the blacks to play, but also the equally dangerous self-deceit with which all men attempt to prevent the realization that "we are liars, and we are murderers." The broad sweeping inclusion articulated in the word "we" dramatizes vividly, compresses in virtually a symbolic way, the mutual involvement in the deadly filth "that passes as whatever thing we feel is too righteous to question, too deeply felt to deny" (p. 44).

The rhythm of the prologue moves from subservience to mastery, from the faltering, uncertain speech at the start to the clipped assertiveness at the conclusion, from the officious servant to the "old blues people…hard as nails, and takin' no shit from nobody." Despite this building pattern of strength and assurance the speaker finally relapses into his former posture of a tired, unsure field hand as he shuffles slowly across the stage to begin the play.

This cyclical structure of the prologue is repeated in the main body of the play where it acquires a forcefully direct and thematically portentous significance. At the play's conclusion Walker appears triumphant: Easley is dead, Grace is dying, and his connection with his past in white society is emphatically severed, symbolized finally by Walker's revelation that his mulatto daughters are dead. But, as Walker exits to join the revolution, he stumbles unsteadily through the door accompanied by the sound of a child crying in the distance. The prophecy anticipated in the Prologue, that the slave is awakened by the faint cries of a child, has been realized, and in the image of "the old man at the beginning of the play" Walker leaves, the slave of his revolutionary passions. By killing his former masters, Walker has exchanged physical thraldom for moral bondage; even as he emerges victorious he has become the oppressor, if only because it is his turn now. The revolution is ironically completed; the final image associates the victorious oppressor and the oppressed victim on the revolving wheel of political fortune. The liberated Walker is still a slave; all that has happened in his racial drama is a change in the "complexion of tyranny."[17]

Not long ago *TDR* published a volume entitled "Black Theatre" where under the rubric "Black Revolutionary Theatre" eight plays by seven dramatists appeared. Ranging from Ben Caldwell's four parodic vignettes of the decadent immorality of white culture to LeRoi Jones's latest offerings, none of these plays viewed, as Richard Schechner aptly observed, "black-white reconciliation as the first item on the National racial agenda."[18] Although these plays express different degrees of militancy, virtually all of them exhibit specific formal desiderata of effective revolutionary drama. None of them is longer than twelve pages; the average length is eight. Most of them are set in easily recognizable locations charged with obvious symbolic import: the street that divides the black ghetto from affluent white America, the jail that houses the oppressive symbol of white tyranny, and the cluttered, infested rooms of America's lower depths. The language of these plays is brutally frank and easily understood, the dialogue depending heavily on the idiomatic and

[17]There is a similar pun in Genet's *The Blacks* (New York: Grove Press, 1960), p. 117, when the Governor forewarns the rebellious blacks of the consequence of their revolution: "My corpse will be on the ground, but my soul and body will rise into the air. You'll see them, and you'll die of fright. First, you'll turn pale, then you'll fall and be dead."

[18]"White on Black," *The Drama Review*, 12 (Summer 1968), 27.

colloquial and employing incantational rhythms of repeated imprecations. Some have stunning choreographic effects as silhouetted
figures move in and out of a burning background or weave rhythmic
patterns around a central scapegoat figure. The characters are
scarcely individuated, but still sufficiently differentiated along
clearly symbolic polarities: vitality/effeteness, sanity/madness,
oppressed/oppressor, moral/immoral, and of course, black/white.
And, most important, the conclusions of many of these productions
are "open-ended," designed to bring audiences only to the threshold
of fulfillment, as explicitly exemplified by playwright Ronald Milner's final stage direction: "Important that it ends like there's a
conversation going on down the steps to—."

John Lahr speaks of these plays as "turning the religious fervor
from gospel dreams of the next world to the revolutionary goals on
earth,"[19] and his religious allusion is instructive. Jimmy Garett's
And We Own the Night is set in the midst of the armed confrontation, the secular Armageddon that heralds the rebirth to racial selfhood. Like many of these plays, its vision is apocalyptic, the final
judgment rendered with a terrible swift sword. Its hero, tempered
by fire and baptized in blood, sacrifices himself in proclaiming his
messianic prophecy that if not the meek then the oppressed shall
inherit the earth. There is much of the spirit of revivalism in this
drama: the haunting rhythms of its incantations, the anticipatory
nature of its language, the enthusiastic participation of the entire
assembly, and the politicized rendition of the archetypal religious
drama—the revolutionary messiah, Christ as warrior, who appears
to lead his people to victory over diabolical oppressors. But the
evangelical energy has been turned to other directions; the heavenly city must be created here and now. Garrett is openly contemp-
tuous of organized religion, "a lie" conceived by white society to
allow him to "shoot you in the back while you're on your knees praying to his God" (p. 67).

If religion is an opiate for the Negro, so is the deluding myth of
white benevolence perpetuated by generations of black mothers who
have unwittingly emasculated their men. One of the most salient
facts about the structure of the black family is its dominating
matriarchy, a fact that assures that "the women's aspiration and
values are closely tied to those of the white power structure and not

[19] "Black Theatre: The American Tragic Voice," *Evergreen Review*, 13 (Aug.
1969), 55-63.

to those of her men."[20] Running through these revolutionary plays is an insistent theme describing an unbridgeable generation gap across whose gulf the new spirituality confronts the old. In Garrett's play, for example, the older generation is depicted as either unable or unwilling to fight, even to die, in order to be reborn. Johnny becomes the focal point of a mythic struggle between generations and their implied socio-political life-styles. In obvious contrast to the pitiable and timid spokesmen of stasis—the ineffectual doctor who attends Johnny, his own Tomish father who remains at home during the fighting, and, most significantly, his mother who worships the white man's charity—is Johnny's comrade-in-arms, Lil' T, who relentlessly goads him to forget his mother for the simple, unassailable reason that "she's too old."

All the impressions that emerge during the conclusion of this play focus on Johnny's spiritual odyssey, an initiation that culminates in the concluding lines with his prideful awareness of manhood:

> *Johnny (Points the gun at her back.).* We're new...men. Mama...Not
> niggers. Black men. *(He fires at her back.)*   (p. 69)

In so many ways Garrett's concluding scene is paradigmatic of the emerging conventions of Black revolutionary theatre. Frequently these plays depict characters as abstract personifications of a new morality, the moral perspective of an oppressed people through whose eyes whites are "evil": "That simple alarming fact of your unredeemable evil. You are all disqualified as human beings...disqualified by your inhuman acts."[21] By murdering his mother Johnny recognizes the irreconcilability between the old and the new spiritualities, and the deed unequivocally affirms that the only alternative

---

[20]Neal, p. 38. The defeat of the dominating matriarch is only one aspect of the conflict between generations so many of these plays depict. See, for example, Salimu's *Growin' Into Blackness*, Ben Caldwell's *Family Portrait*, and Marvin X's *Take Care of Business*, all of which appear in *New Plays From the Black Theatre*.

[21]Jones, "The Death of Malcolm X," *New Plays*, p. 9. Without exception these plays present white society as spiritually decadent, physically impotent, and diabolically treacherous. In two plays of Ben Caldwell's Quartet, *Top Secret or, A Few Million After B.C.* and *Mission Accomplished*, white political and religious institutions are implicated in plots of physical and spiritual genocide. Consequently, those Negroes who wittingly or unwittingly collaborate with white establishments are revealed as subtle and dangerous enemies of black identity. Both Ron Milner's *The Monster* and Herbie Stokes's *The Man Who Trusted the Devil Twice* present Negroes who realize too late the price of their betrayal.

to conserving an oppressive system is to destroy the accepted framework of values. Most importantly perhaps, Johnny's assertion, "We're new men...not niggers," indicates the greatest of all themes in Black revolutionary drama: the protagonist's self-discovery. But the identity crisis, as Garrett's use of diction makes clear, is solved in what becomes a characteristic rhythm of this theatre. Selfhood entails abrogating the white man's derogatory fictions (nigger), in order to embrace proudly a new self-conception (black); and identity signifies not rugged individuality of the singular personal pronoun, but the suppression of self to the pluralism of the community.[22]

Consequently the call for cultural solidarity shapes the subject matter and form these plays take. The plays act out confrontations and spell out a new moral value system for audiences to which LeRoi Jones attributes a "prerevolutionary temperament."[23] In Garrett's play the conflict between the oppressed and the oppressor is always apparent, visually enforced by the bodies of the black youth and the white cop upstage. The spiritually weak but diabolically dangerous whites and those collaborative Negroes who betray their people are exaggeratedly heightened for Garrett disdains any subtlety that might obscure his call to action. His language vibrates from the strident challenges and clipped assertiveness associated

---

[22]The thematic distinction between Negro and black is insisted upon in many of the Revolutionary plays. Ben Caldwell's *The Job* is set in the office of N.O. (Negro Opportunity). Here seven characters gather to be interviewed by a patronizing white man. Six have come to suffer the humiliation of the ritual and to bow and scrape out of the office. The seventh, however, has come to kill the interviewer. Caldwell describes the six characters as Negroes; the seventh "a black man." In *The Man Who Trusted the Devil Twice*, a military officer says, "We have to keep telling him they are Negroes. ... They must be taught that if anyone calls them black to take it as an insult." And in Ben Caldwell's *Riot Sale* an angry crowd is referred to as black. But when forgetting their anger they chase after money fired at them from an "anti-poverty cannon" the directions read, "NIGGERS NOW, they gather money in boxes and run home."

The idea of suppressing individuality within the communal identity has led several black writers to redefine the black artist's relation to society. C. H. Fuller, Jr. (*Liberator*, 7 [July 1967], 14-15) argues that the artist's individuality, creativity, and freedom of expression are of less importance than his functional relation to the community he serves. "Only when we subordinate our individuality," Fuller writes, "to the struggles of our people do we come to know them and their struggles." For the opposing view see Timothy Phoenix, "Black Writers Must be Free," *Liberator*, 7 (Aug. 1967), 10.

[23]"The Revolutionary Theatre," p. 5.

with the revolutionary heroes to the pallid monotones of the older generations. He particularly employs incantatory rhetoric, the effect of which stresses words and phrases which acquire new weight and perspective through repetition. Lil' T suggests the white man's weakening resistance to the Black assertion of power by playing on the word "can't" until his speech builds to a litany of positive achievements in the wars simultaneously erupting throughout the country:

> She can't stop us Johnny. Nobody can. The white man can't. Your mama can't. Nobody. We're destroying the white man. There's wars like this in every big city...Harlem, Detroit, Chicago...all over California. Everywhere. (p. 63)

The staccato rhythm of the short lines is punctuated by the "sound of gunfire in short bursts," so that the word "everywhere" erupts explosively reaching beyond the particularized alley to engulf the world.

Or, again, Garrett's insistence that Johnny's only genuine allegiance is to his revolutionary brothers, not to the outmoded tradition of the family unit is emphasized not only by Lil' T's symbolic victory over Johnny's mother, but visually suggested in their concluding handshake which literally and figuratively makes them *blood* brothers. Once more language reinforces the intended theme. Lil' T tries to nullify the effect of the docile, deluded black mother by redefining home and consequently by rhetorically realigning Johnny's sense of family:

> Home, This is home. This alley and those bodies. That's home. I'm your brother and we live and fight in alleys. This is home. And we'll win against the white man. (p. 64)

Garrett also uses language to condemn simply and effectively the enemies of the revolution. The doctor's speeches are short and hesitant, corresponding aurally to the portrait of timid ineffectuality he represents. But significantly Garrett reserves his most flagrant disclosures for the black mother. After Lil' T has catalogued the indignities black women have suffered at the hands of the white man, Johnny's mother incredulously denies such preposterous charges of white guilt, and then unwittingly confesses to the self-induced blindness of the old spirituality: "But I don't know you." Or in trying to win Johnny back to home and establishment she pleads with him to understand "how I've worked and *slaved* for you all." The charged pun focuses a shared emotional outrage, and effectively undercuts all the good deeds she attributes to white benevolence.

But what is most characteristic of these revolutionary plays is their structure, the fluid, open-ended form these playwrights consciously seek rather than the autonomous *objet d' art* of traditional theatre. Garrett's play begins at night, "the time...of death and dying," and closes with the promise of a new dawn. If Johnny's prophecy that "we're gonna build a whole new thing after this" is to prove correct, then his staged life is merely a prelude to the greater scenario yet to be written. Although his dying gesture is to kill his mother, thereby conclusively declaring his choice for freedom, the implications of that choice are even more crucial. For to determine "who he is" is merely half the battle. Once having made that assertion it follows that for the act to be more than an existential proclamation the audience must be willing to fight, even to die, to destroy that society which attempts to deprive them of their claimed identity. Unlike Jones's play, *And We Own the Night* is calibrated to produce visceral rather than intellectual reactions, spontaneous actions rather than contemplation. Disdaining any of the moral complexities inherent in the dialectics of power or the ambiguously shifting relations between oppressed and oppressor, Garrett's play throws its entire emotional burden into the audience demanding they assume the struggle Johnny's death has only begun.

II

Black revolutionary drama portends radical revisions in our traditional idea of the theatre. From Aeschylus to Ibsen, drama had attempted to establish for its audiences a new or renewed sense of life's order, and by so doing to reconcile the spectator with the system of beliefs of his society. If Western theatre performed any political act it was to conserve the status quo, not only by defending society's values but by its very premises. The very notion of catharsis, an emotional purgation of the audience's collective energies, means that theatre becomes society's buffer sponging up all the moral indignities that if translated into action could effect substantial change. Consequently, by focusing on disorder—the social, political, and moral chaos of an oppressive society — Black Revolutionary Theatre starts in empathy only to convert catharsis into palpable and continuing action.

> Our theatre will show victims so that their brothers in the audience will be better able to understand that they are brothers of victims, and that they themselves are victims, if they are blood brothers. And what we show must cause the blood to rush, so that pre-revolutionary temperaments will be bathed in this blood, and it will cause their deepest souls to move, and they find themselves tensed and clenched, even ready to die, at what the soul has been taught.[24]

Jones's lines make it clear that this drama measures its success by emotional excitation which leads to communal action that not only spills over the fourth wall of the stage, but out of the theatre as well.

As the barriers between actors and audience, the stage and the street, become more arbitrary, the distinction between the play's illusion and the spectators' reality so crucial to traditional dramatic forms becomes correspondingly blurred. Consequently, black revolutionary dramatists are simply not concerned with imitating reality either in the high or low mimetic vein. Garrett's play is again paradigmatic of the way this drama attempts to invert — or perhaps subvert — conventionally accepted tenets of Western theatre. By dramatizing the revolution, the successful emergence of Black nationhood, Garrett aims at a different level of realism, one that proceeds not by imitating actuality, but rather by creating a private reality for its audience.

In an important sense the Black Revolutionary Theatre stands poised between two levels of reality, seeking in Jones's words to "take dreams and give them a reality."[25] These plays demand the audience's consciousness of the brutalizing facts of its existence even while they portray a series of events that appeal strongly to the audience's emotionally felt desire for a different reality. The Black Revolutionary play is only ostensibly about the world "as it is"; frequently it strives to transcend this limited perspective to present a utopian vision of the world as it will be, or should be. And in this idealistic glance forward the revolutionary play seeks to convert that deeply-felt emotional fantasy into external, objective fact through revolutionary action. Paradoxically, revolutionary drama

[24]*Ibid.*, p. 4.
[25]*Ibid.*

seeks to transcend its own form as a play, and if it succeeds it will have elicited a spontaneous response that will take the play out of the theatre onto the streets where it will cease to be an illusion and become actuality itself.

Larry Neal argues that "a main tenet of Black Power is the necessity for Black people to define the world in their own terms. The Black artist has made the same point in the context of aesthetics." The form of Black Revolutionary Theatre is self-definition with a vengeance. The notion of the dramatic form as a self-contained, holistic artifact yields to an idea of the theatre that depends finally on the spectators' act of perception and their integral relationship to the theatrical performance. It is a theatre that demands audience participation to shape the outcome on its own terms if the ordered actuality drama traditionally promises is to be achieved. Thus the lack of "dramatic texture"—allegorical characters, melodramatic actions, simplicity of language, incompleted actions—are intended to negate the formal assumptions of drama, to prevent literary critical formulations from interceding between the audience and the political act.

This is not to suggest that Black revolutionary playwrights are the first to employ such techniques. Brecht, Artaud, Peter Weiss, Jack Gelber, and The Living Theatre, each in his own way, attempts similar revolutionary forms. Indeed, the Black playwright's difficulty in finding new dramatic forms to present his revolutionary message is perhaps best illustrated by the implicit irony of the recent manifestoes of the Black Arts Movement. LeRoi Jones's assertion—

> We will scream and cry, murder, run through the streets in agony, if it means some soul will be moved, moved to actual life understanding of what the world is, and what it ought to be. We are preaching virtue and feeling, and a natural sense of self in the world.—[26]

might in a different context be mistaken for a description of the Dionysian revels which students agree were the genetic and generic roots of Western dramatic tradition. And the intention to preach virtue by the shared communal participation of actors and audiences in an atmosphere emotionally charged by the drama differs only slightly from the community of pious devotion that attended a Medieval Mystery play like the York Crucifixion. In attempting to

[26]"The Revolutionary Theatre," p. 5.

escape "the white form bag," black dramatists have rediscovered the communal impulses and emotional rhythms that gave birth to Western drama. Yet, as Richard Schechner points out, "after all artists must begin somewhere, and a fresh beginning may simply consist in sweeping away what is fashionable."[27]

But it is more than the merely fashionable that this drama rejects. In the intensity of its communal consciousness this drama reveals the alienation and estrangement in Western theatre to be the product not of the human condition but of a despairing civilization. In its bold hyperbole and vital argot black drama has reinvigorated a "poetry in the theatre" and suggests that the cosmic and comic silences of contemporary theatre need not be drama's only medium. And, most importantly, in the imperative urge these dramatists feel for justice and ethical prerogatives, the black revolutionary drama proceeds beyond the "quietistic politics" of which so many critics have complained. Lee Baxandall has brilliantly characterized the political implications of naturalistic drama as providing a "theatre of despairing 'protest,' which scarcely hopes for an audience capable and audacious enough actually to put society to rights."[28] The black revolutionary drama, to the contrary, takes as its premise that not only is the audience capable of effecting significant change, but that it must, and to do so is nothing less than to claim one's identity.

What appears most significant about this drama, then, is that its reinterpretation of traditional theatrical forms reflects its dramatists' reordering of deeply accepted philosophical notions of human existence. The dramatic modes that dominate Western theatre— naturalism and absurdity—are the poles of cause and effect of a scientific and cynical world-view which slavishly imprisons man within vectors of social, psychological, and biological determinants. No longer content with the hermetically closed systems of the Western world, systems which because they are closed are destructively conservative, the Black Revolutionary Theatre forcefully reasserts the freedom of human will, the freedom to act and in acting the capability to transform substantially the texture and tone of modern life.

---

[27]"White on Black," p. 26.
[28]"The Revolutionary Moment," *The Drama Review*, 13 (Winter 1968), 95.

Chronology of Important Events

1821   The African Company organized in New York City by Mr. Brown, company manager, with James Hewlett as leading actor.

1823   *King Shotoway* by Mr. Brown; first known play written by an Afro-American produced by the African Company.

1825   Ira Aldridge arrives in London to begin professional acting career; he performs for forty-two years throughout Europe, Russia, and the British Isles.

1843   Dan Emmett with his Virginia Minstrels, a white quartet, officially introduces Negro minstrelsy on the American stage.

1852   *Uncle Tom's Cabin*, adapted for the stage from Harriet Beecher Stowe's famed novel, begins an unprecedented run of eighty years; a version of the play is performed somewhere in the United States regularly until 1932.

1858   *The Escape, or A Leap for Freedom* by ex-slave William Wells Brown published.

1865   Georgia Minstrels, first Black minstrel troupe, organized by Charles Hicks.

1871   Fisk Jubilee Singers on tour of America and Europe with Negro spirituals.

1870s-   B. J. Ford (1878) and J. A. Arneaux leading Black Shakespearean
1890   actors of the period; they perform in their own Black companies such as the Astor Place Coloured Tragedy Company; Arneaux publishes an edited version of *Richard III* in 1886.

1891   Sam Jack's *The Creole Show* opens in Boston, admitting Black women performers in musical revue.

1896   Worth's Museum All-Star Stock Company founded in New York City by Bob Cole, who begins the first training school for Black performers.

1898   Bob Cole and Billy Johnson team up to produce "musical operettas," their first show being *A Trip to Coontown.*

1900   Bert Williams and George Walker produce their first musical show on Broadway, *The Sons of Ham;* in 1903, their production of *In Dahomey* is taken to London, where it plays a command performance for royalty; their successful partnership ends with Walker's premature death in 1911.

1906   The Pekin Stock Company of Chicago formed by Robert T. Motts; Charles Gilpin in company headed by J. Edward Green; company disbanded in 1909.

1915   The Lafayette Players established by Anita Bush in Harlem; company finally disbanded in Los Angeles in 1932. Scott Joplin's opera *Treemonisha* completed but unable to secure professional production.

1917   Ridgely Torrence's *Three Plays for a Negro Theatre* reintroduces Black actors to the legitimate Broadway professional stage.

1920   Charles Gilpin stars as Brutus Jones in Eugene O'Neill's *The Emperor Jones* at Provincetown Playhouse, New York City.

1920-
1950   During this period repeated attempts are made to establish a viable Black theatre company in Harlem; among the most notable efforts are the Krigwa Players (1926), Harlem Experimental Theatre (1928), Harlem Suitcase Theatre (1937), Rose McClendon Players (1938), and American Negro Theatre (1940).

1921   *Shuffle Along,* the Miller/Lyles, Sissle/Blake hit musical comedy, enjoys record run on Broadway. Howard University (Washington, D.C.) establishes a Department of Dramatic Art.

1923   Willis Richardson's one-act drama *The Chip Woman's Fortune,* first nonmusical play by a Black playwright on Broadway.

1924   Paul Robeson plays lead in Eugene O'Neill's *All God's Chillun Got Wings* produced by the Provincetown Players; interracial casting generates considerable controversy.

1926   The Krigwa Players, intended as a nationwide movement of little theatres presenting Black plays primarily for Black audiences, started by W. E. B. DuBois, editor of *The Crisis.* Paul Green wins Pulitzer Prize for his play *In Abraham's Bosom,* with leading Black actors Rose McClendon, Abbie Mitchell, Frank Wilson, and Jules Bledsoe.

1930   The Negro Inter-Collegiate Drama Association formed by Randolph Edmonds to promote dramatic art among member colleges in the South. Marc Connelly's *The Green Pastures* opens on Broadway with an all-Black cast of some 100 actors and the Hall Johnson Choir singing Negro Spirituals; Richard B. Harrison gives towering performance as De Lawd.

1935   Langston Hughes's *Mulatto* opens on Broadway and establishes a record run for a straight play by a Black writer. The Federal Theatre Project of the Works Progress Administration, through its Negro units in several cities, provides employment for Black theatre artists and technicians during the Great Depression; the project is discontinued in 1939.

1940   The American Negro Theatre founded by Abram Hill and Fred O'Neal; greatest success (which causes its decline) is *Anna Lucasta,* produced in 1944.

1941   *Native Son* by Richard Wright (with Paul Green) produced on Broadway with Canada Lee as Bigger Thomas.

1946   Theodore Ward's *Our Lan'* opens off-Broadway at the Henry Street Playhouse and moves to the Royale Theatre for a limited run.

1953   *Take a Giant Step* by Louis Peterson enjoys critical success on Broadway.

1954   *In Splendid Error* by William Branch opens at Greenwich Mews Theatre in New York; the play contrasts the characters of Frederick Douglass and John Brown against the background of the Harper's Ferry incident.

1957   Loften Mitchell's *A Land Beyond the River* at the Greenwich Mews Theatre confronts the most pressing issue of the day: public school desegregation.

1958   Lorraine Hansberry's first play, *A Raisin in the Sun,* opens in New York to wide critical and popular acclaim; it brings Black audiences to professional Broadway theatre.

1959   *The Blacks* by Jean Genet, in a powerful production by Gene Frankel at the off-Broadway St. Mark's Playhouse, introduces the theatre of audience vilification.

1964   *Dutchman* by LeRoi Jones (Amiri Baraka) at the Cherry Lane Theatre off-Broadway, along with Jones's manifesto "The Revolutionary Theatre," heralds the Black revolutionary drama of the sixties.

1967-
present
A resurgence of Black community theatre groups around the country; most notably in Boston, Buffalo, Chicago, Cleveland, Detroit, Los Angeles, New Orleans, New York, Philadelphia, and Washington, D.C.

1967
The Negro Ensemble Company established with Douglas Turner Ward as artistic director at the St. Mark's Playhouse in downtown New York.

The New Lafayette Theatre founded in Harlem with Robert Macbeth as artistic director and Ed Bullins as playwright in residence; disbanded in 1972.

1968
The National Black Theatre formed in Harlem by Barbara Ann Teer; concentrates on Black communal ritual theatre as advocated by writers like Carlton Molette and Paul Carter Harrison.

James Earl Jones awarded the Antoinette Perry Award ("Tony") for his performance as Jack Johnson in Howard Sackler's play *The Great White Hope*.

1970
Ceremonies in Dark Old Men by Lonnie Elder III just misses, and *No Place to Be Somebody* by Charles Gordone wins the Pulitzer Prize for the best American play.

1971
El Hajj Malik by N. R. Davidson, a play about Malcolm X, directed by Ernie McClintock for his Afro-American Studio Theatre in New York, typifies the best of the sociopolitical theatre presented by scores of Black theatre groups throughout the United States.

1970s
Lavish Black musicals once again attracting huge interracial audiences to Broadway; among popular attractions are *Purlie, Raisin, Bubbling Brown Sugar, The Wiz, Don't Bother Me I Can't Cope, Your Arms Too Short to Box With God,* and *Timbuktu!*

The New York Shakespeare Public Theatre establishes Black and Hispanic Shakespeare companies.

Notes on the Editor and Contributors

ERROL HILL is John D. Willard Professor of Drama and Oratory at Dartmouth College. A published playwright, play director, and actor, he is also the author of *The Trinidad Carnival: Mandate for a National Theatre* (1972) and editor of several collections of Caribbean plays. His articles have appeared in *Theatre Survey, Caribbean Quarterly, Cultures,* and the *Bulletin of Black Theatre* of which he was former editor for the American Theatre Association.

KIMBERLY W. BENSTON is the author of *Baraka: The Renegade and the Mask* (1976) and editor of *Baraka: A Collection of Critical Essays,* a volume in the Twentieth Century Views series. His essays on Afro-American literature and culture have appeared in such journals as *Phylon, Massachusetts Review, CLA Journal, Boundary 2,* and *Black American Literature Forum.*

C. W. E. BIGSBY is a lecturer in American literature at the University of East Anglia, Norwich, England. His publications include, besides many articles, *Confrontation and Commitment: A Study of Contemporary American Drama, 1959-1966* (1967) and *Edward Albee* (1968). He has also edited a two-volume work, *The Black American Writer* (1969), and a collection of Negro plays for Penguin Books.

HUGH F. BUTTS has served as attending psychiatrist on a number of New York City hospital staffs. He was formerly assistant clinical professor of psychiatry at the Columbia University College of Physicians and Surgeons and has taught courses in human development and psychology at Columbia College.

WILLIAM COOK is associate professor of English and chairman of the Black Studies Program at Dartmouth College. He has published poems and articles on poetry and expository writing.

JIM HASKINS has taught in elementary and junior high schools, the New School for Social Research, Staten Island Community College, and the State University College of New York at New Paltz. He is also an educational consultant and the author of several books, including *Diary of a Harlem Schoolteacher, Resistance: Profiles in Nonviolence,* and *A Piece of the Power: Four Black Mayors.*

JAMES HATCH, an associate professor at the City College of New York, is cofounder of the Hatch-Billops Collection, Archives of Black Cultural History, in New York City. He has published three books on Black American theatre.

SAMUEL A. HAY is associate professor of theatre and director of the Africana Studies and Research Center at Purdue University.

HELEN ARMSTEAD JOHNSON has been a professor of English at York College of the City University of New York since 1967. She is also affiliated with the doctoral program in theatre at the Graduate Center of CUNY. She is the founder and director/curator of the Armstead-Johnson Foundation for Theater Research, which was started in 1974 for the purpose of collecting, preserving, documenting, and exhibiting examples of the Black American's contribution to the American stage.

MICHAEL W. KAUFMAN was for ten years on the faculties of Cornell University and the State University of New York where he taught courses and wrote on Shakespeare and modern drama. He has temporarily left the contemplative life of academe to work with the Massachusetts Welfare Department.

BERNARD L. PETERSON, JR. is assistant professor of English and drama at Elizabeth City State University in North Carolina. His articles on Black playwrights have been published in *The Crisis* and *Black World.* He is currently working on a two-volume directory of Black playwrights and composers and their works.

EILEEN SOUTHERN is professor of music and chairman of the Afro-American Studies Department at Harvard University. Her publications include *The Buxheim Organ Book* (1963), *The Music of Black Americans* (1971), and *Readings in Black American Music* (1971), as well as many articles on Renaissance music in professional journals and encyclopedias.

DR. SHELBY STEELE is an associate professor of English at San Jose State University. He has published short fiction and critical essays in *Black World, Obsidian, Western Humanities Review, San Jose Studies,* and other journals.

ROBERT FARRIS THOMPSON is professor of art history at Yale University. He is the author of *African Art in Motion* (1974) and *Black Gods and Kings* (1976) and has published articles in some ten anthologies. He specializes in Black Atlantic art and dance.

Dr. Eleanor W. Traylor is professor of English at Montgomery College, Rockville, Maryland. She has formerly taught African and Afro-American dramatic texts at Howard University. She has been awarded the Melvin Hill Professorship for the spring term 1979 at Hobart College, Geneva, New York.

Darwin T. Turner is professor of English and chairman of the Afro-American Studies Program at the University of Iowa, Iowa City. He has published critical studies on Afro-American literature and drama, as well as American literature and literary criticism, in the *CLA Journal, Southern Humanities Review, Massachusetts Review, Mississippi Quarterly, Iowa Review,* and other publications. He is also editor of *Black Drama in America: An Anthology* and other books on Black American literature.

Selected Bibliography

I. General Works on Black Theater and It's Participants

Abramson, Doris. *Negro Playwrights in the American Theatre, 1925-1959.* New York: Columbia University Press, 1969.

American Society of African Culture. *The American Negro Writer and His Roots: Selected Papers from the First Conference of Negro Writers* (March 1959). New York, 1960.

The American Theatre: A Sum of Its Parts. New York: Samuel French, 1971.

Archer, Leonard C. *Black Images in American Theatre.* Nashville, Tenn.: Pageant Press, 1973.

Belcher, Fannin S., Jr. "The Place of the Negro in the Evolution of the American Theatre, 1767 to 1940." Ph.D. dissertation, Yale University, 1945.

Benston, Kimberly W. *Baraka: The Renegade and the Mask.* New Haven: Yale University Press, 1976.

Bigsby, C. W. E., ed. *The Black American Writer,* Vol. II *(Poetry and Drama).* Florida: Everett/Edwards, 1969.

Bond, Frederick W. *The Negro and the Drama.* Washington, D.C.: Associated Publishers, 1940.

Brown, Sterling. *Negro Poetry and Drama.* Washington, D.C.: Associates in Negro Folk Education, 1937; reprint—New York: Atheneum, 1969.

Bullins, Ed, ed. *Black Theatre* (magazine). New York: New Lafayette Theatre, 1968-1972.

Charters, Ann. *Nobody: The Story of Bert Williams.* New York: Macmillan, 1970.

Cruse, Harold. *The Crisis of the Negro Intellectual.* New York: William Morrow, 1967.

Dent, Thomas C., Richard Schechner, and Gilbert Moses. *The Free Southern Theater by the Free Southern Theater.* Indianapolis: Bobbs-Merrill, 1969.

The Drama Review, Vol. 12, No. 4 (T-40, Summer 1968). The entire issue is devoted to Black theater.

⸺, Vol. 16, No. 4 (T-56, December 1972). Black theater issue.

Emery, Lynne Fauley. *Black Dance in the United States from 1619 to 1970.* Palo Alto, Calif.: National Press Books, 1972.

Farrison, William Edward. *William Wells Brown: Author and Reformer.* Chicago: University of Chicago Press, 1969.

Flannigan, Hallie. *Arena: The History of the Federal Theatre.* New York: Duell, Sloan, and Pearce, 1940.

Fletcher, Tom. *One Hundred Years of the Negro in Show Business.* New York: Burdge, 1954.

Gayle, Addison, Jr., ed. *The Black Aesthetic.* New York: Doubleday, 1971.

⸺, ed. *Black Expression: Essays by and about Black Americans in the Creative Arts.* New York: Weybright and Talley, 1969.

Goldstein, Rhoda L., ed. *Black Life and Culture in the United States.* New York: Thomas Y. Crowell, 1971.

Harrison, Paul Carter. *The Drama of Nommo.* New York: Grove Press, 1972.

Hatch, James V. *Black Image on the American Stage: A Bibliography of Plays and Musicals, 1770-1970.* New York: Drama Book Specialists, 1970.

⸺, and Omanii Abdullah. *Black Playwrights, 1823-1977: An Annotated Bibliography of Plays.* New York: R. R. Bowker, 1977.

Hill, Herbert, ed. *Anger and Beyond: The Negro Writer in the United States.* New York: Harper & Row, 1966.

Hudson, Theodore R. *From LeRoi Jones to Amiri Baraka: The Literary Works.* Durham, N.C.: Duke University Press, 1973.

Hughes, Langston, and Milton Meltzer. *Black Magic: A Pictorial History of the Negro in American Entertainment.* Englewood Cliffs, N.J.: Prentice-Hall, 1967.

Isaacs, Edith J. R. *The Negro in the American Theatre.* New York: Theatre Arts, 1947.

Jahn, Janheinz. *Muntu: An Outline of the New African Culture.* New York: Grove Press, 1961.

Johnson, James Weldon. *Black Manhattan.* New York: Alfred Knopf, 1930; reprint⸺New York: Atheneum, 1968.

Keil, Charles. *Urban Blues.* Chicago: University of Chicago Press, 1966.

Kimball, Robert, and William Bolcom. *Reminiscing with Sissle and Blake.* New York: Viking Press, 1973.

King, Woodie, and Earl Anthony, eds. *Black Poets and Prophets: The Theory, Practice, and Esthetics of the Pan-Africanist Revolution.* New York: New American Library, 1972.

Locke, Alain, ed. *The New Negro.* New York: Albert and Charles Boni, 1925; reprint — New York: Atheneum, 1969.

Lovell, John, Jr. *Black Song: The Forge and the Flame.* New York: Macmillan, 1972.

Marshall, Herbert, and Mildred Stock. *Ira Aldridge: The Negro Tragedian.* Carbondale: Southern Illinois University Press, 1968.

Mathews, Jane DeHart. *The Federal Theatre, 1935-1939.* Princeton, N.J.: Princeton University Press, 1967.

Meltzer, Milton. *Langston Hughes: A Biography.* New York: Thomas Y. Crowell, 1968.

Mitchell, Loften. *Black Drama: The Story of the American Negro in the Theatre.* New York: Hawthorn Books, 1967.

———. *Voices of the Black Theatre.* Clifton, N.J.: James T. White, 1975.

O'Daniel, Therman B., ed. *Langston Hughes, Black Genius: A Crictical Evaluation.* New York: William Morrow, 1971.

Patterson, Lindsay. *Anthology of the American Negro in the Theatre.* New York: Publishers Company, 1967.

Robeson, Eslanda Goode. *Paul Robeson: Negro.* London: Victor Gollancz, 1930.

Sandle, Floyd L. *The Negro in the American Educational Theatre.* Ann Arbor, Mich.: Edward Brothers, 1964.

Southern, Eileen. *The Music of Black Americans: A History.* New York: W. W. Norton, 1971.

Stearns, Marshall, and Jean Stearns. *Jazz Dance: The Story of American Vernacular Dance.* New York: Macmillan, 1968.

Toll, Robert C. *Blacking Up: The Minstrel Show in Nineteenth-Century America.* New York: Oxford University Press, 1974.

Wittke, Carl. *Tambo and Bones: A History of the American Minstrel Stage.* Durham, N.C.: Duke University Press, 1930; reprint — New York: Greenwood Press, 1968.

II. Play Anthologies

Baraka, Amiri (LeRoi Jones). *The Baptism and The Toilet.* New York: Grove Press, 1963, 1966.

———. *Dutchman and The Slave.* New York: William Morrow, 1964.

———. *Four Black Revolutionary Plays.* Indianapolis: Bobbs-Merrill, 1969.

———. *The Motion of History and Other Plays.* New York: William Morrow, 1978.

———, and Larry Neal, eds. *Black Fire: An Anthology of Afro-American Writing.* New York: William Morrow, 1968.

A Black Quartet: Four New Black Plays by Ben Caldwell, Ronald Milner, Ed Bullins, and LeRoi Jones. New York: New American Library, 1970.

Brasmer, William, and Dominick Consolo., eds. *Black Drama: An Anthology.* Columbus, Ohio: Merrill, 1970.

Brown, Sterling, Arthur Davis, and Ulysses Lee. *Negro Caravan.* New York: Dryden Press, 1941.

Bullins, Ed. *Five Plays.* Indianapolis: Bobbs-Merrill, 1969.

———. *Four Dynamite Plays.* New York: William Morrow, 1972.

———. *New Plays from the Black Theater.* New York: Bantam Books, 1969.

———. *The Theme Is Blackness.* New York: William Morrow, 1973.

———, ed. *The New Lafayette Theatre Presents: Plays with Aesthetic Comments by Six Black Playwrights.* New York: Anchor Press/Doubleday, 1974.

Childress, Alice, ed. *Black Scenes.* New York: Doubleday, 1971.

Couch, William, Jr., ed. *New Black Playwrights: An Anthology.* Baton Rouge: Louisiana State University Press, 1968.

Edmonds, Randolph. *The Land of Cotton and Other Plays.* Washington, D.C.: Associated Publishers, 1943.

———. *Shades and Shadows.* Boston: Meador, 1930.

———. *Six Plays for a Negro Theatre.* Boston: Walter H. Baker, 1934.

Hansberry, Lorraine. *Les Blancs: The Collected Last Plays of Lorraine Hansberry,* ed. Robert Nemiroff. New York: Random House, 1972.

———. *A Raisin in the Sun; The Sign in Sidney Brustein's Window.* New York: New American Library, 1966.

Harrison, Paul Carter, ed. *Kuntu Drama: Plays of the African Continuum.* New York: Grove Press, 1974.

Hatch, James V., ed. *Black Theater, U.S.A.: Forty-five Plays by Black Americans, 1847-1974.* New York: Free Press, 1974.

Hughes, Langston. *Five Plays,* ed. Webster Smalley. Bloomington, Ind.: Indiana University Press, 1968.

Jones, LeRoi—*see* Baraka, Amiri.

King, Woodie, and Ron Milner, eds. *Black Drama Anthology.* New York: New American Library, 1971.

Locke, Alain, and Montgomery Gregory, eds. *Plays of Negro Life.* New York: Harper, 1927.

Oliver, Clinton, and Stephanie Sills, eds. *Contemporary Black Drama.* New York: Charles Scribner's Sons, 1971.

Patterson, Lindsay, ed. *Black Theater.* New York: Dodd, Mead, 1971.

Reardon, William, and Thomas Pawley. *The Black Teacher and the Dramatic Arts.* Westport, Conn.: Negro Universities Press, 1970.

Richardson, Willis. *The King's Dilemma and Other Plays for Children.* New York: Exposition Press, 1956.

———, ed. *Plays and Pageants from the Life of the Negro.* Washington, D.C.: Associated Publishers, 1930.

———, and May Miller, eds. *Negro History in Thirteen Plays.* Washington, D.C.: Associated Publishers, 1935.

Turner, Darwin T., ed. *Black Drama in America: An Anthology.* Greenwich, Conn.: Fawcett Publications, 1971.

Ward, Douglas Turner. *Two Plays: Happy Ending and Day of Absence.* New York: Third Press, 1966.

White, Edgar. *Underground: Four Plays.* New York: William Morrow, 1970.